THE NEW TOWNIES OF THE MOOR

NEWTONMORE –
ADVENT AND ADVANCEMENT, 1820 TO 1913.

MARY MACKENZIE

Moyhill Publishing

First Published in 2020 by Moyhill Publishing.
ISBN 978-1-913529-91-8

A CIP catalogue record for this book is available
from the British Library.

Printed in UK.

This book has been published with the support of the Royal Celtic Society:
Safeguarding the languages, history, music and arts of Scotland since 1820.

To find out more about the Royal Celtic Society visit:
www.royalcelticsociety.scot/en/

and for more about Badenoch Heritage visit:
www.badenochstorylands.com

Moyhill Publishing,
1965 Davenport House, 261 Bolton Rd, Bury, Gtr. Manchester BL8 2NZ, UK

Contents

List of Figures iv

Introduction 1

Acknowledgements 6

Ch 1 Emigre's early days, pre Newtonmore. 9
'Ossian' and his son, James Macpherson ~ description of tenement ~ life in the townships ~ map of some pre-1820 settlements ~ threatened evictions ~ Moors of Strone, Clune and Banchor ~ new villages.

Ch 2 The first of the feu, 1820-40. 19
Early leaseholders ~ name of village? ~ 1828 map ~ expansion of village ~ work ~ hardship ~ emigration.

Ch 3 Deprivation Decades, 1840-60. 34
Poverty ~ living conditions ~ wells ~ traditional seasons including Hallowe'en pranks ~ The Disruption ~ the Free Church ~ famine ~ destitution and aftermath.

Ch 4 Railmen and Riflemen, 1860s. 52
The railway ~ John Taylor, eye witness ~ the Volunteers ~ bankruptcy ~ mixed fortunes.

Ch 5 Education and Litigation, 1870s. 71
Queen Victoria passes through ~ a Newtonmore entrepreneur ~ opportunities brought by the railway? ~ bankruptcy ~ disreputable tea merchant ~ schools and schooling ~ right of access to St Bride's Churchyard ~ local societies ~ first Ordnance Survey map ~ evidence of an emerging community spirit.

Ch 6 Borlum, 1880s. 94
Mackintoshes of Borlum and Raitts ~ building lease of James Forbes ~ west end folk including toll keepers ~ Mrs Brewster Macpherson ~ east end folk ~ limited tourist accommodation ~ review of businesses ~ interesting characters ~ first public hall ~ more businesses and characters ~ general election ~ feeing market ~ 1877, Newtonmore Lodge ~ village groups ~ land agitation.

Ch 7 How Stick Skill Stuck, Shinty. 121
The Eilan ~ early 1890s shinty song ~ players (and families) listed or indicated in the song ~ coaching and tactics ~ in-coming families who embraced shinty ~ the longest shinty-playing dynasties in Newtonmore?

Ch 8 Unique Ùnag. 131
The Rose family in Nuide, Glenbanchor and Newtonmore.

Ch 9 Time of the Trowel, 1890s. 139
Death on the shinty field ~ developing The Hotel, Sam's fine establishment ~ Macpherson of Belleville: supporting shinty and the community, County Councillor ~ Church unrest ~ rebuilding and upgrading of village properties ~ a few more visitors 'finding' Newtonmore ~ railway: connections from the west, station burnt, fatal crash ~ societies: golf, curling, cricket, temperance ~ land agitation, Deer Commission ~ churches built ~ from 1895 building feus began to be awarded to residents and incomers ~ finances of building for letting ~ sleeper houses ~ two village characters ~ personal and surnames ~ organisations which supported villagers ~ village celebrations.

Ch 10 Soldierly and Spiritual Strife, Early 1900s. 167
Background to Boer War ~ Newtonmore Volunteers departing ~ their experiences in South Africa ~ welcome home ~ Church schism ~ resolution of schism.

Ch 11 Progression and Processions, 1900-1911. 178
Volunteers return to a different world ~ herding ~ Newtonmore becoming progressively popular with visitors ~ tourist accommodation ~ Village Committee ~ infrastructure upgrades ~ Cattanach bards ~ Gaelic Bible Class ~ Newtonmore hotels ~ bankruptcy ~ house names ~ Johnnie Blair ~ campaign to secure access to Glen Banchor ~ unrest in Europe ~ house building continues ~ talented ladies ~ increasing diversity of occupations and retailers ~ support for young and old ~ more new infrastructure and extension of the school ~ connections to royalty.

Ch 12 The Silver Key to prosperity? 1911-1913. 209
Village Committee's greatest challenge ~ fund raising for new hall ~ Grand Fancy Fair with stall holders list ~ extensive consultation about plans ~ opening of the new hall ~ an up-lifting time for Newtonmore villagers.

Appendix 1 221

Appendix 2 224

Bibliography 226

Index of persons 229

List of Figures

Fig 1 – Map, some pre-1890 settlements in Glen Banchor. 12

Fig 2 – Map, 1828. 23

Fig 3 – House, similar to early Newtonmore house. 25

Fig 4 – 1855 chart of lease holders in 'core' area of Newtonmore. 27

Fig 5 – But and ben style house in Newtonmore. 35

Fig 6 – Rev. Shepherd preaching in the wood at Carrbridge. 44

Fig 7 – First locomotive which pulled wagons from Perth to Inverness. 62

Fig 8 – Shop which Mr Caldwell had owned. 69

Fig 9 – Rev. Kenneth A Mackenzie. 81

Fig 10 – Old graveyard sign. 87

Fig 11 – A bone shaker. 88

Fig 12 – 1871 heads of households in central core of Newtonmore. 92

Fig 13 – Map showing where some 1871 householders lived. 93

Fig 14 – Veranda at end of old Post Office. 98

Fig 15 – Cattanach family, c 1892. 101

Fig 16 – Seven descendants of Donald Cattanach and Ann Mackay, Croftbeg. 129

Fig 17 – Unie. 131

Fig 18 – Macdonald farmstead, Westerton, Glenbanchor. 135

Fig 19 – Ewen Macpherson Cattanach. 139

Fig 20 – The Hotel, letterhead. 140

Fig 21 – Donald Cattanach, catechist. 142

Fig 22 – Anderson's Hotel, Rockview, old Toll House. 144

Fig 23 – Malcolm Cattanach. 150

Fig 24 – East End, from Pine Cottage to the new Balavil Hotel. 154

Fig 25 – Chart for 1897 map. 156

Fig 26 – Map,1897. 157

Fig 27 – Post Office and Main Street. 169

Fig 28 – Volunteers from Badenoch who were selected to serve in South Africa. 170

Fig 29 – Free Church party outside the original Newtonmore Village Hall. 175

Fig 30 – United Free Church party passing Anderson's Temperance Hotel and Ivy Cottage. 176

Fig 31 – Road roller at The Hotel. 182

Fig 32 – Angus Macpherson's shop at Cor an easan. 184

Fig 33 – Am Bèicear Bàn with his horse and bakery cart. 185

Fig 34 – Two-bay Balavil Hotel and gardens. 189
Fig 35 – West End, Pre-1900. 190
Fig 36 – West End, 1908/09. 191
Fig 37 – Group outside Simpson's Temperance Hotel, 1908. 192
Fig 38 – Opening of new road to the station, 1907. 203
Fig 39 – Villagers preparing to welcome the King, 1909. 207
Fig 40 – Construction of Coig na Shee, 1903. 210
Fig 41 – 1887 Bond, cover. 224
Fig 42 – 1887 Bond details. 225

For my sons, Alister, Robert and Andrew

Cùm dlùth ri dualchas ur sinnsre.

Remain faithful to the cultural heritage of your ancestors.

Introduction

Two hundred years ago Newtonmore (*Baile Ùr an t-Slèibh,* The New Town of the Moor) slowly began to emerge on the moors of Banchor, Clune and Strone. This book, written in 2020, charts its early years, the hard times and the more prosperous years, as pre-WW1 it rose to prominence as one of the most popular tourist destinations in the Highlands of Scotland. That success was due to the hard work, foresight and dedication of The New Townies of the Moor.

Newtonmore is a lovely village situated north-west of the River Spey in the Badenoch area of the Central Highlands of Scotland. *Bàideanach* (drowned place) is the historical name for the uppermost third of the broad strath and its hinterland through which the River Spey runs. The main settlements are now in, or near, the flattish valley floor at an altitude of about 250 metres. Before 1800, many of the inhabitants lived slightly higher up in numerous scattered townships on the surrounding moors and foothills. Until 1765, when the Spey was bridged at Ralia, the routes for travellers and armies, into and out of the area, were through Drumochter and along the south-east side of the Spey. Also several hill passes including the Minnigaig and the Slochd were used.

The founding and early development of Newtonmore remains largely a mystery, mainly because there are no records of the original buildings in the General Register of Sasines of Scotland before 1876. An instrument of sasine was a legal document which recorded the transfer of ownership of a piece of land or of a building. The original document is called the feu charter. House and feu purchases in the General Register of Sasines can be consulted in the National Records of Scotland in Edinburgh. Home owners may consult their title deeds to find out when purchases of the land on which their houses stand were recorded on the sasines register. The earliest land purchase i.e. feu purchase in Newtonmore was in 1876. The primary school now occupies that site. From other sources it is known that house building began somewhat earlier in Newtonmore in the 1820s. It is also apparent that pre-1876 buildings in Newtonmore were erected on land which had been leased for 99 years. That land did not appear on the sasines register.

Clues from documentary sources; official records; wills; gravestone inscriptions; articles and obituaries in newspapers; personal family memories and local poetry can be used to help chart the beginnings and give a clearer picture of early Newtonmore. In the remaining paragraphs of the Introduction I try to indicate the sources used, and their widespread nature, in tracking the development of Newtonmore.

We should be grateful to Kingussie Parish Church for their record keeping. Yes, Newtonmore and district were in the ecclesiastical Parish of Kingussie. They still are in the civil Parish of Kingussie. The local parish ministers in the 1790s and 1830s contributed detailed information on all Scottish parishes to the First and Second Statistical Accounts of Scotland. Kirk session records of the Church of Scotland (the Established Church) give some insight into the ways in which the church interacted with the community. Before 1855, many births and marriages and a few deaths were recorded in the Old Parish Registers (OPRs) kept by individual parishes of the Established Church. From 1843 until 1855, the Free Church of Scotland also kept birth records for their Kingussie Parish congregations. When approximate birthdates are given, 'born circa' (born about) will be abbreviated to 'b.c.'. Both sets of church records often included places of residence at the time of the events. Township names were often quoted but individual homes in Newtonmore were not identified. Until 1843 the majority of the people from Newtonmore and district worshipped at Kingussie Parish Church. Many of them are remembered on headstones in the churchyard there, although a few folk are identified in St Bride's Graveyard (Banchor Cemetery), Newtonmore. Towards the end of the 19th century, Kingussie Church of Scotland produced an annual magazine which can be viewed at the Highland Archive Centre, Inverness. The Poor Records kept originally by kirk sessions and after 1845 by county councils offer some extra evidence.

Government documentation which helps to build a picture of early Newtonmore includes the census records gathered every 10 years from 1841. Although those give many details, it is often difficult to pick out individual houses. Occasionally the householder acknowledges being a 'feuar' and this is a great help. A Newtonmore 'feuar' in this case was an individual who held a lease, usually for 99 years, on the land on which he could build his house. Valuation rolls are available from 1855 and sometimes it is possible to relate census information to them. Unfortunately, the earlier valuation rolls do not include individual house names. From 1855, it became obligatory to register births, marriages and deaths. Once again, the early ones note only the place i.e. Newtonmore: towards the end of the 19th century they start to include house names e.g. 1 Kennedy Cottages, Newtonmore. For information about Newtonmore School post 1872, the Kingussie School Board Minutes and Newtonmore School Logbook are very helpful.

The Inland Revenue surveyed all buildings in Scotland in the early 1900s. Their extensive revaluation reports on Newtonmore, noted in the Valuer's Field Books, are undated but seem to have taken place between 1909 and 1912. Detailing the buildings adds a very interesting insight into the living and working conditions of the early twentieth century.

Wills and Inventories give added detail to some of the above records.

Gravestone inscriptions sometimes give a clue to where people lived and thus can help with the understanding of the development of Newtonmore. The only gravestone inscribed in Gaelic (below) gives a wonderful early example of that.

So we know that *Donull Catanach* lived in the Moor of Clune area of the new village in 1842. Using evidence from other sources, it is possible to work out where Donald Cattanach lived. (The last month of Autumn 1842 was October, so Donald died on the 30th October 1842.)

Several villagers who were passionate about Newtonmore left notes on many aspects of life there. One of those was Sir Thomas Stewart Macpherson.

We owe a great debt of gratitude to Thomas, known in the village, in his retirement, as Sir Stewart. Born in Strone, in 1876, he was the eldest child of James Macpherson, tenant of Croftdhu, and Ann Stewart. Their ancestors had lived for centuries in the parishes of Kingussie, Alvie and Laggan. In his youth, Sir Stewart helped his father on the croft, herded cattle, played shinty in the 1st team and was

"THOGADH AN LEAC SO	This stone was raised
MAR CHUIMHNEACHAN BUAN AIR	In memory of
DONULL CATANACH	DONALD CATTANACH
SLIABH NA CLUAIN	Moor of Clune
A DH'EUG AN IOMH LATHA 20D	who died on the 30th (10+20)
DE MHIOS DEIRIDH AN FOGHAIR 1842	of the last month of Autumn 1842
'NA THRI FICHEAD BLIADHNA 'SA H-AON DEUG	aged seventy-one years
AGUS A CHEILE GRAIDH	and to his beloved wife
CATRIONA CHEANADAIDH	CATRIONA KENNEDY
A DH'EUG AN CEUD LATHA DE'N GHIUIN 1865	who died on the first of June 1865
'NA CEITHIR FICHEAD BLIADHNA 'SA H-AON DEUG."	aged ninety-one years

active in village life. He listened attentively to the village elders and their tales of times past and was a life-long supporter of Newtonmore Camanachd Club. He was passionate about his native language, Gaelic, and served a term as president of the Gaelic Society of Inverness. While working as a judge in India, he corresponded regularly with friends and relatives in Badenoch. He had the local paper sent out to India. He often contributed letters to the paper in response to questions raised by the Badenoch councils: the correspondence explained facts which had been forgotten by many in his native area. His son, Niall Malcolm Stewart Macpherson, 1st Baron Drumalbyn, when writing in Creag Dhubh, 1950, of his father's life, reported: "Throughout his years in India my father maintained his connection with Badenoch. My mother declares that when the mail arrived, it was THE BADENOCH RECORD that he used to open first." When Sir Stewart retired to Newtonmore, he was a regular contributor to THE BADENOCH RECORD from 1939 to 1949, often signing his contribution as "TSM". Those initials will identify him in this book.

Among others with long local connections who shared their enthusiasm for Newtonmore with the local paper in the first half of the twentieth century were John Cameron, son of John Cameron, bootmaker, and Mary Bain, and an unnamed correspondent who was probably 'Johnny the Master', son of John Macdonald, head teacher at Newtonmore, and Mary Cattanach. Later anonymous contributors were The Two Cronies, who probably were James Macdonald (1882-1965) and Donald Campbell (1880-1964). Their pride in their native village shone through a series of most interesting articles in THE BADENOCH RECORD describing late Victorian Newtonmore under the title "RANDOM REMINISCENSES by the Cronies at Cnoc-an-fhraoich." Books by Angus Macpherson and the Rev. Thomas Sinton also contain some references to early Newtonmore.

Others who had pride in their village gave very interesting reminiscences to the Badenoch Oral History Project of 1984, when people born as early as 1888 were interviewed.

The estate records for Belleville are long gone but some references to them can be consulted in secondary sources. One was by Charles Fraser-Mackintosh (1828 – 1907), a Highland lawyer and Liberal MP with strong pro-crofter sympathies in Land Agitation who was a member of the Napier Commission. Fraser-Mackintosh, in 'Antiquarian Notes', cites the names of Belleville tenants threatened with removal in the early 1800s. Some facts concerning the early building leases in Newtonmore are listed in one of the copied Belleville estate records and in later sasines.

Many of the above sources will be used frequently in this book. They will not be individually referenced but at the end of each chapter further sources of references may be listed. Quotations will be enclosed by double quotation marks. The original spelling and grammar has been retained in quotations and single quotation marks are used for a quote within a quote. Occasionally words within square brackets have been added to quotations where considered helpful. Long quotations will have the text indented.

In the late 18th and early 19th century, a road to connect Fort William to Pitmain was being planned. Three maps from that project have survived. Along with an 1828 map proposing an alteration of the line of the road from Inverness to Spey Bridge at Ralia, they give a great insight to the development of Newtonmore.

Place-names, apart from Biallid, are as the current Ordnance Survey map spellings except in some quotations. Although the main street runs roughly SE-NW, TSM and also local people into the 21st century talked about going 'west' i.e. to the Laggan Road end of the village and 'east' if travelling the other way. Identification of buildings on Newtonmore Main Street is difficult as those houses were never allocated numbers. Original house names are given when known: current house names are dated to 2020. Gaelic house names are given as displayed. The Gaelic language was loved by many of the older folk and through to the mid 20th century some local funeral services had a Gaelic content. Gaelic was an integral part of the cultural heritage of most Newtonmoracks which strongly directed their feelings and thinking. Although there are currently no Badenoch Gaelic speakers the gentle and hospitable qualities of the Gaels are still evident in their descendants. Many of the older people mentioned in this book were known by their Gaelic names and those names have been included. Some of the Gaelic names look similar to the English version; *Catanach/* Cattanach and some slightly different; *Dòmhnallach /*Macdonald.

The Gaelic words '*suas*' and '*sìos*' are usually translated as 'up' and 'down'. In Badenoch Gaelic they are also used for 'west' and 'east'. This is noticeable on some Badenoch hill and place names. Local examples are *Ordan Shuas* and *Ordan Shìos* near Ralia. *Baile Shuas* and *Baile Shìos* in Glenbanchor are found on page two of 'The Poetry of Badenoch'. Sinton translates them as West Town and East Town. (*Baile* means township.) They are known today as Westerton and Easterton of Glenbanchor.

Money values used are in pre-decimalisation British pounds (L), shillings (s) and pence (d) – L s d. There were 12d (pennies) in each shilling and 20 shillings in each £1. Multiplication of 19th century values by between 70 and a 90 will give a very rough equivalent of early 21st century values.

Acknowledgements

It is with great sadness that I recall the inspiration and support given to me by the late Hugh Stewart, my partner and soulmate, who encouraged me to investigate and write up the early development of Newtonmore. We started writing the manuscript together but, after his untimely death, my enthusiasm for the project dwindled and it took a long time for my interest in it to be rekindled. The wonderful support of friends and family has made this possible.

My interest in Highland history and communities was also kindled and nurtured by Alastair Macleod, former Highland Council Genealogist, and David Taylor, historian and former colleague at Kingussie High School. Alastair's extensive knowledge and understanding of Highlanders is unparalleled as is David's wide-ranging and sensitive research and writing up of Badenoch history.

I wish to express my deepest thanks to David Taylor for his unstinting support, encouragement and historical input. Judy McCutcheon also helped me through the bad times and most willingly shared her Badenoch research with me. Donald and Morag Barr staunchly supported and encouraged me and spent many hours commenting on my investigations.

Many others have shared their research, images and love of Newtonmore and district with me. For that I would like to thank: Sandra Anderson; Margaret Bennett; Roy Brown; Nigel Buxton; Ùna Cochrane; Barbara Cross; Moyra Dawson; George Dixon; Fiona Dorta; Grace Dunn; Chris Fleet; Pam Moir Ford; Graham Grant; Seumas Grant; Irene Green; Allan Macpherson-Fletcher; Anne Job; Dondo Kennedy; Niall Mccreath; Sandy MacDonald; Athol McDonald; Ian and Joey MacGillivray; Sandra McInally; the late Jessie McKillop; Margaret McKillop; the late Alan G Macpherson; Angus and Valerie Macpherson of Biallid; Ewen S L Macpherson; Lady Macpherson of Biallid; Alister MacRae; Ian Moffett; Pete Moore; Sheila Macpherson Noble; the O'Reilly family; Fiona Patrick; Yvonne Richmond; Edie Russell; Rob Ritchie; John Robertson and Ann Wakeling. Casual conversations with local people in village shops and at social functions have also helped: a little comment here and there has added to the overall picture. My sincere thanks for support and hospitality during research go to Ailsa Taylor; Bill Chalmers; and Barbara Bielby who also contributed by skilfully and patiently editing maps and some of the photographs. For his wonderful drawing entitled

"An Artist's Impression of Newtonmore Hall in 1913", I owe thanks to Jim McCutcheon. I also extend thanks to Ross Noble, Bob Powell and Rachel Chisholm of the Highland Folk Museum; the past and present staff at the STRATHSPEY AND BADENOCH HERALD; the Highland Archive Centre; Inverness Reference Library; the National Library of Scotland; the National Records of Scotland and the Clan Macpherson Museum, Newtonmore – all of whom so willing helped and answered my many questions. I extend my apologies to anyone who may have been omitted from this list of thanks. All help was gratefully appreciated but responsibility for any mistakes is mine and mine alone.

Production of this book would not have been possible without the sensitive and patient guidance of David Cronin of Moyhill Publishing and Ian Moffett of Badenoch Heritage. I am deeply grateful to Badenoch Heritage and The Royal Celtic Society for supplying generous funding towards the production of this book. Coincidentally, The Royal Celtic Society was also founded in 1820.

Mary Mackenzie

Chapter 1
Émigrés' early days 1800 to 1820

The village of Newtonmore and its surrounding countryside have a special place in the hearts and souls of countless people from all walks of life and many parts of the world. The district means many things to many people, but little is known of the initial phase of the village and how it developed.

There are no documents or maps which suggest a village in the current location before 1820. However, from at least the 17th century, Glen Banchor, Clune, Strone and Benchar (now Banchor) were populated by families named Cattanach, Kennedy, Macdonald, McIntosh, and Macpherson. By the early 18th century Gordons, MacRaes and Warrens had arrived. These names are confirmed on the Rentall of the Lordshipe of Badzenoche at Vitsonday, 1603; Inverness Commissary Court records; church records and The "Invereshie" Book, which lists the pre-1705 genealogies of the Macphersons.

Tracing the foundations and the 19th century development of Newtonmore is extremely difficult. With many towns and villages that can be done by referring to the Scottish Register of Sasines which shows when lands and properties changed ownership. Estate records often

give that information and may have added detail. However, in the case of Newtonmore, that is not possible for two reasons.

Newtonmore developed on part of the estate of Belleville which was owned by the descendants of one James Macpherson. *Seumas Bàn* (fair-haired James) was born at Invertromie on the 27 Oct 1736. He was educated at the long-established Ruthven Grammar School which earlier in the century, according to Lachlan Shaw, was the only school between "Speymouth and Lorn." Further education was available to very few including some of the sons of minor gentry, ministers, doctors and teachers. James was one of the fortunate ones. At university, one of the subjects he studied was divinity. In the mid 1750s, being too young to enter the ministry, he returned briefly to Badenoch when appointed schoolmaster at Ruthven Grammar.

Macpherson later became a controversial writer, wealthy businessman and MP based in London. He never forgot his roots and in the 1780s and 90s he bought several estates in Badenoch. Those included Phones, Etteridge, Invernahavon and also Raitts, Benchar and Clune. The final three became the estate of Belleville, now known as Balavil. The Belleville Estate included Moor of Clune and Moor of Benchar, both of which had many small townships, along with sections of Glen Banchor. At one time Benchar and Clune had been separate davochs, to use the land measurement unit then commonplace. After the purchase by *Seumas Bàn* they became one estate and the boundary between the davochs became blurred.

Seumas Bàn was perhaps best known for his claim that he translated the ancient Poems of Ossian. During the 19th century, he was often referred to as James "Ossian" Macpherson, although contemporary Badenoch residents spoke of him as "Fingal", after the title of the most famous of the Ossianic poems. James died at Belleville in his big new house on 17 Feb 1796 and was buried, at his own request, in Poets' Corner, Westminster Abbey. The journey of the hearse to London took 18 days and the funeral expenses amounted to more than £700.[1] (That would be around £50,000 in today's money). It is interesting to note that 16 years later the remains of Jane, Duchess of Gordon, made the reverse journey from London. That journey took 23 days. An obelisk to "Ossian" can be seen from the A86 near Balavil House.

Controversy concerning the earlier decedent did not stop with his death. He left two wills, one Scottish (dated 15 Feb 1796) the other English (7 Jun 1793), and entailed his estate.

It took lawyers more than 50 years to unravel those complications.

James Macpherson, the eldest son, inherited the estates but, because of the wills' complexity, he could not sell or feu plots of land in the area that is now known as Newtonmore. Instead, he offered 99-year building leases on plots or tenements. Tenements in this case were long narrow strips of land extending back from the Main Road. Many of them measured about a quarter of an acre with the larger ones covering more than twice that area. Because the early houses in Newtonmore were built on those leased tenements, there is no contemporary record of them in the Register of Sasines.

It is often possible to glean much information about land and property from estate records. Some of those for Belleville Estate were stored locally at 'the big house' and some with solicitors in Edinburgh. Unfortunately, a fire in 1903 at the mansion, by then known as Balavil House, destroyed the estate papers stored there. Those trusted to Edinburgh survived until 1986 when they were lost during the solicitors' move to new premises, although some important research had been done on those papers before that date. The Highland Folk Museum holds a few of those records.

Thus, regrettably, the early history of Newtonmore can never be complete but some can be pieced together from a wide variety of sources. An examination of the Glen Banchor settlements in the early decades of the 19th century will help to set the scene. It will include some of the names and occupations of the inhabitants, where they lived, where they went to school and church, what their houses were like and what sort of lifestyle they had.

Early references to the western end of Kingussie Parish can be found in books, newspaper articles and wills. The people lived mainly in small townships similar to *Bailegean*, the one that has been re-created at the Highland Folk Museum at Newtonmore. The number of inhabitants would vary depending on the amount of land available to support them. The soil would have provided the main live-lihood of the township, which may also have had artisans such as a tailor, weaver, cobbler, blacksmith, miller etc. Not all townships would have had each of those trades. They would have been visited by packmen and traders, and they probably traded some of their own produce for wares.

Many of the people employed in agricul-ture would have been short-leased tenants. They could be forced to, and often did, move on annually. Sometimes they were allowed to stay on another annual lease. Some of them had large families and the parish register shows children being born in different locations as the parents moved to seek out land to support their families.

Life in the townships was precarious. The climate was unpredictable. Often there were several successive years when they had very little decent weather for growing crops. From the 1770s to the 1820s the weather was notice-ably colder and often turbulent. People and their animals often perished during that time. Families had to work hard to survive. They had to be skilful in using any local materials available to them for house building and food production, including cheese and butter. Most of their agricultural yield was used to sustain themselves and to pay their rent, which at that time was levied in produce, labour and cash. The most common way of acquiring cash was through the sale of a cow. In 'The Economic History of Scotland', I F Grant, looking at their system of agriculture with a 20th century perspective, described it as "barba-rously simple". Recent research, however, has suggested a more sophisticated economy than generally credited.[2] Either way, survival depended on long hours of hard work. A large work force was needed for short spells at crucial times of the agricultural year but at intervals there was much underemployment.

People had to make most of their own clothes and blankets by spinning, dyeing, weaving and sewing, although sometimes they sought the help of the weaver or tailor. They had to cut peats for heating and cooking. They learned the skills to entertain at the ceilidh house

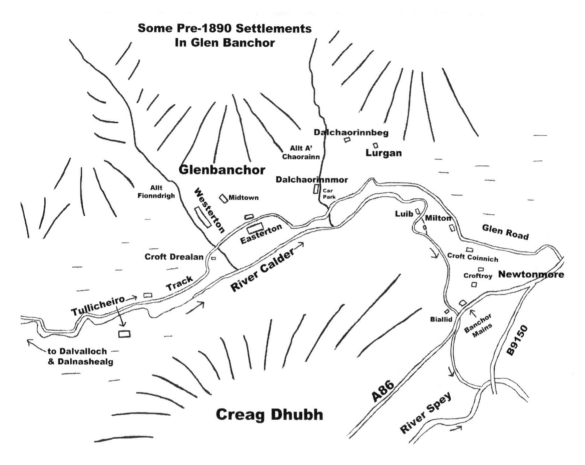

Fig 1 – Some pre-1890 settlements in Glen Banchor. *(M Mackenzie and B Bielby)*

in the community. They tried, where possible, to have their children educated for which they often paid with produce. On Sundays, they regularly walked miles to attend church.

Only one of the landowning families, the Macphersons of Banchor, lived locally on their farm until it was sold to *Seumas Bàn* in 1795. The Banchor family controlled much land and along with other landed gentry were the local elite. In the 1800s it was a deferential society, so their tenants, who had no land and very little money, were clearly subservient to them.

The names of the occupied places appeared in the parish register: many of them have been forgotten through time. In Glen Banchor, working towards the source of the Calder from Newtonmore, the following townships could be found:

Croftroy	Easterton of Glenbanchor
Croft Coinnich	Midtown of Glenbanchor
Milton	Westerton of Glenbanchor
Luib	Croft Drealan
Dalchaorinnbeg	Tullicheiro
Lurgan	Dalvalloch
Dalchaorinnmor	Dalnashealg or Dallanach.

Glen Banchor children usually had to walk to school at Ralia, a considerable distance for some. One ploy to make the long journey seem shorter was song composition. The ditty below gives a fleeting insight into life in Glen Banchor in the late 1820s. The bards were teenagers, John Macpherson and Donald MacRae. (Two of Donald's songs of love are preserved in 'The Poetry of Badenoch'.) *'Mnathan a' Ghlinne'* (Women of the Glen) described how the women in *Baile Shuas* (Westerton) and *Baile Shìos* (Easterton) celebrated the "birth of a son to the *Dròbhair Fiadhaich* [the Wild Drover]", a tenant in Easterton. In this case it seemed to be the women who wet the baby's head: they also smoked their pipes. The song was a local pastiche of one of the same name, well-known. Part of it was passed down through the Macpherson family by *beul aithris* (word of mouth) to William C Macpherson. He recited it to his nephews, TSM and his brother, James Ian, who preserved the words for future generations.[3]

Mnathan a' Ghlinne
'Se mnathan a' Bhaile Shuas ' bha ceart:
Dh'fhuirich iad tacan a dh'oidhch',
'S dar thog iad an t-acair mu dheireadh
Gun chàil an casan an greim.
Mhnathan a' Ghlinne, nach
mithich dhuibh èirigh?

'Se mnathan a' Bhaile Shìos ' bha gasd'
Dh'fhuirich na b'fhaide dhe 'n oidhch':
Bha cuid diubh a' garadh an leinibh
'Us cuid diubh a' cur teine ri pìob:
Mhnathan a' Ghlinne, nach
mithich dhuibh èirigh?

'N sin thubhairt Calum 's e
garsainn 's an uinneig
Na 'm b'fhalbhadh sibh leis
na 'm beil agaibh,
Cha bhithinn s' cho fada 'g a chaoidh,
Mhnathan a' Ghlinne, nach
mithich dhuibh èirigh?

The wild drover was Alexander Macpherson who retained his tenancy in Easterton until 1855, when aged 59, he emigrated to Australia with his family. He would have dealt with many of the small-holders in Glen Banchor and in the numerous small townships at the east end of the glen.

There was an amazing number of those townships nearer to where Newtonmore now is. It is difficult to work out where they were and also whether slight differences in name, did in fact, refer to the same township. Some are named on figure 1 and others on the map in Chapter 2. Unfortunately the location of several is now obscure. Many of them were in the area known as Moor of Clune which was part of the estate of Clune which ran up from the Spey to the top of the Monadhliath. The western boundary passed near where the Laggan Road leaves the village. The march to the east ran from the Spey along the east side of Loch Imrich. It then followed the now disused cattle track up by Glenbrae (north-west of the Highlander Hotel), to Croft of Clune and Croftbeg. The remaining section of the boundary is marked by carvings on a series of natural stones embedded on the moor and the hill beyond. Those stones were rediscovered by Dondo Kennedy in the 1980s. With Dondo's guidance, Christine Brigden and friends plotted, photographed and recorded the stones in the booklet: 'The March Stones of Newtonmore.' Records show that the Clune townships included: Revack of Clune; Craggan of Clune; Knock of Clune; Shanvall of Clune; Croft of Clune; Clachernich of Clune; Mosshouse of Clune; Moorhouse of Clune and Newton of Clune, the last four being on the Moor of Clune. The area immediately to the west, Moor of Benchar, included: Croftduach of Benchar; Moorhouse of Benchar; Croftroy and Benchar Farm.

When James Macpherson, eldest son of *Seumas Bàn*, took over the management of the estates, he radically changed policy to sheep farming and sport to increase profits. From 1801 to 1806 a series of notices which threatened eviction was sent out to the small farmers. Some of the townships' titles in them are slightly confusing. That is probably because it was only a few years since the davochs of Clune and Banchor had been united. The factor seems to have mixed up some of the designations for the townships and does not make it clear which is Benchar and which is Clune. That confusion is evident years later in a number of documents. That not withstanding, it is worth looking at those eviction orders as they give an idea of the numbers of people who made their livings and supported their extended families in the Glen Banchor area. Croftduach of Benchar had two tenants threatened with eviction; Croftroy had four; Croft Coinnich had two. There were seven tenants menaced with removal at Milton; three at

Lurgan; four at Dalchaorinnmor and two at the smaller Dalchaorinnbeg.

Easterton, Midtown, Westerton (NRS, CR8/195), all townships of Glenbanchor, were not listed. They belonged to the Duke of Gordon, as did Strone. However, a Gordon estate rental of 1804 lists 12 tenants at Glenbanchor (also 14 at Strone and Moor of Strone).[4]

Approaching the west end of Glen Banchor, Croft Drealan had one tenant warned of clearance; Tullicheiro had three. An initial glance at the lists suggested there were more tenants threatened with eviction than totals given above. Closer examination reveals that about 12 tenants were served with eviction notices more than once.

Those figures show that at least 41 families lived in Glen Banchor in the early 1800s. Some current Newtonmore residents have ancestors whose names appear on those lists which can be viewed at www.electricscotland.com/history/inverness/chapter36.htm Entries in the OPR and later rental documents confirm that some of those given notice were not removed immediately. Also, the next generation of some families continued in the holdings up to 1841 and later. The 1841 census records 30 occupied places, housing just over 120 people in Glen Banchor compared with the 41 listed in the early years of the century. There were no threatened evictions in the townships at the west end of the Glen: Dalvalloch and

Dalnashealg also known as Dallanach. They had already been converted to sheep farming.

The Spey was bridged at Ralia in 1765. From there the new Highland Road, sometimes referred to as the Military Road, followed a line similar to the present B9150 and A86 through Moor of Clune and Moor of Strone towards Aultlarie. The boundary between Moor of Clune and Moor of Strone was just east of Loch Imrich. On Moor of Clune, which was part of James Macpherson of Belleville's estate, there were, before 1820, several small buildings situated near the Highland Road. There were also several on different parts of Strone, which belonged to the Duke of Gordon until 1821. *Sliabh na Sròine,* which included *Sliabh Dubh,* was near the Highland Road. *Sliabh* was a Gaelic name used locally for a moor. Croftdhu, Croftbeg and several other crofts were at the top of the escarpment. The eastern boundary of Strone followed the Aultlarie north-west from the Spey with the middle section now being marked by the high stone wall between Ballachroan and Strone.

Thomas Sinton identified a hostelry on the *Sliabh Dubh* known as *"Tigh Dhunnach an Tàilleir".*[5] That was probably Duncan Mackay, long-term tenant of Strone, who died in 1842. When Duncan's daughter was married in 1819, his occupation was given as "vintner". Duncan, who lived in a "low-roofed shanty" where the house called The Shieling is now, may have had a handy supply of spirits. In October 1822, his neighbours to the west were involved in a fracas with the Excise. "John, son to Donald Macpherson, *Sliabh na Stron* [sic] and Ann MacGregor, his wife, was born 20 Sept [1822]". He was only weeks old when his mother, Ann MacGregor, and her sister-in-law, Sophia Macpherson, tried to stop two excisemen seizing two ankers of whisky. (An anker was a cask containing roughly six to ten gallons.) The officers had found one anker in a lochan at Moor of Strone; the other, nearby, in Macpherson's barn. At their trial in Inverness in April 1823, Donald, Ann and Sophia were examined in Gaelic. The Inverness Journal reported: "the female prisoners insisted they should only take one; and the officers would not agree to this, the male prisoner said they should have neither, and immediately carried away one anker, and came back for the other. The officers did not oppose him, fearing it would be in vain, as a crowd, principally composed of women, were at hand, and the officers did not know which side they might take; no violence was used; the officers having procured assistance from a neighbouring village, could not find the whisky. The officers had reported to their superior that they were deforced. The jury returned a unanimous verdict, handing the pennels [sic] guilty of obstruction, but the deforcement was not proved." The sentence was a month's imprisonment.

Eviction rather than conviction was the fear of the Clune residents: Revack of Clune; Shanvall of Clune; Croft of Clune; Clachernich of Clune; Mosshouse of Clune and Moorhouse of Clune each had one tenant involved. Knock of Clune had two; Newton of Clune, which seems to have been the largest of the townships, had eight. It is possible that Newton of Clune and/or Newton of Banchor is "Balnoe" shown south of and lower than "Balcraigan" on the Roy Military maps of the mid 1750s. "Balcraigan" is probably the township of Craggan. TSM suggested that *Baile Nodha* (Balnoe), which means New Town, was situated near where the golf club house now is. It was probably synonymous with Newton of Clune. Roy maps can be viewed on maps.nls.uk

Births and marriages were being registered at Newton of Clune from c. 1750 up to the 1810s. The main families living there were Kennedys, Cattanachs and, towards the end of the 18th century, some Gordons. Alexander Gordon and his sons, John and William, were noted in Newton of Clune in 1792. They were also on the Belleville eviction list mentioned above. John and William had children born in Newton of Clune and Newton of Banchor from 1797. Those place names were written by the keeper of the register, but from other evidence, including that of the Rev. Evan Gordon to the Napier Commission and the press in 1883, it seems that Newton of Clune and Newton of Banchor were possibly the same place. The younger Gordons were tenants there until 1820, when the Duke of Gordon's factor received a letter from John and William Gordon, tenants in Newton of Banchor.[6] They pled for "any land" because – "owing to the Newton of the Moor of Banchor they will be deprived of their possessions, for acres for the Tenementers there." William did retain his tenancy until at least the end of 1822. Evan's birth was noted in the OPR: "Son of William Gordon tenant in Newtown of Banchor and his wife Jane McIntosh was born 9 October and baptised 22 November 1822." In 1883, Evan wrote emphatically that he had been born at Balno and not Newtonmore.[7] Included in a notice advertising lets on Belleville Estate in 1826 was "the Hill Grazing formerly attached to Newton of Clune." So, by that time, the brothers had lost the hill grazing which was vital to the economic functioning of the farm. They eventually found ground at Ralia where they lived and worked for many years.

But why did the Belleville estate want to evict their tenants? The answer was that they needed to make the estate more economically viable. Many Highland estates, since about the 1760s, had been in a similar position. The solution the proprietors often chose was to set up villages and clear the hinterland to facilitate charging incomers a higher rent. Local examples of new villages in the late 18th century were the laying out of plots for housing in Kingussie and Tomintoul by the Duke of Gordon and in Grantown by Sir James Grant.

From the 1790s, sheep farming spread north from the Scottish Borders and, with prices high, flockmasters would be expected to pay higher rents than small farmers. The sheep farmers needed large areas of pasture free of small farmers. As a result the latter were being forced to relocate. Commercial shooting was also becoming important to the lairds and once again threatened the livelihood of the small tenants in the townships. The western end of Glen Banchor was a sheep walk by 1800: from then until 1876, the Belleville family repeatedly tried to let the land occupied by the small tenants to big farmers and sporting tenants, usually incomers, for extensive farming and shooting. In November 1805, James Macpherson of Belleville, was advertising "Extensive Sheep Farms" comprising 3900 acres of hill pasture and 440 acres of arable for let. That included all his land from the Strone-Clune boundary west to Tullicheiro as far as the River Calder and down there to the Spey and the extensive Banchor acres. While most of that land was not let in 1805, Tullicheiro was cleared for a sheep farm before 1810.

As others had done before, Belleville and his advisers probably considered setting up villages to accommodate, among others, the small tenants who might be cleared off his estates, which included Raitts, Phones and Etteridge. There were costs involved in the laying out of new villages, but in the long run the profits from the reorganisation would cover those. The rents from sheep and sport were very much higher than those which could be obtained from small tenants and the management costs were very much smaller. In addition there would be an income from annual rentals or feu duties of the properties in any new villages. A plot in a new village was small, so rents of acres near new villages could be increased as the residents needed such land for their milk cows and some produce. New villages also provided a ready supply of men to work on local farms.

Deteriorating conditions made the need to set up villages greater. The majority of the population were subsistence farmers struggling to make a living on poor land in an inhospitable climate. That struggle became much more difficult in the late 1810s. The demand for black cattle had declined after the end of the Napoleonic Wars and any income the small farmers might make from selling a cow was much reduced. The weather was also their enemy with very bad winters from 1816 to 1819: in such situations, with great pressure on stored food supplies, survival was difficult both for both people and their stock. In those circumstances tenants struggled to pay

their rents and became a burden on the estate. Despite all that, the population numbers were increasing. In Badenoch there was a pressing need for new villages for émigrés and others.

Selected further sources used in this chapter:

[1] Gentleman's Magazine, March 1796

[2] Taylor

[3] TSM

[4] NRS, GD44/51/732/30

[5] Sinton, 1906, 154

[6] NRS, GD44/29/3/2

[7] NC, 19/12/1883

Chapter 2

The first of the feu   1820 to 1840

A CAPITAL NEW HOUSE on the Moor of Banchor, Badenoch at the adjoining Roads to Fort William and Perth to let for an INN at Whitsunday first for such a term of years as may be agreed on, consisting of two large public Rooms, four good Bed Rooms with Garrets and a sunk Cellar, Family Room, Kitchen and Pantry with Garrets; Stabling for six Horses, a Hay Loft, Barn and Byre: with a Plot of Ground behind for a Garden. The tenant, if he pleases, may have six Acres of Land, with two Cows's [sic] Grass. The said Inn is well calculated for Shooting Quarters, being contiguous to Belleville's Moors.

Apply to Captain Forbes James Macdonell, Ballochroan.

This advertisement in THE INVERNESS JOURNAL of 14 Mar 1823, was the first suggesting a development "at the adjoining roads to Fort William and Perth". Road and bridge building was encouraged in the early 19th century by the recently established Commissioners for Roads and Bridges in the hope of bringing prosperity to the Highlands. An early priority was the replacement of ferries at Dunkeld by a toll bridge which opened in 1808. That enabled a direct coach service between Perth and Inverness which ran twice weekly in the winter and thrice weekly in the summer. Mail deliveries to Badenoch became more frequent, although a daily mail coach service on the Highland Road was not introduced until July 1836. The road from Fort William to Pitmain caused many headaches for the Commissioners and was eventually completed in 1818. Its junction with the Perth to Inverness road was an obvious place for the development of a village to service the traffic from three directions. Even before the construction of that route to the west, the Duke of Gordon's factor, William Tod, in 1774, had suggested that "Benchar's Lands from their Situation is the Centre of the Country and on the public Road, and their having an inexhaustible Fund of Moss [peat] is the proper place for a village."[1] Benchar was Andrew Macpherson of Banchor, who controlled most of the land on which Newtonmore now stands, also much of Glen Banchor and other parts of Upper Badenoch. After Andrew's death, his son Evan sold smallish parts at the western end of Glen Banchor to Cluny Macpherson and in 1795, he sold the remainder of his Glen Banchor holdings to *Seumas Bàn* (James Macpherson).

The above house was re-advertised in THE INVERNESS JOURNAL of 4 May 1827 –

There is to be let in the VILLAGE OF NEWTOWNMOOR, BADENOCH, WITH IMMEDIATE POSSESSION an Excellent and Commodious HOUSE, with Stable, Barn, Byre, Coach House, Cart Shed, and Garden. The Situation is well adapted for an Inn, being only a few yards from the joining of both the Perth and Fort William Roads, and close to the Market Stance for Sheep and Cattle, which holds four times a year, besides the great advantage of Gentleman Shooters every Season. A Person of respectability will meet with every encouragement.

For further particulars, apply to James Macpherson, Esq. of Belleville, Badenoch; or Captain MacDonell, Clury, by Grantown; if by letter, post paid.

This house with its accompanying outbuildings, clearly designed to be an inn, did indeed become a hotel, but not until 1888. It is now Mains House.

It is interesting to note the mention of James Macpherson of Belleville, as he was the owner of the leased land on which shinty patron, Captain Macdonell, RVB (Royal Veteran Battalion), now at Clury, had built the above-noted house. Perhaps Macdonell had not managed to let the building but he was still promoting its position as one suitable for an inn which would have been the first in the new village.

The advertisements pinpoint a problem that was to beset the new village, as, for many years it had an identity crisis. In the papers from the 1822 court case described in chapter 1, the village was referred to as "Newtonmoor", "Moor of Banchor" and "Newton Moor." 'The Edinburgh Almanac' printed in Dec 1822 listed "Bannocher Village" two miles from Pitmain Inn. Note the phonetic spelling to include the middle vowel which does not appear in the current spelling but is pronounced by local people as 'Banachor'. The Gordon Papers in late 1823 stated: "There are two villages – Kingussie and Moor of Strone. Kingussie containing about 400 inhabitants; the other not more as yet than 50, or 60, but it is increasing." Perhaps it was not surprising that those Gordon Papers would refer to Moor of Strone and no other name for the area. The Ducal family had had a cluster of small tenants there for many years, but no recent jurisdiction over Moor of Clune where Newtonmore was expanding.

In his 1823 advert, Forbes Macdonell used the name Moor of Banchor. The following variations were used in the Parish Register – December 1824, Newton Moor; January and March 1825, Newton More; August 1828, New Village; May 1830, Newtonmore. Anderson's guide book of 1834 said: "About two miles beyond Pitmain we reach the village of Newton of Benchar, commenced not long since, under the direction of the late Mr. Macpherson of Belleville, the proprietor."[2] In 1837, Laggan Kirk Session used Banchor Village and Pigot's Directory listed the Rev. J. Matthewson in Newton moor. From then the village was generally named as 'Newtonmore' although an 1852 guide book used "Newton Moor."[4] Bear in mind that the clerks of the Parish Register and other documents were writing in English and many of the residents reporting to the scribes would have been speaking in Gaelic. TSM wrote that the local people referred to their village as *An Sliabh* (The Moor). That statement might explain a lot. When villagers said that they resided in *An Sliabh*, officials may have added 'Newton' or 'Clune' or 'Strone'. The Gaelic name used in the 20th century – *Baile Ùr an t-Slèibh* – was probably not used by the Gaelic-speaking 19th-century population and is a rough translation of 'Newtonmoor' into Gaelic. Even in the 1980s local Gaelic speakers and some of their families used '*An Sliabh*'.

One of the few documents copied from the Belleville Estate Records was headed: "State of Rents of Belleville, Falling due during the period from 9th October 1861 to 27th June 1862." It listed the years when leases to Newtonmore tenements began, the lengths of the leases and the annual rents. The first leases were awarded at Whitsunday 1820. The tenants named on the 1862 list being Robert Forbes, rent 10s; James Rusell (sic), £1 and Finlay Macpherson, 10s. The 1855 Valuation Roll (the earliest VR available following the Land Valuations (Scotland) Act, 1854) named those proprietors as James Forbes, John Rusell and Finlay Macpherson. James Forbes was the father of Robert and John was the brother of James Rusell. That and later evidence suggests that the first lease-holders in Newtonmore were James Forbes (currently Inverglen), John Rusell (Truim Cottage; Tarlee; Birch Cottage) and Finlay Macpherson (currently Dalchurn). The Forbes plot was the smallest of the three, measuring 51ft along the road and extending back by 226ft. John Rusell's was the largest, being 100ft by 228ft.[3]

In 1821 a lease was awarded to Christine Campbell, 10s, but by 1855, Isabella Clark/Macdonald was the proprietor of that tenement. The Register of Sasines, in some cases, gave details in retrospect of the period from 1820. It revealed that Christine Campbell had died about 1838 and Isabella was Christine's niece.

Also in 1821 Forbes Macdonell obtained the lease to his large tenement at the Perth-Laggan road junction, rent £1.

Four leases were awarded in 1822. The lease to Donald and Isobel Macbean cost them 10s. annually. A lease was granted for the school which probably did not come into use until 1829 and was rent-free. Miss Ann Macpherson, the elder sister of James of Belleville, was given a lease at an annual rent of 10s but there is no record of her ever living in Newtonmore. Proprietors of new villages sometimes gave building sites to their friends and a plot for a school as ways of encouraging others to have confidence in moving to what was expected to be a thriving village. A most interesting lease was granted that year to Robert Warren, a young man whose family had been tenants of one of the two holdings at Croftdhuac since at least 1787. His father, Charles, had been one of those threatened with eviction in 1806, but the Warrens had continued to farm at Croftdhuac. Robert's largish tenement, on the Laggan Road, at the east end of his croft, cost £1 per annum. That arrangement allowed him to live on the land he was working but gave him the security of a 99 year lease and the ability to pass on the lease to family members. It remained in the family for three generations.

The 1862 document showed one lease being awarded in 1823, naming the tenant as Alexander Rose, 10s. However, Alex was born in 1825 so his tenement must have been awarded to someone else. In the Register of Sasines, in 1905, the then Rose lease holder, named the original lease holder as James Rusell, Dellifour, near Grantown. His lease was dated 1836 but had been granted in 1823 for 99 years. As explained above, the original Rusell leaseholder was probably John Rusell. The 1841 census showed John Kennedy living in the house. By 1851 his son, Donald, was the head of the household and gave his occupation as "feuar" as did Donald Cameron and John Macpherson. Although they were lease holders, not feuars, they were obviously proud to be home owners. The lease must have been transferred from Rusell to Kennedy after 1836.

The number of early leases was confirmed in a letter to THE INVERNESS COURIER in 1883. The Rev. Evan Gordon, b. 1822, wrote: "When I was born and for some years after, there were no more than about half-a-dozen houses in the village." Some of the rents were twice as expensive as others. The tenements which had a rent of £1 were larger and were subdivided. Robert Warren eventually had two small semi-detached houses on his plot and John Rusell had several.

The next tranche of leases was not awarded until 1829, but a map dated 1828 (Fig 2), drawn to show a proposed realignment of the Highland Road, is very useful in giving an impression of how Newtonmore developed.

That map indicates where the early buildings in the new village were situated but does not show the gap wherein the school and the 1829 leases would be developed. Three leases were awarded in 1829; four in 1830 and one in 1833. All were on the north side of the road in the

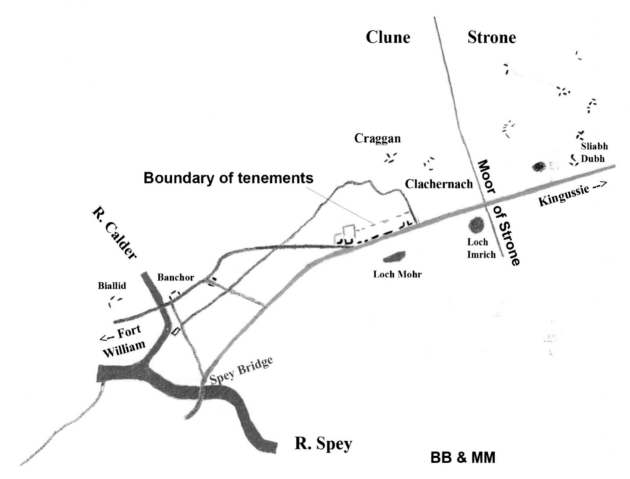

Fig 2 – Map adapted from NRS RHP 11683 by Mary Mackenzie who claims © copyright of this amended version. Additional names and structures from a variety of sources have been added to the original 1828 version. The tenements were built on from 1820. Forbes Macdonell's U-shaped building is prominent at the road junction with Robert Warren's west and Miss Macpherson's east of it. The townships pre-dated them. The crofts of Duncan Mackay and Donald Macpherson (see Chapter 1), were east of the un-named lochan. *(Courtesy NRS)*

space between Old Glen Road and Glen Road. In 1834, when Finlay Macpherson obtained another lease to the west side of Old Glen Road, all the building land from Mains to Glen Road had been allocated.

The positioning of the tenements suggest some organised planning in the development of Newtonmore. However other evidence suggests that development was fairly haphazard and poorly thought out.

In most cases when new villages were being planned a foundation advertisement, including the name of the proposed village, appeared in newspapers or local leaflets. Such an advert would have confirmed the name but none has been found for Newtonmore. In many new villages a plot of agricultural land was allocated for each tenement but not in Newtonmore. From later evidence it appears that the land which John and William Gordon lost for "acres for the Tenementers" was let out in a large block to a few people who then had control of what happened to it. As a result many tenementers could not use it for grazing. That land, Newtonmore Grazings, now the golf course, was not cultivated and became degraded year by year. Also, part of that land was subject to flooding on a much greater scale than now-a-days. A most important requirement for a new village is some sort of industry to give the residents employment and an income. There is no evidence to show that Belleville made such

a provision. Scrutiny of the Register of Sasines in some cases gave details, in retrospect, of the period from 1820. Those records revealed that the original "leases" were often suspect and sometimes non-existent.

The only detailed description of an early building was that of Captain Macdonell's. Miss Macpherson's adjacent house must have been fairly substantial as by 1851 it was a two-storey inn. The existing buildings at Moor of Strone were small, older style houses. They were not enlarged and upgraded to slated, stone and lime construction until late in the 19th century. The majority of the houses on the new tenements were small with few windows and low doors. The attic space was very low with no skylights. In the mid-1840s, Malcolm Cattanach, slater, b.c. 1822, bought the leases for two adjacent tenements from the sons of the original 1829 lease-holders, one of those being *Donull Catanach*. During his evidence to the 1892 Royal Commission (Highlands and Islands), Malcolm, aged 74, said: "I have two one-storey houses in Newtonmore." Malcolm related that the original lease-holders had "built them [their houses] with stone and lime, perhaps seven feet high, and thatched them with divots and straw. I put a little more height on them, and slated them." Those buildings were similar in size. In the revaluation notes of the 1910s one is described as having two rooms and two closets downstairs with two attic bedrooms upstairs (by that time the low attic would have had a skylight). Malcolm's two buildings are now known as *Seann Dhachaidh* and Sunnyside, the description being of Sunnyside. Malcolm lived in *Seann Dhachaidh*. In 1871 he occupied it with his wife and nine of his family. The early houses in Newtonmore were built straight onto the moor on heavy boulder footings. Along the lines of the walls, rocks were dug into the ground: like icebergs, only the tips of the large

structures could be seen above ground level. The tops of them can still be seen in front of some of the houses in the oldest part of the village. A few were excavated in 2015. They each weighed about 3cwt. The floor would have been earthen or paved with large slabs. From at least 1847 onwards it was the practice to whitewash some of the houses.

There are no photographs of original Newtonmore houses but they were probably similar to the one below.

Fig 3 – House, similar to early Newtonmore house? *(Mary Mackenzie and Barbara Bielby)*

It is probable that those early tenementers who had a building trade constructed their own houses. Finlay Macpherson was a mason; James Forbes a carpenter and two of the sons of *Donull Catanach* were masons. John Rusell, a mason from Cromdale, had in 1819 given detailed estimates for the building of a traveller's room and stable at Strathmashie. By 1827, John was farming a large acreage at Kincraig. When he died in 1859, his Grantown-based brother, James, became the lease-holder of the large tenement in Newtonmore. It is possible that neither of them ever lived in the Newtonmore properties but thought of them as investments with earnings from letting.

Building tradesmen, including John Eason, would have been available from 1799 when Kingussie was being set up. John was recorded as a mason in different contracts throughout the area, including at Glenmore. There, in 1821, he appraised the mason work on the house at *Beag Ghleann* for the Duke of Gordon who was installing a new deer forester, John Macdonald, from Laggan. As time went on, more people required the roofs (of their properties) to be slated. Slating was a trade new to the area and three Cattanach brothers, William, Donald and Malcolm, whose father had been evicted from Milton around 1835, monopolised it. *Calum Catanach*, uncle of the brothers, was said to have been the first in the area to practise slating. In 1820, he was a slater working from his croft in Strone. He probably learnt his trade on some of the early buildings in Kingussie and on the houses of landed proprietors, perhaps at Belleville where the Cattanachs are said to have been tenants at Raitts. They quarried the slate at Carn Macoul, near Loch Dhu, in Glen Banchor. That heavy stone-slate can be seen on the roof at the rear of a few houses in Newtonmore and Kingussie. Some of the slaters stayed overnight in basic lodgings in the Glen. Others who trekked in daily "carried a 'piece' – consisting of mealy pudding and black pudding – known as 'marrack'."[5] One of the methods they employed to crack weak lines into thinnish slices was to pour in water. When it froze, expansion would cause the cracks. They used sledges to haul the slates down to the Calder. They then transferred the heavy slates onto carts for the bumpy journey to Newtonmore. It was strenuous work.

The first VR (1855) for Newtonmore is the earliest document which listed those who leased tenements there. It included that year's lease holders of the early houses which were built on the north side of the road from Glen Road to the Laggan Road. Working from east to west locals and incomers could be found (Fig 4). Some of the listed properties had more than one family living in them. That area of the new village was quite a heterogeneous wee place with less than half the lease-holders

	Occupation	Born	Notes
Francis Halliday	merchant	Dumfries	He was assigned part of the original 1830 lease in 1849 by Alex Macpherson, Craggan.
Alexander Macpherson	crofter	Tullicheiro, Glen Banchor	Crofter in Craggan. Lease split between Francis Halliday and Alex Macpherson.
William Caldwell	merchant	Edinburgh	Original lease of Lachlan Macpherson, 1830, was transferred to William in 1849.
Donald Kennedy	feuar	Kingussie Parish.	Original 1823 lease was to John Rusell, born Cromdale.
Alexander Davidson	weaver	Insh	Lease of 1822 was to Donald & Isobel Macbean, Dunachton.
Primary School			It is not listed in the VR because it was free of a feu duty. Lease dates to 1822.
Malcolm Cattanach	slater	Milton, Glen Banchor	He bought leases for two houses from original 1829 tenementers.
Allan McDonald	drover	Perthshire	His lease was dated 1829.
John Rusell	farmer	Cromdale	Lease granted in 1820. The buildings in the row were rented out.
John Macpherson	game-keeper	Nuide	The 1830 lease was to William Cattanach, slater.
Isabella Clark		Laggan	The 1821 lease was awarded to Christine Campbell, aunt of Isabella.
James Forbes	carpenter	Raitts	James was the original 1820 lease holder.
Finlay Macpherson	farmer	Biallid	The leases date to 1820 and 1834. He was farming at Invernahavon in 1855. His houses were rented out.
Mrs Margaret McKenzie	inn keeper	Cromdale	She rented from the leaseholder, Miss Macpherson of Belleville.
Misses MacBarnett	annuitants	Ballachroan	Lived in Moray; nieces of Forbes MacDonell; house let for shooting quarters.
Alexander Gordon	small farmer	Newton of Clune	Lived at Croftdhuac. Brother-in-law of Rob Warren who leased the feu in 1822.

Fig 4 – 1855 lease holders of the early houses
between Glen Road and the Laggan Road on the north side of the Main Street. *(M Mackenzie)*

having been born nearby and five having been born more than 40 miles away.

So why did those folk take on leases in Newtonmore? Business opportunities might have been the attraction for Francis Halliday, William Caldwell, Alexander Davidson, John Rusell, Margaret McKenzie and Forbes MacDonell. Scarcity of land must have been the reason for some others moving to Newtonmore. In the 1700s, most people in Badenoch made their living on the land. In the early 1800s, that was becoming increasingly difficult. Population numbers were rising and the land could not support everyone. Also large chunks of land were being given over to sheep farming and the small tenants had to find somewhere else to live. In 1851 there were 78 families living in 57 houses in Newtonmore. Of the heads of the households 60% were born in Kingussie Parish; 12% in Laggan Parish and 13% in Alvie Parish, some on Raitts, which James Macpherson of Belleville cleared in the early 19th century. James Forbes had children born at Raitts from 1799 to 1814. However, his youngest son, Duncan, was born in Newtonmore in the early 1820s – perhaps the first child to be born in the village.

From 1830, tenements were offered in other areas of the village. That year, a Strone mason, Donald Cattanach, obtained the first tenement on the south side of the Highland Road, in the area where Meadowbank stands. Four years later, Donald leased an adjacant plot. That gave him tenements from where the Village Hall is situated to Tir nan Og. Donald, b.c. 1810, was a crofter who lived and died in Strone. Did he build the houses for his retirement or to make some money by renting them? One of Donald's sons, Alexander, a mason, later based in Kingussie, took on architectural work and designed many of the late 19th/early 20th century buildings in Newtonmore.

The early 1830s also saw the village expanding in the area around where the Balavil Hotel now stands. Working west from Balavil Brae, the leaseholders were Alvie carpenter Alexander Wilson (1831); John Kennedy, carrier, Kingussie (1834); John Gray, weaver in Nuide (1831); Laggan man, James Mackenzie (1833) and John Macdonald, born at Croft Drealan in Glen Banchor (1834). Working east from the Balavil Brae four leases dating to 1831 were taken up by John Cattanach, tailor, Strone; *Calum Catanach,* slater, Strone; Ranald Macpherson, plasterer, born Invertromie, but lived in Kingussie before 1831 and a local mason, John McIntosh whose lease was in the area where Greystones currently stands. In 1833, James Davidson, who had raised his family in Croft Coinnich in the 1810s obtained a lease west of John McIntosh. The rental for each of those 1830 to 1834 leases was £1. Perhaps Belleville Estate was short of money.

In Dec 1834, Miss Macpherson of Belleville advertised farm leases in areas near the village and also: "Building Leases of 99 yrs will be given to industrious Tradesmen and others in the thriving village of Newtonmore, where ample Pastureage has been provided for the Cows and Horses of the Villagers." Perhaps that advert generated some interest as in 1835 David Watson, road contractor, was granted a lease just east of Balavil Brae. There was also further development on the south side of the Highland Road, with leases going to Donald Cattanach, slater; Duncan Grant, carpenter; Donald Macpherson, tailor; and John Mackay, all young men who lived in Kingussie Parish. But, Miss Ann's advert was misleading. Newtonmore was not thriving and there was only a limited supply of poor quality grazing available for use by some of the residents.

Miss Ann Macpherson had inherited Belleville Estate after the death of her brother, James, in 1833. She was born c. 1778 in London and educated at boarding school there. She had lived for a time in Edinburgh and probably knew very little about running a Highland Estate. From 1833 to 1836, Sir David Brewster and his wife, Juliet Macpherson, half-sister of Miss Ann, lived with the new laird at Belleville. According to his daughter, Margaret, Sir David threw himself into "reforming the way the estate had been run" and introduced "a new reign of order and business habits."[6] During that period, many of the leases which had not been written down were formalised.

No more leases were granted before 1841. The emergence of Newtonmore can clearly be seen in that year's census. All the 35 tenements that had been allocated since 1820 had been developed but many of the small buildings thereon were home for more than one family.

Those early years were hard for the residents who must have struggled to survive. Many who had grown up on small farms learnt a trade to help sustain them in their new style of life. Money was tight, jobs were scarce and short-term, and the weather caused seasonal lay-offs. Some of the villagers found work on the bigger farms such as Banchor, Biallid or Nuide, but that was often seasonal. People took work wherever they could get it. Often villagers travelled south or east to obtain short-term work in domestic service, construction projects or harvesting crops. Strone-born Ewan Macpherson's description of such work was recorded by his grandson, Ian Macpherson, the author known locally as the '*Othaichear*'. In the period after the Napoleonic Wars, Ewan, b. 1803 "walked with his sisters and many other young women and boys over the Grampians through Gaick to cut the harvest in Forfarshire. They went barefoot like savages, with a poke of meal at their hips to make brose for themselves, and a plaid rolled round their shoulders in which they wrapped themselves when they lay down at night to sleep in the heather. Once the corn was cut in Forfar they progressed north to Aberdeenshire for a second harvest."[7] They came home "over the Lecht Hills past Tomintoul, barefoot in the sleet and cold of autumn, to help with their own harvest in Badenoch. They were always in plenty of time to help at home. The stooks often lay in the fields and were covered with snow at Christmas." Some employment was available locally at peat cutting, dry stone dyking, tree planting, building embankments on the Spey, or in road repairs, or seasonal work with the sheep farmers or shooting tenants.

Belleville had set up a residential village but failed to create opportunities for regular employment for the residents. He did spot an opening to make some money for himself. A notice in THE INVERNESS JOURNAL of May 1824 advertised that grass parks at "NEWTONMUIR, near the Bridge of Spey … worthy of the attention of Drovers", would be let at a roup to be held there on 1 June. Local people, who desperately needed land to augment the very small areas of the tenements and help them provide for their families, must have been disappointed at being overlooked for it. Overnight-stances for drovers were at a premium and locals would not have had the cash to compete with the droving fraternity

at the auction. Those same parks would have been the site of a cattle tryst to be held on 26 Oct 1824 on "Moor of Banchor." There followed several advertisements promoting the establishment of cattle markets to be held four times per year at Newton-moor from August 1825. The site was on Banchor Farm: "Newton-moor possesses peculiar advantages as the site of a Cattle Market. The proposed stance is extensive and dry; and it is situated at the junction of the Parliamentary Road from Fort William to Pitmain, with the Great Military Road from Inverness to Perth, and within half a mile of the bridge over the Spey." At that time there were no toll charges on the Highland Road, but a toll bar was erected at Spey Bridge in September 1827. No contemporary reports of those marts have been found. It is therefore difficult to know how successful they were. Droves from the west cut off at Feagour, heading for Dalwhinnie and therefore bypassing Newtonmore. Droves from the north, if not using the Glen Tromie route south, would have been used to the Kingussie markets which had been established 20 years earlier. After the introduction of tolls, some droves from the north-east would go along the north side of Loch Gynack and ford the Spey near Invernahavon. Judging from later newspaper adverts, it seems that one-day markets were held sporadically at Newtonmore with between one and three per year being advertised up to

1859. In 1849 many of the bigger farmers in Badenoch advertised that they would only attend the April and October markets in Newtonmore. They would attend those in Kingussie "at every other period of the year."[8] In Newtonmore a horse fair was occasionally held and from 1860 to 1865 there were up to five one-day fairs advertised annually but after that the frequency of markets dropped to two per annum. By the end of the 19th century, only one sale per year was being advertised for Newtonmore. By 1870, the market stance had been moved to a six acre site on the south side of the main street, running east from the present school to opposite the Balavil Hotel. However, in the 1820s and 30s, some trade from the markets would have been a fillip to any villagers who could offer overnight accommodation or necessities. The adults and children would have looked forward to the buzz created by the drovers, their entourage and the animals. The Highland roads were in poor condition for many years and that limited the number of strangers passing along the main route north. The sound of a coach and horses, which by 1826 was at least a twice daily event, would have been a diversion from the tedious grind of trying to keep house and home together.

Had the new village flourished, there would have been opportunities for merchants, tradesmen and publicans, but it did not attract industry. That meant no wealth coming in to sustain the population.

The weather also caused many problems which seriously impacted upon living conditions. In THE INVERNESS COURIER of 15 Feb 1821, the Rev. Mr McDonald of Alvie summarised conditions current in Badenoch at the time when the early leases in Newtonmore were being awarded: "the almost total failure of the Potatoe [sic] crop, on which the poorer classes depend as their principal food for three fourths of the year; the great fall in the price of Cattle and Sheep, the staple commodity of the country [area], during the whole of the last season, and more particularly towards the conclusion of it; together with the general poverty of the country." Bad weather had adversely affected the years before that. Donald MacBarnett, farmer at Ballachroan, had complained of "the serious losses which I sustained both in crop and sheep during the severe seasons of 1816 & 1817". The weather was again very bad in 1818, 1820, 1822, 1827, 1828, 1829 and 1831. In 1827, Mrs Macpherson of Belleville, wife of the laird of Newtonmore, despaired about the "horrendous winter we have had in this unhappy poor poor Country … I never saw such a Season bad in every way … The loss of Sheep in some places has been almost beyond belief".

After a brief respite in the weather, the years 1835-8 were particularly bad: the people suffered great poverty and poor health attributable to poor nourishment. The corn and potato crops were extremely poor in both quality and yield. Early in 1837, as the severity of the famine across the Highlands and Islands became widely known, funds were donated from throughout the UK. A Famine Relief Committee, set up in Glasgow, dispensed across the whole region some £50,000 which had been contributed in a few months. In August, that committee distributed 62 bolls of meal in Kingussie Parish along with a donation of 25 bolls from 'Old Biallid', Capt. Lachlan Macpherson, tenant of Biallid. During the next two years, Kingussie Kirk Session listed "Extraordinary Donations" of over £125 received from the widowed Duchess of Gordon; Mr Baillie, proprietor of Kingussie; Miss Macpherson of Belleville and the Inverness Committee. From 1837, the number of Newtonmore folk named on the poor roll increased annually and by 1840, 15 were claiming. In Kingussie, which had double the population of Newtonmore, 12 people were listed on that 1840 poor roll. The names on the poor list were read out from the pulpit in the 1830s.

In 1838, about 150 people from Badenoch sailed to a new life in Australia. William McBain, a shoemaker in Newtonmore, his wife and young children considered themselves lucky to be part of that group. Many more had hoped to go including *Dòmh'Il Phàil*

(Donald Campbell) a celebrated local bard who immortalised that emigration in the song *'Gu 'm a slàn do na fearaibh'*. Some of the reasons he gave for emigration told of how the area had suffered. He said that they were going to a country "where no cold will they feel": that they would "experience no want": that their rents would be "trifling" and they would not have to worry about finding the money to pay them. In one verse he wrote,

> *Gu 'm fàg sinn an tìr so,*
> *Cha chinnich aon nì ann;*
> *Tha 'm buntàt' air dol 'dhìth ann*
> *'S cha chinn iad le fuachd.*

> We'll depart from this region,
> Where nothing will flourish,
> The potatoes are ruined
> And won't grow for the cold.

Conditions in the Highlands did not improve. On 5 Aug 1840, THE INVERNESS COURIER, reported that the Famine Relief Committee had warned "that distress continued to prevail owing to the partial failure of the potato crop, and the want of fuel. In consequence of wet weather not a single peat had yet been got in."

It was amazing that the pioneer settlers of Newtonmore had survived the early years of the village but worse was to come in the Hungry '40s.

Selected further sources used in this chapter:

[1] NRS, GD44/43/127/14

[2] Anderson, 1834

[3] Register of Sasine

[4] Murdoch

[5] Cronies

[6] Gordon

[7] Macpherson, 1935

[8] IC, 13/9/1849

Chapter 3

Deprivation Decades   1840 to 1860

This is a very poor village, there being no manufacture or other employment to support the inhabitants. The neighbouring division is also thickly populated for its extent with the very poor. If anything in the way of assistance to enable a few of them to emigrate could be devised, it would certainly be of great importance.

That chilling statement was noted on the 1841 census of Newtonmore by the Supervisor of the Enumerators, Mr. Andrew Rutherford, a Kingussie schoolmaster.

In 1841 the population of Newtonmore was 222 and many of the houses were occupied by more than one family. Most of those houses would have been the size of Greenbank, one of the single-storey houses opposite Loch Imrich. The wide plot there was developed over many years, with the two attached houses east of Greenbank being erected first. Much later those houses had extra height added to them. That tenement, which had been leased in 1831 to John McIntosh, was one of the first four leases granted east of the Balavil Brae. The others were for tenements in the areas of the current buildings at Granite House, Bhun-a-Mhonadh and Rose Cottage: all those original houses would have been similar to Greenbank. A 1904 report about early Kingussie said:

"Most of the houses in the village sixty years ago were very small buildings, consisting of a but and ben, and perhaps two small attics above."[1] Those single-storey buildings with low attics in the roof space but no attic windows would, of course, have had no central heating, electricity, sanitation or running water. In Newtonmore, the residents would have collected water from Loch Mohr (sic) which was situated behind the houses on the south side of the main street or perhaps the burn, *Caochan Staile*, which ran alongside Old Glen Road. Many local wells were valued for the quality of their water. Those were sited in Glen Road, *Fuaran Lag an Dromain*; near the junction of Golf Course Road and Station Road, *Fuaran Tom an t-Silidh*; below the Craigerne, *Fuaran Geal*; near Moor of Strone, Lac a Chitchi (La kitchy). The crofters at the east end of Strone fetched water from the *Allt Làraidh*. Croft Dhu, Croftbeg, Croft of Clune,

Craggan and Knock of Clune all had wells. *Fuaran Bhrìghdeig* was beside the Calder, below the falls near Banchor.

The New Statistical Account (NSA) for the

Fig 5 – Late 19th century image of the but and ben where Maggie Cameron was born (Ch 8). Each of the cottages with adjoining doors had a room and closet downstairs and two small rooms in the loft. When first built the roof would have been lower and thatched with no skylight. *(Y Richmond)*

parish submitted in 1835 and a description of life in Kingussie in 1844 gave some idea of the living conditions the New Townies had to endure. The NSA reported: "The common food of the peasantry consists of potatoes, and oatmeal in its various preparations, with now and then a little butcher-meat, cheese and milk." Most people would have grown their own potatoes. "Oatmeal … sold for about 20s" for "nine stones" … "beef, 5d. or 6d. per lb; cheese, 7s." Butter cost 9d per lb and mutton was 6d per lb. "Day labourers received in summer 1s. per day with, and 1s. 6d. without, victuals; and women 6d. or 9d., according as they supply themselves with food or not; when engaged at harvest work, they receive 1s. per day, with victuals. Mason's work, at from 2s. 3d. to 2s. 6d. when hired by the day, and carpenters at 2s." So, the joiner could have bought about a pound of meat; a pound of cheese and six pounds of meal with his day's wages. (Today, a joiner could buy much more with his day's pay.) Wages were similar in 1844: "Women were employed at the Kingussie Peat Moss at 9d and 1s per day, while men received 1s 3d and 1s 6d. Many women from Newtonmore walked all the way to and from the moss – a distance of fully six miles – putting in a hard day's work for that miserable sum, and yet people seemed as happy then as now." ("1s." is a shilling: there were 20s. in a pound. There were 12d (pennies) in one shilling.)

In the 1841 census, many a man living in Newtonmore gave his occupation as an agricultural labourer but in that census several occupations were lumped together under one heading. 'Agricultural labourers' could have been farmers, shepherds, ploughmen or other land workers. There were also two cattle dealers and two gamekeepers. Serving the public there were three shoemakers; two tailors; two hand-loom weavers; a teacher; a merchant; a road contractor and an inn-keeper. A former Gordon Highlander was listed as a pensioner. He would have fought in the Napoleonic Wars and was receiving a British Army pension. There was no welfare state and no state pension. Where female occupations were given, there were many "female day labourers" along with six female servants and a dressmaker. Two women and one man were listed as begging and one female as a pauper. Some did not state an occupation. The building trade was upheld by three masons; a labourer; three carpenters; a plasterer and two slaters.

Three young Cattanach slaters were mentioned in chapter 2. They served their apprenticeship with their uncle *Calum Catanach*, b. 1775, who had been working in that trade since at least 1820 and probably earlier.[2] Slating was the domain of that Cattanach family. William Cattanach, elder half-brother of Donald and Malcolm, had been a slater from 1826. William was soon joined in the trade by Donald and later Malcolm. In 1841, Malcolm was living with his widower father, John, in a rented house in Newtonmore. Donald was lodging with relatives in Strone in 1841, but may have been the lessee of the house in which his father was living. Donald's and Malcolm's mother, Isabella McIntosh from Milton, had "died in child-bed" when Malcolm was nearly five years old, c.1826.[3] Those four Cattanachs were the only slaters in Kingussie Parish in 1841 and 1851. In many cases the occupation given at a census was only an indication of what a person did to support himself. Malcolm was known also to have been a baker whose oven was in an outhouse in his back garden. Malcolm gave his occupation as slater and farmer in 1881.

A few of the tenementers managed to rent small areas of land around Newtonmore at Clachernach, Newton Parks, Croftdhuac and small parts of Banchor. Behind their dwellings they had basic outhouses which were byres for a cow or two and barns for hay and other fodder. Robert Forbes, a schoolmate of Malcolm's, also had several occupations: at various times he was a labourer, a butcher, a plasterer and an inn-keeper. The inn-keeper in 1841 was Alexander Wilson, who had leased land next to the Balavil Brae in 1831. His hotel was not given a name in the census.

Because Kingussie had been in existence 20 years longer than Newtonmore, it had, in

1841, more facilities and a greater range of tradesmen, including blacksmiths, a cooper, a wright, a baker and a butcher. It had several inns: a medical practitioner, a surgeon, a midwife, a sheriff's officer, an excise officer, a public notary, a post master and for the ladies, two milliners as well as several dressmakers. The church, minister and beadle were in Kingussie, and Newtonmore folk had to travel there for worship, mostly by foot.

Newtonmore was still a very rural society in the early 1840s. Many of its inhabitants had been brought up in small farming townships around Badenoch and still practised some animal husbandry. The weather and the seasons would have been very important to them and their year would have been marked by events relating to those. The following traditional Celtic quarter-year events which roughly coincided with the seasons and the agricultural calendar would have been recalled by the older inhabitants. Candlemas was at the beginning of February; *Bealltainn* or Beltane in early May; *Lùnasdal* or Lammas in August and *Samhuinn* or Hallowmas in November. Originally those were pagan festivals. After the arrival of Christianity in Scotland, the pagan and Christian rituals ran parallel. As time went on and the festivals became more Christian, there were still traces of the pagan beliefs.

Most people look forward to Spring with its new life and warmer weather. Candlemas, which was traditionally the start of spring, was celebrated on St. Bride's Day in early February. For Badenoch, that seems very early to celebrate spring. To the people of Newtonmore, St. Bride's Day might have been extra-special because of the long association of the area with that saint. Within the burial ground at Banchor there are remains of the ancient chapel to Brighid. It is thought to date from the sixth or seventh century. The Rev. Lachlan MacEdward, in a talk to the Badenoch Field Club in 1960, suggested that St Bride was St Bride of Kildare, who died on 1 February 525. Affleck Gray in his 'Legends of the Cairngorms' wrote of *Latha Fhèill Brìghde* – St Bride's Fair Day – being celebrated on 12 February, OLD STYLE (OS). It was OS because the area retained the Julian calendar which differed by 11 days from the NEW STYLE (NS) Gregorian calendar now used. Legend has it that the Mill of Banchor was idle on St Bride's Day lest the miller invoke the curse of a witch who lived at Loch an Ovie.

Beltane (*Bealltainn*), the start of summer, was celebrated at the beginning of May. In 1840s Newtonmore, the date observed was 12 May (OS). Young people in Kingussie celebrated Beltane on 12 May in 1903, but by 1913 they were using 1 May (NS). When Pennant toured the Highlands in 1772 he watched long, elaborate Beltane celebrations which varied slightly in different areas. Those included herd lads throwing pieces of Beltane bannocks over their shoulders to placate the predatory eagles and foxes.

Beltane was still being celebrated in Newtonmore in the early 1900s. By then, the bannocks could be bought at the bakers but some were still homemade. Jimmy Guthrie, who came to Newtonmore in 1905, described going to Craggan to roll his Beltane bannock. *Marsag* (Marjory Cattanach) also rolled hers there. They always kept back "little bitties" and put them on the rocks for the cuckoos. Was that a folk memory of the herds' appeasement of predators? Bannocks were used in other celebrations, for example, at Baptisms, Christmas, New Year and the other quarter-year events. Beltane bannocks were different in that the ingredients included eggs. In the journal 'Folklore' in 1895, Janet Davidson, Kingussie, aged 81, described how they were made: "Bannocks were baked the evening before Beltane … They were made of oatmeal in the usual way, but they were washed over or 'watered' with a thin batter composed of whipped egg, milk or cream, and a little oatmeal. Before being laid on the … gridiron, the upper side was rubbed over with this batter. When the underside was sufficiently baked or 'fired', the bannock was turned, and the underside was now rubbed over with the batter. The bannock was then allowed to hang over the fire on the gridiron till fully baked." Catching

sight of the 'Beltane flower', *lus buidhe Bealltainn*, the marsh marigold, is thought to bring luck to the viewer. Margaret Bennett in 'The Oxford Companion to Scottish History' wrote: "At dawn everyone arose to welcome the sun and to wash in the May dew, thought to have been the holy water of the Druids, but, according to oral tradition, believed to assure beauty." Beltane has survived into the 21st century as May Day.

It is not clear if *Lùnasdal* or Lammas was important to the people of Newtonmore. In the Oral History Project of 1984, when people born as early as 1888 were interviewed, no-one mentioned that quarterly event. In mid August 1850, "The Lammas lamb market was held" in Kingussie, so the term was still in use at that time. The Celts called the festival Lughnasa. They celebrated and feasted "to ensure that the god of prosperity would overcome the god of blight and secure a good harvest for his people." In many parts of 19th century Scotland it was celebrated as a fair-day. According to the journal of Patrick MacGregor, he attended the Kingussie Lammas Fair on Tues 13 Aug 1833.[4]

The final quarter day was *Samhuinn* or Hallowmas. By the end of the 19th century it was being celebrated as Hallowe'en in Newtonmore. That festival was prominent in the folks' minds. It was seen as marking "the end of the half year containing the long days of summer and the beginning of the dark and cold second half of the year."[5] In the dim and distant past, *Bealltainn* was a Celtic fire festival, as was *Samhuinn*. F. Marian McNeill in 'The Silver Bough' recalled that the bonfires "were kindled at dusk … to combat the powers of darkness that were now in the ascendant … and to burn the witches." Also "Hallowe'en was the great flitting-time of the fairies, who moved in procession from one fairy-hill to another to the music of bells and elf horns." Newtonmore has its own fairy hill, *Sìdhean Mòr Dail a' Chaorainn*, locally known as Johnnie Blair's Garden. Many hills in the Highlands are named '*Sìthean*'.

In early Newtonmore, it was the young men who celebrated *Samhuinn* /Hallowe'en.

An anonymous series of articles depicting life in Newtonmore in the last two decades of the nineteenth century appeared in the local newspaper in the 1940s. The author was almost certainly *Seonaidh a' Mhaighstir*, John Macdonald. John, born 1875, was a son of John Macdonald, schoolmaster in Newtonmore, and his wife, Mary Cattanach, who herself was the granddaughter of John MacMaster, the first village dominie. John related how, for weeks before Hallowe'en, the boys collected bushes, "depositing them in a deep hollow at *Cnoc an riach*." The day before Hallowe'en, the bushes, along with wood and peats, were "built up into a big *Samhnag* on top of the famous Cnoc. On Hallowe'en night, the

Samhnag was lit by the oldest available male inhabitant, and shone beautifully in the dark November night. Other bright bonfires could be seen at Aultlarie, Strone, Craggan, Ralia, Glentruim and Catlodge – all blazing merrily – a joy to all youngsters, aye, and to grown-ups as well." John went on to describe how most of the boys dressed up as a "bleckie" calling at every house for his Hallowe'en. "Most householders responded handsomely with gifts of apples, nuts, 'pieces', and occasionally money… It must be recorded that on very rare occasions some of the more mischievous boys almost *invited* the close attention of the village constable, who, however, very kindly and often turned a blind eye on these irregularities." Jimmy Guthrie remembered that "The blaikies used to go out until there was a big row when the policeman was struck, resulting in a 'big court case in Inverness'." F. Marian McNeill told of a Ross-shire man recalling that, those "who took the lads' pranks badly had extra attention the following year." Perhaps Sarah Rose in Newtonmore merited that.

"HALLOWE'EN AT NEWTONMORE: Mobbing and Rioting"

was a headline in THE KINGUSSIE RECORD of 17 Dec 1910, reporting that court case in Inverness. "It was alleged that on the night of the 11th November (Hallowe'en OS), J. Guild, mason; J. Logan, labourer; and D. Macdonald, postman, formed part of a riotous mob, and obstructed two policemen in their duty by pulling them about and striking them with sticks and a potato masher, whereby Constable John Cowper was rendered unconscious: also wilfully destroying two gates." The incident happened at Heather Cottage (currently Dalchurn) the home of Miss Sarah Rose. In the long report many villagers were named as having given evidence, some of it contradictory. One gate had been removed and a spar broken. Earlier the crowd had been running about the Main Road with a cart. "Sheriff Grant put the case before the jury, and concluded by saying that there could be but one feeling, and that was regret that what was a perfectly harmless and innocent evening's amusement should have degenerated into a row, resulting in severe injuries to one of the policemen." The three accused were found guilty of mobbing and rioting and were sentenced to 60 days in prison or fines of £10. That, "the fines were paid" by previous public subscription, suggests that those three were perhaps considered by the villagers to be scapegoats. Those high-spirited youths matured into energetic young men who worked hard for the community, supporting hall events and shinty committees. Sgt.J Logan was awarded The Distinguished Conduct Medal for "conspicuous gallantry and devotion to duty" during WW1. The youth of the village played Hallowe'en pranks well into the 20th

century and as late as 1928, they celebrated that event on 11 November. They took and hid carts, sometimes removing the wheels; they tied door knobs with rope and then knocked on the doors; they removed and hid gates; they blocked the tops of chimneys with turnips. Some of the older people in Newtonmore can still recall such pranks.

In season, the country people would have celebrated the safe harvesting of the crops before the autumn frost damaged them. The fact that they thought in Seasons is obvious on the gravestone of *Donull Catanach* in Banchor. He died in October: the gravestone notes it as "*Mhios deiridh an fhoghair*" – the last month of autumn.

Although it was not a quarter-year event, Hogmanay, which heralded in the New Year, was a very important and enjoyable time. For many, the following day was the only official annual holiday from work. Highland hospitality was foremost at that time of year. In preparation, the women and girls cleaned their houses "with the aim of beginning the year in the best possible condition." Bleckies and bannocks again featured. Those bannocks were thick and made of oatmeal without eggs. The young men, bleckies, went out New Year guising, but it was a much smaller celebration than at Hallowe'en.

Gunshots were fired at midnight to mark the beginning of the year. It was traditional to visit family and friends to wish them well in the next twelve months. They shared specially prepared dishes made by the women with locally-produced ingredients. They enjoyed drams, music and reminiscences. As has been noted, life for the New Townies was very hard. Along with the traditional Hogmanay celebrations, they must have fervently hoped for some improvement in their circumstances.

Around that time the local lairds gave hospitality to their tenants and useful gifts to the poor. They also sponsored the New Year shinty matches and donated post-match refreshments: a treat for all in the community. The most widely reported of those contests took place at Cluny. There, most of Laggan and many from adjacent areas including Newtonmore, were treated to a game, some drams and traditional food by "Old Cluny", Ewen Macpherson, chief of the clan from 1817 to 1885. Cluny, a fluent Gaelic speaker, lived at Cluny Castle and thoroughly immersed himself in local customs. He was involved in, and often the leader of, many organisations which helped with the improvement of Badenoch. Other local lairds also "gave" ball-plays at New Year.

The lairds of Newtonmore were the Macphersons of Belleville. When they had an important event it was often celebrated by the people of the village. One such event which celebrated the Free Church wedding of the eldest grandson of *Seumas Bàn*, James Brewster, was described in detail in THE ELGIN COURANT of 28 Feb 1845. The tenants lit a bonfire on Craggan and the dancing was led off by four of the old men followed by four young men, all "handsomely dressed in the full Highland costume." Upwards of 500 attended and there was "an abundance of usquebaugh [sic]." At a late hour "They retired to Mr Wilson's Hotel, Newtonmoor, headed by their piper, where a happy evening was spent. Many excellent songs were sung, particularly one by Mr Donald Macpherson, cattle-dealer, Knock, composed by himself for the festive occasion. At length all, peaceably and much gratified, retired to their respective homes. At Belleville, similar rejoicings took place." The paper claimed that the above celebration mimicked a similar event which took place when the Belleville laird bought Strone.

Miss Ann Macpherson of Belleville and Cluny supported the Free Church.

Christianity had an importance now long lost. Each parish in Scotland had a parish church. The Church Patronage (Scotland) Act, administered by the state, required the heritors or major landowners to finance church buildings and appoint ministers. Those landowners supplied the ministers with a house and a glebe and paid their stipend. The heritors and the state, therefore, controlled the church. Although it was Presbyterian, and should have been administered both locally and nationally by the ministers and their elders, because of the above Act, that sort of control was only nominal. Many Highland ministers were mouthpieces for their heritors and paymasters. Few people could read in English and fewer had access to the Bible. They therefore could not consider the Scriptures for themselves and had to accept what their dictatorial ministers told them. In the 1830s, throughout Scotland, change was afoot. The Scottish Bible Society made Gaelic Bibles available for a small charge. Kingussie and Newtonmore parishioners were fortunate that their minister had vision and empathy. He encouraged them to read the Scriptures and think for themselves. Evangelical preachers toured Scotland, preaching the Word and impressing on the people that they need not accept the tyrannical diktats of their ministers. Those preachers were supported in many communities by *Na Daoine* (The Men): lay preachers and thinkers who considered that the church, in a different form, could give better spiritual nourishment to the people. The following parishioners of the charismatic-leaning Kingussie ministers, John Robertson and George Shepherd, became leading Men who brought evangelistic thoughts to the ordinary people: Donald Rose, Glenbanchor; schoolmasters John MacMaster and Gordon Meldrum and Donald Cattanach, slater and catechist. The evangelical-minded ministers strongly disagreed with the so-called Moderates who ran the church and accepted the

links with the state and the lairds. The minister in Laggan, Donald Cameron, had Moderate leanings and strongly objected to young Donald Cattanach being invited to James Tolmie's house in Balgowan in 1837 to catechise many who came to unofficial services there. Mr Cameron expressed grave concern about that "schismatical" behaviour.[6] Other churches, the Baptists and the Congregationalists, began to emerge from the turmoil and both became established in Kingussie. The Baptists in Kingussie parish were led by the Rev. William Hutchison, who lived at Drumguish.[7]

At the General Assembly of the Church of Scotland, on 18 May 1843 in Edinburgh, over one third of the delegates walked out in protest against political control of the Church's affairs. In a brave and bold move they broke away to form the Free Church of Scotland. Eventually about 470 of the 1200 ministers of the Church of Scotland joined the Free Church. The Rev. George Shepherd, minister of Kingussie Parish, signed the Act of Disruption. He was following his convictions, but thereby lost his livelihood, his church, his glebe and his manse. Many Highland clergy suffered likewise. To continue serving their communities, they had to work extremely hard with the congregations who had followed them to build new churches and manses. That Kingussie parishioners were supportive, was shown by a report in THE INVERNESS COURIER that on Sunday 28

August 1843, the first Free Church "Sacrament was dispensed" in Kingussie with approximately 2000 present and preaching all day. The Established Church records showed that their local congregation after The Disruption numbered a dozen.[8] A hundred years after the upheaval, TSM commented that Kingussie Parish was fortunate "in that the resident landed proprietors … and the native farmers adhered zealously to the Free Church, and prominently Cluny and Miss Macpherson of Belleville… . With amazing energy and liberality the congregation had before the end of 1844 built their large and comfortable church (the first building on the Ruthven Road)."[9] The Free Church at Insh had no building or minister. For many years, Donald Cattanach, slater and catechist, Newtonmore, ministered to them in the open air. The protective plaid they wove for him is now in the collection at the Highland Folk Museum. Donald also led services at Rothiemurchus.

George Shepherd undertook the onerous task of overseeing several churches from Laggan to Carrbridge where he preached all year round in the woods (Fig 6 overleaf).[10]

The journeys made by those men were often very difficult and draining on their health. Mr Shepherd also led occasional evening services in the woods at Newtonmore.[11] TSM recorded that in Kingussie: "large and enthusiastic congregations attended the services (held very often in the open)." John MacRae, Kingussie, whose father Duncan belonged to Glen Banchor, became the Procurator Fiscal at Kirkwall.

John recalled that, when a young boy, he had accompanied his father to an open-air service at the churchyard beside Ardbroilach Road: "One of my earliest – indeed I may say my earliest – recollection … one hot summer Sabbath afternoon … sitting with my father upon a tombstone … listening, along with a crowd of others, to a minister preaching from a tent." He recalled that many of the "congregation were from the uplands of the parish – Strone, Newtonmore, Glenbanchor etc"[12]

Spiritual hunger and thirst were thus satisfied. Their physical equivalents also required sustenance. Although many of the men in the village had trades, they also needed to rent land to help feed themselves and their families. They would have hoped to produce fodder for their milk cows and grow turnips, oats and potatoes for themselves. Because of scarcity of land, the potato crop which gave a higher yield than the others, was the most important for nourishment for the families. For their crop production to be successful, they needed suitable weather. As has been stated previously – during the 1810s, 20s and 30s there were many years when the elements were adverse and countless people struggled to survive. In August 1840, the Kingussie Kirk Session noted: "the great

DUTHIL.*

Fig 6 – Free Church service in the woods. *(Annals of the Disruption, 414)*

poverty of the people arising from the failure of the Crop for the last three years."

The early 1840s brought no respite from bad weather. Because of late rains, the harvest in the areas around Insh was still not in by 11 Nov 1840. That was *Samhuinn,* when the people would have hoped to celebrate the safe winning of the crops needed until the next growing season. Alvie Kirk Session reported that 1842 and '43 were difficult growing years and a drought in 1844 made for poor growth.

The Poor Law Inquiry (Scotland) report of 1844 contained evidence from their meeting in Aviemore in August 1843. George Shepherd, parish minister in Kingussie since 1825, reported that he had been responsible for distribution of the poor funds which came from church collections and "fines of delinquents [sinners]."[13] He confirmed that in 1842 one of the heritors, Mr Baillie, and concerned individuals had given more than their usual donations but that when the funds were distributed: "The highest ordinary allowance does not exceed, on average 10s. a year … There is no provision made for nutritious diet to the poor in time of sickness, by an assessment; and there are no funds in the hands of the session from which such can be supplied." He added that the poor managed to get some extra money by knitting stockings, harvest work and begging from house to house. "People in the parish are exceedingly kind to them." … "Those who are

not able to go about are very badly off … They depend upon what people send to them, and what the session [church] give them." He said the paupers and lower class of labourers live on meal and mainly potatoes for a great part of the year. "The labourers, from their connexion [sic] with the farmers, may get milk oftener."

John Murray, Esq., M.D., Kingussie, George Shepherd's nephew, also gave evidence to the Commission in 1843. Young Dr Murray, the sole medical practitioner in the district which included Newtonmore and covered an area with a radius of 20 miles around Kingussie, told the committee "There is no fund in any of the parishes" which he could use "to furnish proper diet to the poor when labouring under sickness." He found "that a great many of the diseases in this district originate in, or are aggravated by, the poverty of the people, such as continued fever and stomach affections." He saw "many of the cottars and the paupers ill off in point of food." The poor had wooden bedsteads with heather or straw mattresses and "Sometimes no blankets, but their own body-clothes or some other covering used as a substitute – sometimes blankets that are whole, and sometimes blankets that are in rags."

Dr Murray was also concerned that: "There is no allowance by any of the parishes for attendance on the poor or medicines for them." Often he had to supply the medicines from his own means although two of the proprietors gave him a small allowance "for attending the poor upon their own estates." A further regret was: "There is no provision for vaccination."

Both witnesses agreed about the housing of the poor, Dr Murray saying that "their houses are generally turf houses, and in very bad repair; in the villages, their houses are of stone and lime." Many of the poor could only afford to rent run-down properties or huts on the outskirts of villages in areas such as Clachernach and Strone. A later Belleville estate report recommended demolition of such properties.

Potatoes formed a very important component of the diet of the majority. They were cheap, easy to grow and gave a good yield compared with other crops. The people must have despaired when the crop of 1846 was destroyed by blight. In most good years there was no surplus, therefore no reserves of food. Buying in of meal was a painful necessity in bad years.

Kingussie Kirk Session spent many hours in January 1847 discussing the ensuing crisis. They were fortunate to have recently received a bequest of £100 from Elizabeth Macpherson, widow of a previous Kingussie minister, the Rev. John Anderson. Their main concern was the terrible suffering of many of the labouring class "not upon the Poors' Roll", due to "the almost total failure of the potatoe [sic] crop – the high price of provisions – and the severity of the Winter." They resolved to use £50 to provide "meal, money or Seed Potatoes as may be considered best hereafter." Since 1845, the "Poors' Roll" had become the responsibility of the new Parochial Boards and the church awards would have been extra to any other relief given.

The community expressed their concerns at a meeting of villagers from Kingussie, Newtonmore and Lynchat in February 1847.[14] They reckoned that 10 lbs of oatmeal per week was "necessary for the support of each individual" and worked out that about 3000 bolls would be needed to feed people until the next harvest. They resolved to elect a committee including two from Newtonmore and to open a depot there. That store was dilapidated by 1863 and, from then, Newtonmore was supplied with meal from the Kingussie depot.[15]

The extent of the misery was evidenced in a document headed "List of Destitute families in the United Parish of Kingussie and Insh appointed by the local committee on the 23rd March 1847 to obtain relief in meal from the £100 sent by 'The Central Board of Management for Highland Relief' in Edinburgh." No-one would have wanted to appear on that list. Only those who were impoverished were eligible for help. Thirty seven heads of households in Newtonmore were awarded relief, roughly half the families there at that time.

The list included two tailors; two slaters; two carters; two needleworkers; a shoemaker; a plaisterer (sic); a carpenter and a 75-year-old herd. The others were listed as laborers (sic) and included 21 women of whom eight were widows. To earn their relief in meal, each claimant had to perform tasks set by the board. The 80-year-old carpenter, James Forbes, had to cultivate his garden and 48-year-old Donald Cameron had to repair his thatch and whitewash his house. The quantity of meal awarded varied according to the number in the house and their ages. It was supposed to sustain them for a month. The eldest claimant was an 84-year-old labourer, "Widow John McIntosh". She received 35 lb. of meal in return for whitewashing her room and putting her garden in order. The gardens were vitally important as a source of food. Ranald Macpherson, the 58-year-old plasterer who had a big household to support, was given 185 lb of meal. Some of the others who received assistance were: 60-year-old Lachlan Rose; William Cattanach, 48, slater; William Stewart, 32, shoemaker; Donald Macpherson, tailor and 50-year-old Angus Kennedy. Young father, James MacLaen (sic), 34, claimed for himself, his wife and two young children. In 1842, James had married Janet Ross, a servant to James Mitchell at Ribigill, Tongue. Mitchell was a well-to-do sheep farmer. He had been born in the Parish of Kingussie,

as was Maclean. The Macleans' eldest child was born in Tongue Parish in 1843 and their second child, Betsy, was born in Kingussie Parish in 1845. Returning to his home area, James set up trade in Newtonmore as a carter. He did not have time to establish his business before disaster struck in the form of potato blight. Some of the 37 claimants were also being supplied with meal and money from the churches in Kingussie. That was badly needed as the amounts of meal provided could "barely sustain basic physiological function".[16]

An eyewitness account from journalist Robert Somers, who visited Badenoch about the end of October 1847, was very discouraging. Of Newtonmore, he said: "Here the propertyless, the dependant, and the wretched of the parish, are gathered. Small pieces of land are attached to most of the houses; but few of them are larger than ordinary village gardens; while the only external support given to the trade of the place is derived from a number of small crofters, who are located on a rocky acclivity that stretches back behind the hamlet."[17]

Following the distress of 1847, potato blight receeded, but yields were poor and the fear of that disease a constant worry. The remainder of the Elizabeth Anderson bequest was used during the next two years for coals and meal for the poor. The church was also able to disperse a donation of five guineas from John Grant, Esq of Malta and interest from a bequest by

Allan Macpherson, merchant, Kingussie. Local proprietors continued to give gifts to the poor for many years. The Relief Board gave support until the autumn of 1850. During the 1820s and '30s people from Newtonmore could have supplemented their income by obtaining short-term work in other parts of Scotland. Potential earnings from such temporary migration were greatly reduced in the late 1840s. A sharp fall in the price of black cattle and a slump in the industrial economy of the Lowlands made seasonal work less easy to find.

After those traumatic times the villagers struggled on and tried to rebuild their lives with mixed success. James Forbes was recorded on the 1851 census but died before 1855, however his children made important contributions to an expanding Newtonmore. Donald Cameron died in 1860. His wife, Nell, survived him for 25 years, living with her son, Ewen, hotel keeper at Kinlochlaggan. Ewen's brother, Angus, emigrated to Canada in 1868 with his wife, Isabella Stewart, and their five children, all born in the Newtonmore area. John McIntosh's widow, Mary, was not recorded on the 1851 census.

Ranald Macpherson died in Newtonmore in 1855. Many of his descendants were well known and well loved in Badenoch. Several of them were plasterers locally and some had an adventurous spirit. His son Alexander, a shoemaker, emigrated to Australia soon after his father's death. In 1860, Sandy nearly lost his life when working as a saddler for the infamous Burke and Wills expedition which intended to forge a route through central Australia. His salary of £120 per year must have seemed like a fortune to his siblings in Newtonmore where a farm grieve received £20 per annum. When Sandy eventually escaped from the outback, he was almost unrecognisable, wizened and weighing 8 stone. In 1865, he moved to New Zealand in search of gold. One of his four younger brothers, Duncan, b.c. 1842, enlisted in the 79th Cameron Highlanders. During a spell in India he was promoted to senior colour sergeant. On his return, he was offered the post of instructor in the Inverness Company of the Inverness-shire Rifle Volunteers by Cluny Macpherson, Lt-Col of the Battalion. After 15 years service, he retired and set up a small shop in Inverness in 1887 – D Macpherson, Gun and Fishing Tackle Warehouse. He was later joined in the business by his young nephew, John, son of James Macpherson, tailor, Newtonmore, who, after serving his apprenticeship, bought the business in the 1890s and built it up to what became John Macpherson, Sporting Stores. Duncan moved back to Badenoch and was proprietor of the Royal Hotel, Kingussie, for many years. Angus, an older brother of Sandy, the saddler, had two adventurous plasterer sons, Ranald and Lachlan. In the late 1880s, when in their 20s, they emigrated to the United States and settled in the burgeoning town of Minneapolis. Also there were Newtonmore brothers, Alex and Donald Cattanach, masons, and their sister, Juliet. The Macpherson brothers returned to Newtonmore in the early 1890s and by 1893 had set up what proved to be a very successful business – R & L Macpherson, plasterers. Later in the decade they relocated to Kingussie.

Lachlan Rose, William Cattanach and William Stewart all lived beyond their allotted span of three score years and ten. Their heirs were well known in Newtonmore and beyond, having careers in medicine, piping, business and the railway. Several played an important part in the development of Newtonmore in the 1890s and 1900s with a significant input to village life and shinty.

Angus Kennedy (*Aonghas Ruadh*) survived to 1873. After his death, his wife and most of the family re-located to Edinburgh from where they kept closely in touch with their native area. Charles Kennedy and his sister, Christina, each obtained villas in Newtonmore around 1900. Before that Charles and his brother, Alexander, travelled north for shinty.

James Maclean and Janet Ross had at least six more children. In 1851, the Maclean family was living in rented accommodation. By 1854 James, along with others, had obtained rented land at Clachernach which provided keep for his horse. In 1856, he was able to lease a tenement and build the family home. It still stands proudly in the Main Street, opposite the school. Many will remember his namesake – Jimmy Maclean, B.E.M.[18] and his lovely garden. Jimmy was the cheerful lollipop man who, in the 1980s, carefully escorted our children safely across the road to school. A view of the west gable of the house reveals the roof line of the original single storey building. After working away from home, Jimmy returned and added height and rooms to the house.

Donald Macpherson, tailor in Newtonmore from at least 1838, his wife, Kate MacGregor, and four children emigrated on *The Chance* which left Liverpool on 24 July 1852, arriving in Melbourne three months later. It was a perilous journey which 46 of the passengers, one in ten, did not survive. Berkeley Hutchinson, surgeon, was the government doctor on *The Chance*. All his children – Arabella Ann, Robert Burns and Arthur Vincent – died on board in September. They were the great grandchildren of Robert Burns.

Many young people from Badenoch, including some from the Newtonmore area, emigrated in the 40s and 50s. They had heard of family and friends making a good life for themselves in Australia and Canada where there was plenty of land and good job opportunities. From the mid 1850s news of the gold rush in Australia lured many away.

In 1851, in the enumeration district which

stretched from Moor of Strone to Croftdhuac, 78 households living in 57 houses were listed. Conditions were cramped and at least 27 people were paupers. Those facts suggest that there was still much deprivation.

New life brings new hope and many children born in the troubled times of the 1840s went on to make their mark. The Newtonmore blacksmith, George McCook, had two children born then: Joseph became a gamekeeper in the Ben Alder area and an infamous bothy there bears his name. There were many fallacies about the bothy, one being that Joseph hanged himself there. The late Donnie Wilson, Blargie, was adamant that his grandfather, Joseph, had died peacefully, in his bed, in 1933, at the East End of Newtonmore. Donnie said that some of the stories had been spread by Finlay McIntosh, gamekeeper, and Ian Macpherson, novelist, to discourage deer poachers from using the empty cottage in the 1930s. Hannah McCook and her husband, Alexander Macpherson, had at least 11 children, known as "the Hannahs". Several surnames were borne by many in Newtonmore at that time, Macpherson being among them. Families were often known by their byname. Macdonalds and Cattanachs were also legion and attracted bynames. Seven of the children of Malcolm Cattanach, slater, were born in the 1840s. The eldest son, John, *Am Bèicear Bàn,* (the fair-haired baker), became very well known throughout Badenoch.

The children of the 40s and 50s were born into and grew up in a community which was described by one writer as "by no means distinguished for progressiveness."[19] The years of famine and poverty seemed to have drained the spirit of the people. That the Parochial Board continued to provide for the poor is evidenced by their regular adverts throughout the 1850s. Several times each year they advertised for up to 100 bolls (each containing 140 lbs) of oatmeal. Some short-term work might have been available in 1857 embanking the Spey meadow grounds of Newtonmore and Strone[20] but the community received an economic blow in the summer of 1859 when the Newtonmore (Glenbanchor) Shootings remained unlet on 11 August.[21] The money usually brought into the local economy by shooting parties would have been sorely missed. Dozens of men and women would have lost out on associated employment opportunities. The tenants of those shootings usually rented the largest house in the village: the one advertised by Forbes Macdonell which his nieces, the Misses MacBarnett, had fallen heir to. The following spring, they advertised that house for sale, the description being almost identical to the original adverts of the 1820s.[22] The second biggest house in Newtonmore, that of merchant William Caldwell, was also for sale.[23] Did the fact that neither was sold indicate a lack of confidence in the future prosperity of Newtonmore?

The indebtedness of many Badenoch people was revealed in 1859 in the "Inventory of the Personal Estate of John Russell, sometime Tacksman of Kincraig."[24] John had a healthy bank balance but a very long list of people who owed him money. The roll of debtors was differentiated into three categories. Those were 11 "good" debts which, it was hoped, could be repaid; 28 were classed as "doubtful" and 85 "wholly irrecoverable" debts. John's properties in Newtonmore passed to his brother James. The total value of the estate was £4877, equivalent to around £400,000 now-a-days.

The less affluent of Newtonmore just survived the 40s and 50s. Despite the hardship, the population rose from 222 in 1841; 284 in 1851, to 344 in 1861. A change in fortune was needed if the village was to prosper.

Selected further sources used in this chapter:

1. KR, 9/7/1904
2. PJ, 14/10/1899
3. Royal Commission (Highlands and Islands), 14/8/1894
4. BR, series, Sept 1949
5. Grant, 1995, 359
6. GB0232,CH2/394/2, 85
7. Andsell, 45
8. GB0232,CH2/1419/5, 1906
9. BR, May 1943
10. Brown, 414
11. The Witness, Edinburgh, 28/8/1847
12. Glimpses, 123
13. NSA, Kingussie, 78
14. IC, 10/3/1847
15. GB0232, C1/7/15/1
16. www.clone.caledonianmercury.com/tag/medicine
17. Somers, 31
18. 1989 New Year Honours
19. Evening Telegraph, Angus, 25/8/1877
20. IC, 30/4/1857
21. IC, 11/8/1859
22. IC, 20/3/1860
23. IC, 26/1/1860
24. NRS, SC29/44/10

Chapter 4

Railmen and Riflemen   1860s

THE INVERNESS ADVERTISER, 6 July 1860, displayed an invitation to purchase shares in the Inverness and Perth Junction Railway Company. "The proposed undertaking will complete a direct through line of Railway between Perth and Inverness … It will thus form the last section of the great central line from London, and enable a passenger to travel without change of carriage from London to Inverness in sixteen hours… The line … will command the whole through traffic in passengers, cattle, sheep, fish and general produce … this alone will yield an ample return on the Capital. Beside this traffic, and the ordinary local traffic of agricultural and pastoral districts, a very large amount of traffic will arise upon the line throughout its whole length, in the imports of coal and lime, and the export of timber from the great forests in the immediate neighbourhood of the Railway." A month later the same newspaper reported that Mr Mitchell, CE (civil engineer), and staff were surveying the proposed line.

The movers and shakers behind the proposal were the many big landowners through whose properties the line would pass. "Every one of the fifteen Inverness and Perth Junction Railway (I & PJR) directors in 1861 was a Highland Landowner or estate commissioner." Their motivation was that the railway could bring shooting tenants and their retinues to the estates and also export their livestock in good condition rather than sending them on a long drove during which they would lose condition. They also hoped it would open up the country to trade. Local proprietors on the provisional committee were James Evan Baillie of Kingussie and Cluny Macpherson. The latter owned much of Nuide as well as several estates in Laggan Parish in 1860. Miss Ann Macpherson of Belleville, who owned three estates, Etteridge, Phones and Belleville, through which the railway would run, was not on the committee. She was over 80 years of age but she supported it by buying "Sixty shares of £10 each."[1]

This was third time lucky for the backers of a direct railway from Inverness to Perth avoiding the longer route via Aberdeen, then the only route available. A direct line, via Drumochter, had been proposed in the mid-1840s but it was rejected because the height and gradients made that proposal unworkable. The proposals had been revived in 1853 and meetings held in Pitlochry, Kingussie, Grantown and Inverness. Cluny Macpherson was chairman of the provisional committee. Finding finance for the scheme proved too difficult, so they chose to build a line from Inverness to Nairn, being the first part of the longed-for direct Perth to Inverness line. Meanwhile, the great road and rail engineer, Joseph Mitchell, who had surveyed the land, was determined to push forward a scheme which would work.

Mitchell's very detailed survey and proposals of 1860, 'PLANS & SECTIONS OF THE INVERNESS & PERTH JUNCTION RAILWAY', can be viewed in Inverness Library. The south Badenoch section of the route will surprise Newtonmore folk. Near Etteridge, the planned line would have swung east through Glenfernisdale passing Loch Etteridge and Phones almost following the line of the Wade Military Road. Continuing roughly north-east through Nuide Estate the proposed route passed south of *Balinver* (Inverton) before crossing the River Spey. It would then have run north of the Dell (shinty pitch) and crossed Ruthven Road and the River Gynack. The track would have continued diagonally across the flood plain towards the east end of Kingussie and passed obliquely over the ground where there are now allotments. The nearest point to Kingussie would have been at the village's south east corner, south of the parish church. Those plans would have accompanied the application to parliament for approval of the line. On 22 July 1861, the Government authorised "An Act for making a Railway from Forres to Birnam, near Dunkeld … to be called The Inverness and Perth Junction Railway"

Communication links are vital to the development of a community. One of the big spurs to the development of Newtonmore was the opening of the Fort William-Pitmain road and its intersection with the Perth-Inverness road: but Newtonmore was still difficult to access. The road network was in poor repair and journey times, for the mail coach and carriers, were very long. There were regular stage coaches to Perth and Inverness but no scheduled link to the west. Most tourists did not venture north beyond Blair Atholl and Pitlochry. According to Mitchell's 1860 plan, Newtonmore would have been by-passed. Had that been the case, would Newtonmore's population have decreased rapidly, as did Tomintoul's or would Newtonmore's desperate plight have increased even further?

That was not the first proposition to bypass Newtonmore. George and Peter Anderson, in the third edition of their well-researched and comprehensive 'Guide to the Highlands and

Islands of Scotland' (1850), made a similar suggestion: "At Ettridge Bridge … the old military way left Glen Truim and proceeded in a direct line eastwards through Glenfernisdale … keeping all the way along a fine gravel terrace, and considerably shorter than the present line of road, which makes a detour to secure a foundation of rock for a bridge across the Spey [at Ralia] … near Kingussie … a wooden bridge has recently been erected south of the west end of the village, communicating with the south bank of the Spey … and if the approaches to this bridge could be well protected from the over-flowings of the river, the public road should cross here by a stone bridge and proceed southwards by the direct line through Glenfernisdale."

The building of the 104-mile I & PJR line was an impressive feat of engineering and construction. It was completed in less than two years; an amazingly quick time considering the many hazards which had to be overcome. Lady Seafield cut the first sod at Forres, Morayshire on 17 Oct 1861. The work was put out to tender in various sections, with the final two sections comprising the stretch in Badenoch from Kinrara Post Office to the county boundary. Gowans and Mackay won the contracts for both sections.[2] Unusually, two contiguous sections were awarded to the same contractor. The advantage, in this instance, was that if bad weather hindered work on one, the

work force could be redeployed to the other. That was a very important consideration when attempting a massive civil-engineering project over Drumochter summit and alongside Insh Marshes during the winter of 1862.

THE EDINBURGH GAZETTE, 14 Nov 1862, listed an application by the I & PJR Company to make eight deviations from their authorised line: one of them ran through Badenoch. That route started just over a mile east of the Kingussie Parish Church, on the Alvie side of the parish boundary, finishing a quarter mile south of Balsporran Cottages.

The top priorities in Mitchell's 1860 plan were probably focused on the engineering challenges and instructions from the board to keep costs to a minimum. He seemed to have given little thought to the convenience or future prosperity of the villages: on that plan, Dalwhinnie and Newtonmore would have been completely by-passed and the Kingussie Station could have been built only at the east end.

The crofters in Strone (Donald Macpherson; John Cattanach; James Stewart; Donald Cattanach; James Macpherson; Alexander Macpherson, junior; John Macpherson; Alexander Macpherson, senior; Widow Cameron; John Clark; Widow Gordon and John Kennedy) in the autumn of 1862, were advised by Belleville, their landlord, of works over their pasture by the I & PJR Company.[3] The crofters had grazings on the east Dell, now part of Newtonmore Golf Course. The deviation application and the crofters' notification suggest that, at the last moment, the company had decided to re-route to the present placing: that gave Newtonmore a rail service. When the railway plans were drawn up, station siting seemed to be open to negotiation. Some lairds whose properties the railway traversed wanted stations on their land. Robert Macpherson of Glentruim, an enthusiastic backer of the railway, might have found a station near Etteridge suitable. However, Ewen Macpherson of Cluny, a director of the I & PJR Company, would surely have preferred a station on the north side of the Spey, given that he was also involved in promoting a railway from Fort William to join the I & PJR.

The work of constructing the railway must have made a big impact in Newtonmore. Because it happened in 1862/63, the census does not give any idea of that impact. Information may be gleaned from Statutory Records, VRs, written accounts, newspaper reports, Kirk Session Records, Poor Records and Testaments. There was only scant mention of the railway in many of those documents, giving just a brief glimpse into what was happening.

There must have been short-term job opportunities on the railway for local men. That would have been especially welcome in the winter when jobs were particularly hard to obtain and when men were often laid off for long spells because of the weather. The rush to get the railway open meant that the workforce laboured through most of the winter weather. THE INVERNESS ADVERTISER, 25 Nov 1862, reported that at the Kingussie feeing market, agricultural wages had to be increased because so many men were labouring on the railway. The navvies earned £1 per week, three times that of a male farm servant at Belleville. The Newtonmore carters, James Maclean, Donald McIntosh, and crofters with carts would have been very busy. Newtonmore's small businessmen: Malcolm Cattanach, baker; William Caldwell and Christina Kennedy, merchants; Donald McKenzie, tea agent; Paul Grant and Alexander Wilson, inn-keepers; and Widow Catherine Halliday, stoneware merchant and hawker would have had opportunities to improve profits. There must have been an increase in work opportunities for tradesmen such as masons: Angus Cameron, Donald Cattanach and John McIntosh and carpenters Duncan Grant and another Donald Cattanach. Bootmakers, Alexander Rose, William Stewart and Duncan Gordon and those in the clothes business, weaver Alexander Davidson and tailors Finlay McIntosh, James Macpherson and John Cattanach, must have gained customers. Possibly the thatcher, John Buie, the Cattanach slaters and Angus Macpherson, plasterer, were also able to pick up extra work.

The blacksmith George McCook probably missed a golden opportunity through illness: on production of a medical certificate, in Nov 1862, he was awarded 12s. and two stone of meal/month by the Kingussie and Insh Parochial Board to support himself, his wife and son. Young Hannah McCook, by then, was working as a servant at Gaick.

Downsides of the construction of the railway included reports throughout the strath of navvies causing trouble after long evenings spent at the local hostelries. One newspaper suggested that, because of disturbances by drunken navvies in Kingussie, more police or mounted dragoons were needed. It also appears that during the two-year building period there was an increase in the number of illegitimate children conceived. Occasionally, local churches noted such an occurrence. In October 1863, Cromdale, Inverallan and Advie Kirk Session Minute Book recorded: "George Torrie, timekeeper on the Inverness and Perth Railway at Newtonmore … and Jane McGillivray residing at Dalvey … confessing that they had been guilty of the sin of fornication." Their daughter, Jane Maria, was born at Dalvey, 23 March 1863.

Many of the construction workers lived in wooden huts specially erected for them. Others were accommodated in the villages, putting pressure on availability of lodgings. Margaret Mackay, pauper, Kingussie, had her rent paid by the Kingussie and Insh Parochial Board. Their Minute Book noted that they refused to pay the rent for Margaret as her room had been taken by some labourers employed by Mr Gowans, railway contractor. The board instructed that other accommodation should be found for Margaret.

Statutory Records provide some evidence of local men working on the railway. Ann, daughter of Donald Cameron and Isabella Mackenzie, died on 7 Feb 1863. Her father's occupation was given as a railway surfaceman, although he had been a farm worker living in Newtonmore when she was born in 1855, and also in the 1861 census. Donald continued as a railway surfaceman until his death in 1895, aged 69. Donald was the only local man living in Newtonmore in 1871 who was working on the tracks. Some local girls married the workers: Isabella Forbes wed John Tolmie, a native of Edinkillie Parish, early in 1863 at Banchor. Their eldest child, Ellen, was born in Newtonmore on 14 Dec 1863. Her father's occupation was given as a railway porter at Dalwhinnie. John Tolmie had progressed to being a railway inspector in Lanarkshire by 1881.

Contemporary reports said that about 10,000 men were employed on the construction of the railway. Many of them, including Irish navvies, moved around the country to such jobs. Craggan lass, Isabel Macpherson, married a 28 year old Irishman, Thomas Gibson. He found work on the highland railway line construction and, on its completion, worked on the tracks, initially as a foreman platelayer in Newtonmore and then as a railway surfaceman, living at Inshlea, Etteridge.

Another young construction worker was John Taylor from Ross-shire. He later published a book of his poetry and in the long introduction described some of his experiences while toiling for the contractors. Because John's is one of the few eye-witness accounts, it is worth quoting from it at length to give a flavour of the conditions of the construction workers (punctuation and spelling are John's):

I started on the Highland Railway between Glentruim and Dalwhinnie, where I got employment as a common labourer. I lodged with an old woman in a little turf house, and had for my bedfellow a waggon-driver, who was also my fellow-lodger there; while in the same humble shieling there were two other lodgers besides, consisting of an old English navvy and his wife... Here, for lack, of other accommodation, we had on an average no less than five miles to come and go every morning and evening to our work, — only this inconvenience was got over so far by our being carried out and back in the contractor's carts.

No doubt some temporary huts were thrown up near the works for the use of the men, constructed of the roughest materials, and in most cases after the most primitive fashion; and in these the greater number of them were put up, and allowed to accommodate themselves as they best could... But some rough scenes were to be witnessed among them at times, particularly on pay-nights, as may be supposed; or, indeed, on any night when drink was to be had. Then fighting and blasphemy became the order of the day. And not unfrequently it was the same even on Sabbaths; indeed, it was no uncommon thing for the people returning from the churches at Laggan on that sacred day to witness sights of the most revolting description when passing near the huts ... I got employment, from the summer of 1863, at plate-laying and slope-dressing, until after the railway was opened for traffic, in September of the same year, and afterwards, during the winter, finishing off the line with ballast, etc. Our task was then filling waggons with stones, gravel, and other suitable material, and driving it, with the help of an engine, for many miles along the rails to the various hollows that had to be filled up. This was attended with considerable risk and danger for the workers, owing to the insufficiency, in many cases, of the new-laid rails, which were not as yet properly settled down or duly levelled; nor were the 'box-waggons' very suitable for such use. Consequently a train of such waggons might be seen, heavily laden, with three or four men atop of each, flying along the line, and dancing up and down in the most perilous fashion imaginable, with the engine propelling them from behind, which made the danger all the greater. And one day in particular, I myself made the narrowest possible escape with my life, when thus employed upon a train of waggons that was driven off the rails. The engine-driver and the gaffer had been drinking pretty hard that day, nor ceased till they had emptied some bottles of brandy betwixt them. They went dashing recklessly along with the waggons as described, and the engine-driver being unfit for his work, the gaffer, who was nothing better, tried to manage the engine, when at last the whole of the waggons, with men and material, were pushed clean off the metals. Down went the whole, helter-skelter, in one pitiable heap of wreck and ruin! The men, after being tossed about and torn among the wheels and broken waggons, were carried to their lodgings on 'bogies' and carts. Many were sorely crushed and bruised; some were sent to the Inverness Infirmary, and some died soon after. At another time the waggons I wrought at were dashed off the rails through sheer carelessness on the part of the engine-driver; they were thrown some yards away from the line, and smashed to pieces. Nor can I to this day recall without horror the ghastly spectacle I then beheld of the men, some of them young, healthy fellows, crushed and mangled in much the same way as I have mentioned before. This occurred near Kingussie, and I remember the inhabitants turned out and gathered around us like a market. Another danger for us, after the line was opened for traffic, was that occasioned by the trains passing us while at work. In this way my gaffer at the plate-laying, having fallen across the rails, had his head as completely severed from his body as if it had been decapitated with the headsman's axe! At Kingussie, the Spey not unfrequently broke out over the railway banks, not only inundating the works, but carrying great portions of them away. Then the men were turned out by night and day to repair the damage, often under the pelting rain, and wet to the skin. And after many hours at such work, it was rare that we had comfortable lodgings to retire to for food or rest. For my own part, the accommodation I had in the village was of the very worst description — no fire to warm or dry you, be you ever so wet and cold. Indeed, I have seen me go for weeks here with never a dry coat on my back and as for my lodgings, the place where my bed stood was not only confined, but in wet weather the rain came dripping freely through the roof on bed and floor, so as scarce to allow me space to dress in. So much exposure to wet and cold, and so little comfort within doors, was very disagreeable, and not very favourable for my constitution, which was not robust at the best, and so I was forced to look out for other quarters. I accordingly changed my lodgings, and found it a change considerably for the better, in as-much as the house was warmer and more commodious… I was then obliged after a time to leave this house also, and go to one of the railway huts or barracks, with the carters and waggoners. In the back-side of the hut were six beds in a row, occupied by twelve men, or two in a bed. The only conveniences I had here were being near my work, and having fine roaring fires of nights, by which I could sit and dry myself when wet, and read when inclined. The carters are generally found to be somewhat clannish in their own way, not caring to have any in the same hut with them but such as are of like occupation with themselves. Their spare time was usually employed in telling stories of the feats of strength or dexterity performed by themselves or others of their acquaintance, the qualities, good or bad, of the horses they wrought with, or of the masters they had served. Some of them were dog-fanciers, and kept dogs for fighting or poaching, or both; and these they kept chained beneath their beds, to be let loose only when occasion required. Of these, too, the qualities, exploits, and pedigrees formed a favourite subject of discourse. These men I found, however, to be more peaceable on the whole than the navvies generally are in huts, and less addicted to drink. They were exceedingly kind and accommodating to strangers passing the way.

Thomas Sinton, who later published 'The Poetry of Badenoch' and 'By Loch and River', gave a brief, youthful account in the latter book of the building of the railway. His father was the tenant farmer at Kerrow, east of Kingussie. Young Thomas and his elder brother took a keen interest in the works as they passed by on their way to school in Kingussie. He commented that the navvies were "odd-spoken". At that time Gaelic was common in Badenoch. The boys would have heard English in school but little variety of accents or Irish Gaelic. Along with a large crowd, they were thrilled to witness the arrival of the first steam train. It was actually "a small service engine, that was being drawn by horses to the scene of its first operations in Badenoch, which was a long cutting beyond Spey Bridge." It ran on light rails, was used for tugging wagons or for shovelling, and was referred to as "the coffee-pot." Thomas had a favourite meadow below the farm. He was very upset by the intrusion of the railroad through it: "an indescribable charm was broken … noble firwood … torn and devastated to make way for a rude embankment of naked sand and gravel."

The highways in Badenoch would have been very busy as much of the materials and gear for the railway construction would have been brought to the sites by road. THE INVERNESS COURIER reported on 26 Feb 1863: "The rails etc. for the Badenoch section of the line have been landed at Gairlochy Locks on the Caledonian Canal. The people of the surrounding district of Lochaber have had constant work carting the same for some months back." Cluny Macpherson was very concerned because his wood along the roadside at Aberarder was being denuded by some of

the Lochaber men filling their empty carts on the way home. At least one enterprising local lad, 22 year old Affleck Fyfe from Balgowan, gained employment by carting rails from Gairlochy. Since the Badenoch stretch was the last to be started, some of those supplies could have come part of the way by rail from the north or south.

Cluny probably sold wood to the railway company for use during the construction. Morrison and Laurence, wood merchants, Inverness, worked a sawmill at Cluny in the 1860s. Large numbers of sleepers and fence posts were needed: also, the bridge which crossed the Spey near Newtonmore was a timber trestle about 300ft in length. That bridge was under threat in the severe frost in the winter of 1881 when the rivers were frozen. A squad of railway surfacemen had the difficult job of breaking "the ice on the Spey above and below the bridge … so as to give egress to the ice to pass through the arches of the viaduct, should a sudden thaw set in." The bridge was replaced by a steel one in 1885. Money was tight, so all stations were wooden and basic, except for Blair Atholl which, on the demand of the Duke, was stone built by 1869.

After all the planning; after all the upsets; after all the hard work; after all the heavy drinking, the great day arrived when the rail track was complete from Inverness to Perth by the shorter route. That very important landmark in Highland and Badenoch history was widely reported by many newspapers. Some of them waxed lyrical about the beauties of the countryside through which the railway passed; some gave great detail about the engineering involved (cutting, embanking, bridging, tunnelling) and some promoted the benefits to local people, visitors and freight. THE INVERNESS ADVERTISER described the local area: "Kingussie … is a substantially granite-built inland village, having two branch banks and a local courthouse. The hotel is one of the best kept on the route. It is impossible to overrate the importance of railway communication to these central districts… . Passing the unattractive village of Newtonmore, where the Fort William road branches off, and we trust the Fort William railway will soon branch off … the line of the railway crosses the Spey … a little below the Highland Road bridge by a trussed timber bridge of eight spans of 32½ feet each." The report went on to describe the rugged land in the Drumochter area and "the navvies' temporary shanties, with their groups of ragged, half-clad urchins." Reductions on the price of coal were detailed: "the saving to a substantial farmer will not be short of £30 per year, while to such an establishment as the Kingussie Inn we have heard the saving estimated by competent judges at not less than £100."

There was general excitement in the town of Inverness on 9 Sept 1863, with "flags flying freely from the Railway Works, the Station Hotel … and from the Royal Tartan Warehouse in the High Street which also had a colourful banner: 'The Highland Capital and the Capital of the Empire, success to the Through Transit. Clann nan Gaidhil an gualibh a cheile.'."[4] The slogan translates: "Children of the Gaels shoulder to shoulder." There had been a lot of pressure from the shareholders to open the final phase as quickly as possible to enable them to start earning revenue. Joseph Mitchell was concerned that there had not been time for trial runs of trains on the line or the telegraph system built alongside the line. That system was used by railway servants, the name then given to railway workers, to send communications between signal boxes and stations.

The first train from Inverness carried passengers, while a goods train departed from Perth.

Neither reached its destination on time. The goods train had between 20 and 30 wagons and its small locomotive, Scottish Central Railways, Engine No. 9 (SCR 9), could not manage the long, steep climb from Struan to Dalnacardoch.[5] The engine drivers, with tubs and pails, in the dark, carried water from the River Garry and eventually got up enough steam for the locomotive to proceed. The trains behind it were now running very late: those included the morning trains from Edinburgh to Inverness which left at 6.25 am and 9.15 am. The first passenger train from the south eventually got to Inverness after midnight.[6] Failure of the telegraph system on part of the line caused problems for the passenger train from Inverness. That train could not proceed beyond Kingussie until the telegraph system was restored. Any excited residents of Newtonmore who might have been waiting to see the first trains must have been very disappointed. THE INVERNESS COURIER's report on the following day concluded: "It took a great deal of time to bring order out of the confusion that ensued, but ultimately all came right, except the loss of time, and no other accident

occurred. Today the trains are in good working order, and have been well filled with passengers." There were teething problems: want of water; lengthy waits for trains to pass on the single track; engines not equal to the work; telegraph workings defective and trains too heavy. Nevertheless, the service was in demand and one goods train was reported as having 61 wagons. The Inverness Courier, 24 September, reported that the trains were "now running with utmost regularity."

Although a regular train service was up and running, the contractors were engaged for a further year after the opening of the line. The track had to be maintained, the adjacent

Fig 7 – Locomotive SCR No 9 offered very little shelter to those in the cab *(S Anderson)*

areas had to be stabilised and finished off and stations had to be built. John Taylor described the dangers of some of those jobs. As well as several fatalities on the track, a young civil engineer employed by Mr Gowans drowned while swimming in the Spey in July 1864.[7]

Equipment and excess material had to be removed and sold, as had the horses. In Edinburgh on 16 Sept 1863: "One of the most important auctions of Clydesdale horses that ever took place in this district came off on Wednesday … There were no fewer than 120 first-class horses offered for sale by Messrs Gowans & McKay, railway contractors, owing to the completion of the Dalwhinnie and Kingussie contracts" on the I & PJR. "Clydesdale draught horses and mares, mostly four, five, and six year olds were all of remarkable beauty and symmetry, young and powerful, and in excellent condition … large attendance at the sale … good prices were obtained. Two horses were sold at £52, which was the highest price… The sale realised in all £3042.10s."[8] Another group of 110 "First-Class Clydesdale Draught Horses & Mares, Mostly 4, 5 and 6 years old" had been sold in Falkirk the previous month. Excess equipment was offered for sale at Kingussie Station in March 1864. Offers were invited for a locomotive engine; 300 waggons; 20 cranes between one and three tons; service rails; blacksmith's tools and equipment,

harness, barrows, hut furnishings and other railway materials.[9]

Newtonmore's first station-master, Mr Meicklejohn, was appointed in July 1863. He relocated from Brechin Station, where he had been a booking clerk. Railway servants moved around regularly for promotion. A Mr Allan followed by a Mr Sim were for short spells in charge at Newtonmore. Towards the end of the decade an Aberdonian, Alexander Duncan, was installed as station-master or station agent. His house was part of the small station building. New names, new skills and new genes, all arriving in Newtonmore.

The mobility and commercial opportunities offered by the railway were highlighted in a DUNDEE COURIER report on the Highland and Agricultural Society's Show which took place in Inverness at the beginning of August 1865. In those days the annual show moved venue each year. The last time it had been held in Inverness was in 1856. Part of the report contrasted the ability of people to attend the show before the railway era and after its construction. Exhibitors, stock, implements, judges, buyers, farmers and the general public all had easy access by rail to the three-day show. A railway siding had been erected near the 20-acre showground at Seafield Farm, currently Inverness Retail Park, "preventing the necessity of driving the stock through the town." The Dundee newspaper reported:

"the number of entries was never exceeded, save at the show held at Glasgow two years ago … accommodation of any description is at a premium." Exhibitors came from many parts including the North, Argyll, and some from across the Border. For Inverness, the 1865 show brought an economic boon. Badenoch gentlemen on the show committee included Duncan Macpherson, Bank Agent, Kingussie, who adjudicated the swine and Cluny, convenor of the Banquet Committee and judge of the black-faced sheep. Cluny had a good working knowledge of that breed and was for many years president of the Badenoch and Rothiemurchus Farming Society. That society had evolved from the Badenoch and Strathspey Farming Society formed in 1803: a sensible change since farming practices in Badenoch and Rothiemurchus were different from those in Strathspey. The final day of the show was "the shilling day" for the public. The Highland Railway often offered special tickets for such events. People from Newtonmore, which was still largely an agricultural society, might previously have been unable to attend the event. They would have taken advantage of the specials and enjoyed meeting up with old acquaintances with similar interests.

The railway also made travel much easier for the recently formed Inverness-shire Rifle Volunteers who were raised on 3 June 1861:

the battalion's local section was the 6th Badenoch Company. The muster roll listed at least 47 Badenoch men who enrolled in 1861, including nine from Newtonmore.[10] Capt. Robert Macpherson of Glentruim, Lt. Lachlan Macpherson, Nuide, (later of Corrimony) and Ensign Neil Stewart, Biallid, also enlisted. Their experience in the regular army should have been helpful to the new recruits. Cluny, who, in the early 1830s held a commission in the Black Watch, was their first lieutenant-colonel and commanded the battalion for 21 years.

"At the first muster parade held on 31 August 1861, Cluny addressed the Volunteers in Gaelic and complimented them on the progress they had made with their drill."[11] The Muster Rolls show that by 1870 at least 42 men from Newtonmore, and its immediate hinterland, comprising 20% of all recruits from Alvie to Laggan, had taken the oath of allegiance. Those included a baker, a hawker, labourers, a mason, merchants, the policeman, a porter, a post office worker, a shepherd and the head teacher of Newtonmore School. The Volunteers were part of a national Volunteer Force, established in May 1859. Organised on a county basis, it provided a national home defence army as Britain considered itself threatened by invasion. The Inverness-shire Rifle Volunteers evolved to become the 4th Battalion, The Queen's Own Cameron Highlanders (Territorial Force) in 1908.

The 6th Badenoch Company had several local sections: the main rifle range was at the Dell, Kingussie. Cluny's land behind Drumgask Farm in Laggan housed one and the Newtonmore range was on the Dell, the butts and targets being on the southerly slope of *Toman Rèidh*. Ranges at Dalnavert and Kinapol were opened much later.

The uniform for the seven companies, by 1863, was "Elcho grey doublets with green collar and piping, plain glengarries with company badge … and black waist-belts." They were allowed to wear their local tartan, so the 6th wore the Hunting Macpherson; the Inverness Corps wore trews. "The sporrans were grey goatskin (white for officers), and the hose red-and-green mixture with green tops."[12]

The Badenoch Volunteers, in their first decade, gained mention in various newspaper reports with W Kennedy and M Cattanach among the prize winners for rifle shooting. Capt. Macpherson of Glentruim gave great encouragement to the men and drove them in a four-in-hand to local competitions. He offered prizes at shooting events including competitions on his private range. Miss Macpherson of Belleville also supported the Badenoch Company, donating £40 to their funds and prize money. The new railway made it possible for the various companies to meet and run shooting competitions. The Badenoch team competed regularly in Inverness, often winning prize money to enhance their funds. They won £15 for gaining fourth place in the company tens in a simultaneous rifle match against teams from Scotland and England in April 1865. The first Friday in June 1865, on their home range, saw a 10-man Badenoch team beat teams from 1st Company Inverness and 2nd Company Lochaber. "At close of firing the competitors were hospitably entertained to dinner, in the Gordon Arms, by the Badenoch Volunteers – Captain Macpherson of Glentruim presiding."

Badenoch Volunteers were also called upon for ceremonial occasions. There were great celebrations in Badenoch when Cluny's eldest daughter, Caroline, married Capt. George Fitzroy at Cluny Castle on 11 Jan 1866. A bonfire was lit on every height near Cluny Castle and the Badenoch Volunteers presented arms when the young couple passed through Kingussie.

The name of the Badenoch Volunteers was made famous throughout Britain by a young man who, although born in the Loch Rannoch area, had many relatives, on both sides of his family, living locally in Laggan, Strone and Kingussie. Angus Cameron, born 1847, son of Patrick Cameron and *Seònaid Phàil*, came north to work with his elder brother, Archie, a merchant in Kingussie. Their mother, Janet Campbell, was a sister of *Dòmh'Il Phàil*, the Gaelic poet. Angus, who was 5ft 6in tall, enrolled with the Badenoch Volunteers in 1864. Despite having no experience as a marksman he took to musketry very quickly and started winning provincial prizes. He qualified, in 1866, for the renowned Queen's Prize at Wimbledon and travelled to London by train with fellow Badenoch Volunteers, Serg. Munro and Pte. McHardy. Angus won the Queen's Prize and was presented with the gold medal by the Princess of Wales. Along with the prize money of £250 he was given the Whitworth rifle he had used to win. Before Wimbledon, Angus had only shot with an Enfield rifle. When the victor arrived home by train on Mon 23 July, he received a rapturous welcome. The Volunteers, including a contingent from Newtonmore, carried him shoulder-high to the Drill Hall, where his health was proposed by Lt. Lachlan Macpherson, Nuide. This was followed by a picnic and dancing at Ruthven. Angus received invitations to participate in shoots in many parts of the country and in 1869 he became the first person to win the coveted Queen's Prize for a second time. Later that year, Angus and many of his fellow Badenoch Volunteers including Lt. T. A. Cameron won individual prizes at the annual Highland Rifle Association meet at Inverness where an unnamed Badenoch team of five, which may have included Newtonmore men, won the Claymore Competition. Angus continued to feature in competitions throughout the country until, in the autumn of 1875,

he left Kingussie to set up in business in Blair Atholl. His shooting career came to an end as there was no Volunteer company there. Angus is buried in the 'Cameron Burial Ground' at Camghouran on the south shores of Loch Rannoch with his ancestors, some of whom still have descendants living in Newtonmore.

Badenoch lost another of its crack shots in 1870 when the Rev. T. A. Cameron, schoolmaster, and a very popular young man, was called away to become assistant minister at Glasgow Cathedral. Thomas retained his links with Badenoch when he later married Jemima Clark of Dalnavert. He volunteered as a military chaplain during the Boer War in 1901, aged 59. During his busy time in South Africa he may have ministered to some of the sons of his former Kingussie pupils who were serving there with the Volunteer Company.

Membership of the Volunteers was challenging, rewarding and often good fun. The young men made a big commitment in terms of service to their country, time and expense. They had to pay a small membership fee in advance and contribute towards their uniforms. They could be fined for, among other things, "being absent from the regular Parades without a sufficient reason – 6d, talking or laughing in the ranks during drill, after being warned once – 6d, discharging the rifle accidentally – 5s." However they would have enjoyed the camaraderie, the challenges and the annual week-long summer training camp. A camp booklet of "Battalion Orders by Lt-Col. Cluny Macpherson, commanding Inverness-shire Highland Rifle Volunteers" makes interesting reading. Discipline was strict and hours of duty were long with reveille at 5 am and morning parade at 6 am. They cooked their own meals in messes of six. The breakfast ration was, half-pound weight of bread, two eggs and a pint of tea or coffee. For supper they were allowed a half-pound of bread; a quarter-pound of cheese and a quart of bitter beer, or a pint of beer or stout. Men on guard were allocated three-quarter-pounds of meat and a half-pound of bread or potatoes for dinner. There was also a canteen at the camp where "all necessaries can be bought." After a busy day, there was an evening parade before supper and lights out at 10.45 pm.[13]

According to the Muster Rolls some men stayed in the Volunteers for many years while others left the service fairly quickly. Dr John MacRae, a young man with Newtonmore connections, enrolled in the Badenoch Volunteers in late 1867. John became the doctor in Laggan in 1870, having initially worked with Dr Orchard in Kingussie.

Dr John Crawford Orchard, a native of Paisley, had joined the Badenoch medical service in 1860. Three generations of the Orchard family gave great service to the community until the mid-1970s when

"Boysie", the popular grandson of John Crawford Orchard, retired from the practice. The Orchard medical dynasty would see great changes over those years with arguably the biggest being the introduction of the National Health Service in 1948, followed closely by the greater range of available medicines and advances in treatments.

Transport also changed. Dr John, in the 1860s, might have gone on horse-back or been driven by his groom to his Newtonmore patients. His son, Dr Edward, "used cross country skis to reach snow-bound patients decades before skiing became a pastime in Badenoch."[14] By the end of the century the doctor in Laggan was using a motor bike with side-car for some of his visits. Early in the 20th century, the doctor was often one of the first people in an area to possess a motor car. Perhaps the first big challenge for Dr John would have been the influx of potential patients from many parts of Britain to work on the construction of the railway. After the departure of the navvies his workload would have become lighter.

The economy of the Strath must have benefitted from the railway building activity but in Badenoch during the first two thirds of the 19th century conditions were difficult; sometimes extremely difficult. In the first half of the century many business failures had been reported in Kingussie. Robert Somers in 1847 had commented on such bankruptcies among the traders of Kingussie. He blamed: "the ruinous system of long credit, commonly entailed upon small dealers by a poor population." In the 1860s Newtonmore had its share of bankrupts, among them: John Macpherson, cattle dealer, Strone, in 1860; Alexander Thomson, stoneware merchant and licensed hawker, Newtonmore, in 1863; Donald Cattanach, jnr, merchant, Newtonmore, in 1868. The Parochial Board was still buying in meal for distribution to the poor in 1866. In 1869, Lt.-Col. David Edward Macpherson of Belleville (who had succeeded his aunt in 1862) showed his concern by donating £5 to church funds to be used to help those on his Newtonmore estate who were on the poor list. The funds were distributed to 23 households in Newtonmore and nine in the crofts. An example of Lt.-Col. Macpherson's support was related by the Rev. Dr Mackenzie in the church magazine of February 1906, long after the death of that laird: "I had expressed regret to him that I should have to trouble the Heritors to execute some repairs in the Manse: 'Why', he asked, with genuine surprise, 'should you express regret for that? The money is not ours; we are simply its curators, whose duty it is to put it to the use for which it was intended.'"

After the death of William Caldwell, merchant, Newtonmore, on 31 May 1864, several of his creditors attempted to recoup their losses including David Shirres, warehouseman in Aberdeen and William Kynoch, merchant, Forres. An application by Edinburgh warehousemen J. and J. Robertson for sequestration of William's estate was made in the Court of Session. His business must have been in trouble. When it was advertised for sale in THE SCOTSMAN, 30 July 1864, the Trustees were Mr Kynoch and a Mr Forbes of J. and J. Robertson. The advert gave a flavour of the type of business he was running in Newtonmore. The stock included drapery goods, groceries and ironmongery. Mr Caldwell was a shoemaker in 1841 and two of his employees lived with him and his wife. He was listed as a "Grocer & Shoemaker, employing 3 men" in 1851. Two of those, Charles McIntosh and Duncan Gordon, were apprentice shoemakers living with the Caldwells. William's building, which included his six apartment home and "commodiously fitted shop", was larger than most in the village except for the MacBarnett house at the cross roads. Although both buildings needed upgrading, MacBarnetts' was assessed at double the price of William's which had value similar to Paul Grant's inn. The building which replaced William's is attached to Rosemeade and currently occupied by two eateries.

The "Inventory of the Personal Estate of William Caldwell, merchant, Newtonmore" revealed the reasons behind the problems his business had encountered.[15] It named at least 270 debtors of whom fewer than half lived in Newtonmore and its immediate vicinity. Many were from the Glen Truim area, some from Loch Ericht, Uvie, Cluny, Crathie and several from Loch Laggan. A few from Invertromie, Gordonhall, Inveruglas, Belleville and Kingussie were on the list. At least 10 of those people also appeared on the 1864 list of 53 debtors of the Estate of William Mackintosh, Merchant, Kingussie. The debtors list of another Kingussie merchant, Peter Gordon, had more than 220 and included some railway

Fig 8 – Men outside the shop which Mr Caldwell had occupied. *(Y Richmond)*

workers. Some people, but no Newtonmoracks, appeared on all three of those lists. Debts owed to William Caldwell and Peter Gordon ranged from a few pence to about £20. William Mackintosh's grocery and bakery business may have been a bigger concern as his debtors owed from a guinea to £190. The lists gave a fleeting glimpse of a few of the navvies and some interesting names including Irish born "Abraham Metzenburgh, Newtonmore." His association with the village appears to be fleeting as he can later be found on the census in various locations in Scotland and also in court cases in connection with his business ventures as a rag merchant in Inverness and the bankruptcy of his Glasgow-based brother while Abraham was conveniently in Chicago. The lists also reveal that many shoppers from the Newtonmore area used shops in Kingussie, so William Caldwell did not have a monopoly on their trade.

William's tenement and buildings were bought by medical student, John MacRae, born in 1843. His father, Kenneth, an Edinburgh businessman, was born and brought up on the outskirts of Newtonmore. John's mother, Jessie Macpherson, died young and John was raised by Duncan Cameron and his wife, Jessie McEdward, in Kingussie. It was Duncan who arranged the purchase for John MacRae. John let out the house and shop. The first tenant of the latter was Donald Cattanach whose 1868 bankruptcy is noted above. The next merchant was Peter Thomson from Errol, Perthshire, in 1870. By 1872, James Macpherson, tailor, was trading there. John MacRae retained the property until the late 1880s when William Cattanach Macpherson became the lease holder.

It would seem that the railway had not brought many benefits to the merchants of Newtonmore, although it would have brought in their stock in a cheaper, more reliable way. As well as reductions in commodities mentioned above, the '*Othaichear*' wrote that imported meal which had previously cost 45s for a boll, reduced in price to 15s when transported by rail. After its inauspicious inception, conditions on the railway improved a little. Stone houses were built for some of the station-masters. Station buildings were still small wooden structures each costing about £80. The line received a boost to income with the transfer of the mail service from the long route via Aberdeen to the shorter over Drumochter. In 1865, the Inverness and Perth Junction Railway amalgamated with the Inverness and Aberdeen Junction Railway to become the Highland Railway.

Newtonmore had mixed fortunes in the 1860s. While the railway brought a promise of prosperity, merchants had a difficult time. Some merchants became bankrupt and there is no evidence of increasing prosperity among the others. That, along with the large number

on the poor list, suggests the people were also struggling. However, perhaps the coming of the railway would prove to be the first link in the chain of events which would lead to a flourishing of the village.

Selected further sources used in this chapter:

1. NRS, SC29/44/11
2. IC, 5/7/1862
3. TSM Archive
4. IC, 10/9/1863
5. Strathspey & Badenoch Herald, 2/8/2018
6. Glen, 101/2
7. DC, 14/7/1864
8. DC, 18/9/1863
9. EEC, 5/3/1864
10. HFM – muster roll
11. IC, 5/9/1861
12. Grierson, 309
13. GB0232, D343/2
14. Scarlett, 72
15. NRS, SC29/44/12

Chapter 5

Education & Litigation

When the Inverness and Perth Junction Railway was opened, THE SCOTSMAN of 10 September 1863, iterated the initial expectations of many people: "The great advantages which the successful achievement of such an important undertaking promises to realise to the public cannot be too highly estimated … there can be no doubt that it will have great influence in stimulating industry and trade." Sadly, ten years later, those forecast advantages were not noticeable in Newtonmore. THE GLASGOW HERALD of 10 September 1873 ran a detailed report of the visit of Queen Victoria to Lochaber. The Monarch also wrote of that trip in her journal.

Queen Victoria and Princess Beatrice were travelling from Balmoral to Inverlochy Castle via Stanley and Kingussie. The Royal entourage left Ballater at 8.40 am in their "own comfortable train." The group included John Brown and the Queen's wardrobe maid, Mrs Annie Macdonald, whose late husband had come from "Newton More" (sic). At Stanley Junction it took about seven minutes to transfer the train from the Caledonian Railway to the Highland Railway. When passing Blair Castle, the Sovereign remembered that as a

young widow, just days after the line opened, when journeying to Balmoral, she had taken a diversion to visit the dying Duke of Atholl. The Queen noted Dalwhinnie Station but, because of mist and heavy rain would have been unable to see eight occupied "surfacemen's huts" alongside the railway north of the Drumochter summit. Those huts, several of which had only one window, were probably wooden shelters left there after the construction of the railway. They accommodated 31 people in 1871.

The party arrived at flag-bedecked, Kingussie Station at 2.35 pm in the rain, and were greeted by "The Master of Lovat, Lord Lieutenant of the County, and Cluny Macpherson." The local volunteers, commanded by Captain Cumming, provided a guard of honour. In Ruthven Road and the High Street, between 800 and 1000 people cheered as the procession passed. The Queen was driven under three floral, triumphal arches which had been erected, at the station, at the Free Church and where the road turned west to Fort William. Her carriage, a "sociable", was drawn by "two splendid horses" supplied by Mrs Hobb of the Duke of Gordon Hotel whose son, Richard, rode postillion. It was followed by a waggonette and several other carriages.

No such welcome awaited the Queen at Newtonmore, which was described as "a straggling and dirty looking village" by the newspaper. Peter MacBey, land surveyor, had suggested to Belleville in 1872 that the appearance of Newtonmore should be improved. MacBey recommended trees to screen the waste ground and hide some of the "old huts close to the Public Road" which "look very ill". Several areas were planted including four acres of the market stance. That reduced it to a two acre strip which now stretches from the bowling green to the Balavil Hotel carpark. The Queen, however, passed through before the screening was effective and commented on "the very poor long village."[1] It was not reported if anyone in Newtonmore turned out to cheer Her Majesty as the convoy of carriages swept through. Perhaps Isabella Macdonald was at her door at the west end of the Main Street, hoping to catch a glimpse of her daughter-in-law, Annie, who was in the waggonette. Isabella was the lease-holder of a low thatched house, which had two rooms with a window. The Braeriach Hotel is now on that site.

Kingussie was the station of choice for many people travelling to Badenoch and also those heading for Lochaber and the West. Newtonmore, with a wooden station building and a small siding with a turntable, had the lowest specification of the three stations in the parish. Dalwhinnie Station was wooden but very soon it had a stone-built station-master's house. It also had a turntable and a facility to water the locomotives. The next watering place was Kingussie, which had a siding with housing for two shunting engines and another siding with a crane. Kingussie Station had several wooden buildings and, by 1870, a stone-built station-master's house. The buildings included refreshment rooms and toilets. Lavatories were very important as the carriages did not have any nor did they have heating. Such facilities made Kingussie Station attractive to travellers. For those journeying further, Kingussie was the terminus for the Fort William coach: passengers could also travel by stage going towards Aviemore. The mail coach to the west had commenced in October 1864. It left Fort William at 5.30am to connect with middle-day trains going north and south from Kingussie. The single fare was 10s, outside or 14s inside. Cluny's family was often reported as using Kingussie when visiting Laggan. Kingussie Station was the local one listed on advertisements for special rail outings, e.g. a New Year excursion to the North.

The near-by Duke of Gordon Hotel had an excellent reputation. There were two or three inns in the village and a variety of largish retail outlets. In contrast, Newtonmore had two small inns and fewer shops; very small affairs.

Kingussie would have seemed the obvious choice for the traveller and certainly seems to have benefitted from the railway a great deal more than did Newtonmore.

Judging from national advertisements, Kingussie people were quicker to spot the business opportunity, afforded by rail travel, of letting out houses to holiday-makers. By 1870, at least five houses in Kingussie were available each year, the earliest being advertised in 1866 by Glenbanchor born Donald MacRae. In 1869, THE SCOTSMAN advertised: "BADENOCH – to let, Furnished, a Farm-House near Kingussie – Two Public, Four Bed Rooms, Kitchen, Pantry, & etc. with Garden. Paul Grant, Aultlarie, Kingussie." Paul Grant seems to have been the only person advertising seasonal letting in the Newtonmore area before 1880.

Paul, from Alvie Parish, may have been Newtonmore's earliest entrepreneur. In 1856, the 30-year-old had obtained the lease of the Inn at the west end, named Craigellachie by a descendant, but in 1857 known as Grant's Inn. The rent was £9 per annum. He also paid nearly £20 annually to rent various pieces of nearby agricultural land to supply grazing and forage for the inn's dairy cows. In 1862, Paul was granted the lease of a half-acre building plot across the road from Grant's Inn at an annual rent of £19. Three years later, Paul Grant, Newtonmore Inn (previously Grant's Inn) was advertising for tenders for a two storey-house to be built there.[2] Heath Cottage was being erected on the building plot and Paul had also obtained a 99-year building lease of land to the east of and contiguous to the first plot. The annual rent for the larger area was £22. He then diversified into farming and was tenant of Aultlarie by 1868, the annual rent being £25. Paul's total rental payments were rather large and he must have worked very hard to meet them. He would have had income from the small inn and from the farm, also from the seasonal letting of Aultlarie Farm House and long-term letting of Heath Cottage. The 1862 Belleville accounts give some insight to wages and payments at that time. The farm grieve at Belleville was paid £20 per year: the rates for male farm servants ranged from £13 to £17. The wage for the ground officer, Donald Cameron, was £32: the gardeners received £20. Mary Fraser, the dairymaid, was paid £8. In the spring of 1862, Paul and 27 others bought oats from the estate at 23s per quarter and Paul paid 6s for three bushels of bere (similar to barley). In comparison, the Sherrabeg shepherd, Archibald Kennedy, was paid £39 per year in 1876.

Paul did much of the work himself, supported by his parents, who lived in his properties, and his wife, Janet Cattanach, who grew up in Newtonmore. Both of Janet's brothers had emigrated to Australia, but she had sisters living locally. One, Anne Cattanach, married Ewan Macpherson, a shepherd whose portrait, which can be admired in the Clan Macpherson Museum, was painted by Kenneth Macleay as part of a series commissioned by Queen Victoria and published in 1870.[3] Anne and Ewen were the grandparents of the '*Othaichear*'. Ewen's seasonal migration was described in chapter 2. Anne's sister Isabella (Mrs John Macpherson) brought up her family on their croft in Strone. John Macpherson, a local bard who was joint author of *Mnathan a' Ghlinne*, was known locally as the Cock of Strone. He was a cattle dealer who twice became bankrupt, unlike Paul, who seemed to steer his businesses to success.

Paul, son of John Grant and Janet MacBean, was powerfully-built, dynamic and industrious. In 1841 he had left the family home at Dunachton and was working at Pitmain Farm. In 1851 his occupation was given as a 'strapper' at Atholl Turnpike, Pitlochry. That job entailed controlling the coach horses when they were changed. He quickly returned to Badenoch and his occupation in 1857, when his daughter, Jessie, was born, was coachman (to Miss Ann at Belleville) and innkeeper. By 1863 he was domiciled in Newtonmore, working his Inn. Despite his many business interests he found time to be an active member of the long established Badenoch and Rothiemurchus Farming Society. In 1883 a bout of bronchitis proved fatal for the energetic Paul who had not yet reached 60. He left successful businesses which his children continued to build up. Paul, junior, and family worked the farm. William, who later emigrated to South Africa, was proprietor of the inn, where he was followed by his brother Benjamin. The inn would become a house and shop and for a while was an outlet for Ben's Inverness business, The Tartan Warehouse. Heath Cottage was developed into the magnificent Craig Mhor Hotel by the energetic and resourceful Tom Grant and his sister Maggie. Their nieces, Jessie and Katie Cattanach, daughters of Ewen Cattanach and Janet Grant, followed them in the hotel.

Provision of tourist accommodation was one example of Badenoch people embracing the opportunities brought by the railway. Judging by the number of shooting lodges being built after rail travel started, landowners must having been doing well with their sporting lets. Rental for the Newtonmore (Glenbanchor) Shootings increased from £170 in the late 1860s to £250 in 1872 and £368 by the end of the decade. The estates employed more full-time and seasonal, stalkers, ghillies, kennel-men, deer-watchers, fox-hunters, water ghillies, domestic staff, pipers, and gardeners. In Newtonmore and district in 1861, there were three gamekeepers and six in 1871. A new keeper at Ralia at the later date was former shoemaker Charles McIntosh whose descendants would be keepers there for three generations. All the building trades received contracts from the estates for the original buildings and some for regular maintenance. Building materials were more easily brought in by train: Ballachulish and Welsh slates started to be used instead of the much heavier Glen Banchor "stone" slates. It would appear that Newtonmore masons were using local stone. In 1871, several men in Newtonmore were employed as quarrymen. There is much evidence of their work in the birchwood above Craggan. Local retailers would have benefitted too by the increased influx of wealthy shooting tenants. The latter brought new ideas to the villages and were sometimes generous to the indigenous population. They often gave scholars treats or prizes and some of the poor were gifted coal or venison or other desirables.

Though some of the local tradesmen profited, the benefits did not seem to filter through and enhance the prosperity of the village. Some form of industry would have greatly helped to improve things, but James Macpherson did not make provision for such when the village was being set up. Perhaps train access to markets encouraged young Thomas McIntosh from Pitlochry to open "a charcoal and tar factory" in the then wooded area at Balvattan in 1872. *Seonaidh a' Mhaighstir* (John Macdonald) was told by Robert Forbes (b. 1858) that it used birchwood and also gave employment to the carters. Unfortunately, in 1874, the factory was badly damaged by fire. Tom's losses amounted to £400 and five tons of charcoal worth £28. He moved to Ardclach, Nairnshire.[4] An earlier entrepreneurial venture was the building of a small distillery just west of Newtonmore in the 1830s. It is not known if any whisky was ever distilled there, but the projected capacity of the still was 80 gallons.[5] In the 1851 census, at the western extremity of Newtonmore, there are houses listed as "distillery" which had paupers living in them. Was that the re-use of redundant buildings? Andrew Macpherson of Benchar had a scheme which would have combined agriculture and processing. In 1771 he stated that: "The flax trade is the only branch of Manufacture that properly occurs to me, which could with the greatest ease be immediately established."[6] Manufacturing of flax into linen is labour-intensive and would have provided employment in the cultivation and pulling of flax, the retting process, scutching at the mill and spreading on the bleachfields. There would have been extra work for weavers and especially for spinners. The extensive river flood plains would have been good flat areas for bleachfields, but Benchar did not pursue his scheme. It is interesting to note that the flax and distilling industries were also tried in Kingussie which had been planned to support industry but where both failed.

During the early 1870s there were several local bankrupts including Donald Kennedy,

Newtonmore; John Macpherson, Strone; and Donald MacRae, Kingussie – the latter two being the young bards of Glenbanchor. By 1851, MacRae was a writer and accountant practising in Kingussie. He employed at least two clerks and several servants. He also retained his interest in the land, renting several big local farms. He bought property in Kingussie and soon after the opening of the railway was advertising tourist accommodation. Property and tourist accommodation may also have been the cause of the bankruptcy of John Bentick, Innkeeper, Newtonmore in 1879. John was the son-in-law of Alexander Wilson, long term proprietor of the Inn at the Balavil Brae. THE SCOTSMAN ran the following advertisement in June 1877:

MR BENTICK, proprietor of the Belleville Arms Inn, Newtonmore (Inverness-shire), finding the number of Visitors yearly increase, begs to intimate that he has taken on lease a Large and Commodious HOUSE (Spey Lodge), situated at the West End of the Village, and about five minutes' walk from the Railway Station. Tourists and Visitors, Botanists and lovers of nature, will find the district unrivalled.

SHOWER AND SPONGE BATHS
ALL THE COMFORTS OF HOME
CHARGES MODERATE

"Spey Lodge", which had served for many years as the lodge for the shooting tenant, was the lovely property erected by Forbes Macdonell at the crossroads. Bentick and MacRae recognised the potential for tourism but possibly overextended their finances in a bid to provide accommodation for visitors.

Another character with unrealistic ambitions was Donald McKenzie, Moor of Strone, whose claim to fame was that he was the first tea merchant in Newtonmore. In early September 1877, he appeared at Inverness Circuit Court: "Accused of 15 different charges of falsehood, fraud and wilful imposition." He had defrauded tea merchants in Aberdeen, Glasgow, Brechin, Burntisland, Portobello, Inverness and several in Edinburgh. THE ABERDEEN WEEKLY JOURNAL ran a long report, quoting the evidence of the merchants and mentioning a previous conviction. The sentence of "18 months' imprisonment, 12 months to be with hard labour" did not act as a deterrent because, in 1880, he was again convicted of similar offences; the sentence this time being "five years' penal servitude". McKenzie, former toll keeper, had suggested that he was a reputable businessman, but one witness told the court; "He has no shop. He hawks the district with tea. His house is simply an old Highland hut."

Although the edifices in Newtonmore were often described in uncomplimentary terms, the village seems to have been lucky in the provision of school buildings. A school was opened in the centre of the village in 1829, the first teacher being John MacMaster from Coirebeag, Locheilside. He had taught during 1828 at the school at Ralia, succeeding its dominie of 22 years, Alexander Macpherson.[7] Alex had a son and great-grandson who followed him into teaching and some descendants still live locally. Ralia School, "a thatched building constructed of turf", served up to 150 pupils from "Dalanach, Presmucrach, Noidveag, Lochanovie, Glenbanchor and Allt-larie." Contemporary Badenoch country schools often used redundant buildings with mud floors and a smoky chimney. Scholars took in a peat for the fire. The new stone-built school was much more substantial than its predecessor at Ralia. Older Newtonmore residents remember it as "The Beehive". When the school moved the tall building became a shop and dwelling. The building was recalled as having been, in the 1930s, "a big old house with a warren of rooms."

Both those schools were run by a charity, the Society in Scotland for Propagating Christian Knowledge (SSPCK). That was formed "in 1709 for the purpose of founding schools 'where religion and virtue might be taught to young and old' in the Scottish Highlands and other 'uncivilised' areas of the country." The curriculum included Christian knowledge, reading, writing and arithmetic. It was later expanded to incorporate some vocational skills in agriculture, spinning and weaving. In rural areas, SSPCK schools were a much needed addition to those run by the Established Church, which, with support from a tax on landowners, provided a school in every parish. The NSA of 1835 for Kingussie parish reported: "there is one parochial school, two seminaries supported by the SSPCK, one which is a female school, and one supported by the Glasgow Auxiliary Society." The parochial and female schools were in Kingussie: the Auxiliary Society's school was at Nuide. Sometimes a bright young man set up a side (or "adventure") school in an area remote from other school provision. In the journal of his early life, Alexander MacBain, born 1855 in Glen Feshie, reported that a young Newtonmore man by the name of Kennedy had set up an adventure school in Finnag in 1862/63. Another Newtonmore lad who held a side school was William Cattanach (1812–1881, later an Edinburgh Baillie) who, aged 14, founded one in Glenbanchor. Until late in the 19th century fees for schooling were charged. Fees for children from the poorest families were often subsidised by the Kirk Session or by the teacher. The fee at Ralia when Alexander Macpherson was the teacher was 2s per quarter.[7] Some of the pupils paid in kind. Thomas Sinton wrote: "The father of my informant was a miller, and paid fees for his family in meal."[8] That miller was probably Robert Stewart, Milton. In the preface, Sinton acknowledged the help given to him by Mary Stewart (Robert's daughter), formerly of the Mill of Banchor. At the Ralia School: "Among the schoolmaster's requirements were the 'fugies' or recreant cocks at the cockfighting match held on Shrove Tuesday."[9] I. F. Grant wrote: "It was almost the invariable custom for the dominie … to arrange a cockfight for his pupils … he also received the corpses of the cocks that were killed. Those that refused to fight were stoned to death and a charge of a bodle (a half-penny Scots) was made for a throw at them." Dr Forsyth, b. 1825, who wrote a memorable account of life in Abernethy Parish, had taken part in cock fighting in his youth. He recalled that girls were excluded and "The last cock-fight in Strathspey is said to have been held at Cromdale about 1837." The parish and SSPCK schools were subsidised to the extent that the master had a regular salary. The side schools had to support themselves. Such schools often lasted for the winter months only: most children and some adults were then able to attend.

Cockfighting was not mentioned in the report of the aptly named John Tawse, SSPCK school inspector. Here is a copy of his beautifully scripted statement:

Newton Moor 23 March 1833

This school is in the village of Newton immediately crossing Spey Bridge it is in the Parish of Kingussie and about three miles west from Pitmain Inn. The Revd Mr Shepherd met me here. The school had been examined last week by the Presbytery when 87 scholars were present. There were 112 on the list and 75 were present today. They had no intimation of my intention to be there. I found the school in remarkable [sic] good order, and the scholars in all the different classes remarkably attentive. They went through their different exercises in a very satisfactory manner. There were 30 at arithmetic, some of them far advanced and all of them showed great proficiency. Mr Macmaster is a most respectable faithful and diligent teacher and very much esteemed in the district. The people are very poor & it would be desirable if some addition could be made to his salary. He has been long in the service of the society, and in the different stations in which he has been placed he has uniformly maintained the same character.

There is a regular Sabbath evening School here which is numerously attended and in this respect Mr Shepherd said Mr McMaster [sic] services were very valuable.

All the accommodations are furnished here and at present are in very good order.[10]

Mr Tawse returned to Newton Muir [sic] when he visited the school with the Rev. Mr Shepherd on Mon 25 July 1836. He praised Mr MacMaster, who by then had been removed by the Society to Stornoway: "excellent and esteemed, particularly efficient at the Sabbath evening School and religious instruction." The inspector was glad to find that Mr MacMaster's successor was equally esteemed and efficient in all respects. When the school was last inspected, the school room and the teacher's accommodation were "by no means what they should be." A school room and dwelling house had been added. The new room was "49ft by 18ft … furnished in the most substantial way, and very well lighted." Part of the floor was yet to be finished: "the contractor is bound to have it finished by the beginning of September … it will be one of the best school rooms on the establishment of the Society. The dwelling house is above the school house and affords ample accommodation. It consists of four rooms all well finished. There is a good garden behind, which is already partly and in the course of being enclosed." He praised the new teacher, Abernethy-born, Gordon Meldrum, who had arrived about 12 months before, and the work of the scholars. Mr Meldrum had the confidence of the minister and the people with his Sabbath evening School being "numerously attended." Mr Tawse was "satisfied that this school is fully answering the purpose of the Society." He noted: "the additional building was done at great expense and the teacher had to pay 50/- [50s., one sixth of his salary] for alternative accommodation." The inspector requested that the money should be reimbursed as they could not expect the teacher to pay it out of his "small salary" of £15 per annum. The number of pupils in his charge varied from 91 to 134. The Society was very aware that the salary they could afford to pay was very meagre: "while from the increasing poverty in [the] Highlands, less is obtained in the way of school fees than what was obtained formerly. It is obvious that such a scant salary is quite inadequate for a teacher."[10]

After The Disruption of 1843, the SSPCK were in a quandary. Their masters and catechists were expected to be members of the Established Church. Many of them, including Gordon Meldrum and the catechist for Kingussie Parish, George Urquhart, moved to the Free Church. Newtonmore quickly became a Free Church School but continued to use the buildings on the north side of the main road. Inspections were then carried out by a committee of the Free Presbytery of Abernethy. When they visited the school in March 1851, they found that most of the 134 pupils on the roll were present. They were examined in English reading, grammar, arithmetic, history, geography and religious knowledge. "Prizes were awarded to those who distinguished themselves for scholarship and good conduct." The examiners were full of praise for the children and Mr Meldrum.[11]

Gordon Meldrum was obviously a hard worker and was only 54 when he died in 1863. He was succeeded by one of his former pupils, Peter Kennedy who lived with his widowed mother, Isabella Cattanach, on the corner of Glenbanchor Road. Peter died, in his mid-twenties, in January 1867. James Cattanach kept the school going until John Macdonald, a native of Moray, who had just finished training at the Glasgow Free Church Training College, was appointed by the Free Church Committee in January 1868. About that time, the Free Church School transferred to new buildings in the grounds where Newtonmore School still stands. When the school was extended in 1910, the Rev. Dr. Kenneth A Mackenzie, chairman of the School Board, recalled that the original school on that site had been built with half the costs being borne by the landowner, Col Macpherson of Belleville "a liberal landowner, the residents contributing the remainder."

The "new" school is described in the Ordnance Survey (OS) name book notes which accompanied the cartography of their first edition map: "Free Church School. Applies to a neat and substantial building used as a school house. Besides the scholar's [sic] fees the schoolmaster enjoys the benefit of the Government Grant. The usual elementary branches of education are taught and the average attendance is 106. There is also a Gaelic service held here on Sunday evenings."

The Free Church ceased to run the school after the Education Act of 1872, which made schooling compulsory for children aged 5-13. An exception was made for children who were ten and over. They could leave school if they had gained proficiency in grade five. Kingussie School Board became responsible for local control and funding of the schools in the parish. Elections for the School Board took place every three years. Men and women with property worth more than £4 per annum were eligible to vote. In Newtonmore, about two thirds of the property had the requisite value, with women occupiers in a handful of them. Fewer men and no women could vote in General Elections and in that of 1877 there were only 102 people in the Parish of Kingussie and Insh who were eligible to vote.

The men elected to implement the act in Kingussie Parish, the first School Board, were John Bruce, agent, Highland Railway, Kingussie; Donald Cattanach, slater, Newtonmore; William Cumming, Dochfour's factor; the Rev. Neil Dewar, (who had become the Free Church minister after George Shepherd's premature death in 1853); Dr John MacRae, Laggan, with the Rev. Kenneth A Mackenzie, parish minister,

Kingussie, as chairman. Kenneth Mackenzie had a special interest in education and proved to be an extremely hard worker and inspirational leader both to the Board and to the many young people he encouraged to reach their full potential.

Implementing the new system with reams of regulations demanded a lot of understanding and hard work. The Board were responsible for three schools in the parish: Newtonmore, and two in Kingussie. They also shared responsibility with the Laggan Board for the schools at Glentruim and Dalwhinnie, and had to work

Fig 9 – Rev. Kenneth A Mackenzie. *(J Robertson)*

with the Alvie Board to provide for children who lived in the Lynchat area. They had to apply to the Scotch Education Board for funding for building schools at Dalwhinnie and Kingussie and to negotiate with the Deacons' Court of the Free Church Congregation of Kingussie regarding the transfer of their school in Newtonmore to the Board.

The first recorded meeting of the Board was on 10 Mar 1873. They elected their chairman and organised an educational census of the parish as demanded by the Scotch Education Board. At their next meeting 11 days later, they set out a basic timetable for the school day: before 10.30 there was to be half an hour of religious instruction given by the teachers. Secular education was to finish at 15.30 with an hour being allowed for an interval. "The whole duties of the day" were "to be concluded with religious exercises." That meeting also set the school fees at 1s per quarter for English. There was an extra shilling charged for each of the following subjects: mathematics, drawing, Latin and all languages. The upper limit was 5s per quarter. The teachers were paid according to the "value of their certificate." They also received money from school fees. Occasionally some parents had to face action in the Small Debts Court for arrears of fees. The Board did react to difficult circumstance and, in February 1879, when the pupils of Newtonmore School owed the Board 13s 6d: "The Board considering the severity of the season and the want of work deem it unexpedient to take any further steps at present to recover said fees hoping that when spring advances most of these will be paid up." The payment of fees was not abolished in Newtonmore until October 1889, when the teacher surmised that "Attendance should be better."

The results of the census determined staffing levels. Kingussie had 190 children in the 5-13 age group, while Newtonmore had 134. Under the new regime, a teacher of industrial work was sought. John Macdonald's wife, Mary, daughter of Donald Cattanach, slater, and granddaughter of John MacMaster, was appointed with a salary of £10 per year. She may have been the Mrs Macdonald who was employed by the Free Church as a sewing mistress. The employment of pupil teachers (PT) continued. In theory they should have been a great help to the head teacher, but John had to supervise and mentor his young assistants. Donald Rose had been a PT since at least 1870 and was to be paid £20 per annum until his term expired on 1 Aug 1874. Donald was followed by John Duncan, who was the son of the station-master at Newtonmore and Allan Mackintosh, Kingussie, as pupil teachers. John became a minister but Allan stayed in the job for a year only and then enlisted in the army. John Duncan had previously been a monitor at the school (a junior post to PT) and was

succeeded by Angus Macdonald from February 1876. The minute of 13 Oct 1876 noted: Mr Angus Macdonald appointed monitor "and to be Pupil Teacher there on passing HM Inspector's Examination." His salary was £10 per annum for Monitor and £10 per annum "for first year as Pupil Teacher with an annual increase of £2.10s afterwards, and half the amount earned by him under Clause 19 E Scotch Code."[12] After Angus came his cousins, Alexander Rose, followed by Ewen Rose. The monitors and pupil teachers were mostly around 15 years old when appointed, although Donald Rose was younger. In May 1875, the School Board minutes noted that Widow Rose (mother of the above Rose brothers) was to be employed to clean Newtonmore School, salary £1 per year.

The school was built on land owned by Belleville, who, after some months of negotiations, sold the three-quarter-acre site to the School Board in 1876 for £197.17s. The processing of the purchase was difficult because of the entail on Belleville Estate. The sale of the school ground was the first sale of land in Newtonmore.

School inspections were an important but intrusive part of the new regime. Donald Withrington in 'Going to School' quoted a reaction to the official inspection thus: "under the direction of cast-iron codes, the annual inspection developed into an organized series of terrors … Any flaw was visited by the most terrible of punishment – a loss of grant. Every failure could be computed in terms of L.s.d." The Newtonmore school log book reported frequent, often unannounced visits, from various members of the School Board. Often the weekly notes in that book listed achievements of each year group. The Board and the head teacher kept a very close eye on levels of attainment. Withrington concluded that "The iron rule of the inspectors, mirrored in the painstaking efforts of teachers to meet their every requirement, too often transferred a dull and humourless rigidity to the classroom." Inspectors' reports were mulled over at the local board meetings in Kingussie and the amount of grant gained was announced.

Financial considerations were regularly on the agenda of the Board. They tightly controlled spending but frequently agreed small amounts for equipment, maintenance and the supply of coal. In August 1874: "It was resolved to erect the Newtonmore Teacher's dwelling attached to the south gable of the school, and to have a small classroom in it, opening of [sic] the school… The privies to be at the south end of the Garden." A year later William Laurie, architect, accepted tenders for the erection of a classroom and teacher's house at Newtonmore. Two former pupils were among the tradesmen engaged: Angus Macpherson, plasterer – £38 and John Cattanach, slater – £75. 4s. The Board had to

borrow the total cost from the Public Works Loan Commissioners. A water supply had been omitted from the specification and despite an appeal: "A letter was read from the Department stating their Lords [of Her Majesty's Treasury] were unable to reopen the case with the view to any increase of the grant of £883.11s.9d for the Newtonmore School in order to bring to it a water supply." The introduction of a water supply would have improved the health of the scholars but 'their Lords' did not seem to consider that. The debate about supplying water to the school flowed on for several years. During that time some of the village houses received a basic water supply which came from Knock via a new reservoir near Glen Road. William Leslie, blacksmith, was appointed as inspector for the first year, 1878.[13] He was paid 9s 6d but by 1891, Alexander Rose was being paid £3 per annum as water manager. Several water pumps were also installed on the street. Despite water pipes running nearby, the school did not receive a supply until 1880. Problems with the associated drainage arose in 1882 and James Kennedy, Newtonmore, was engaged to repair the drain and cesspool at the school. That year the teacher's dwelling house was finally connected to the public water supply.

The extra classroom in the school house would have been very welcome but at certain times of the year it may have been under-used as the number of children attending school varied greatly. Those variations were caused mainly by children staying away to help with various agricultural jobs. Parents could request to withdraw children aged 9 to 13 during the summer months. Bouts of illness such as whooping cough, scarlet fever and bronchitis also caused many absences. On 5 Nov 1875, the head teacher, himself a father of young boys, wrote touchingly in the school log: "One little pupil Thomas Gibson died of fever." The school was closed from 5 to 26 November: "on account of fever in district." That affected the teacher's salary as he would not receive fees during the closure. Early the following year, the School Board addressed that problem: "On account of Fever the Newtonmore School had been closed for three weeks, and the attendance small for a considerable period: School fees consequently cannot amount to the usual sum this year. The Board therefore resolve that the Salary of the Teacher of that School shall be sixty-pounds [£60] out of the rates, with Ten pounds for the rent besides, and half the Capitation Grant earned for the current year ending fourteenth May 1876, and until further notice. The above to be paid half-yearly with the exception of the Grant which shall be paid when received from the Department." The minute of 15 Mar 1876 said that John Macdonald's salary, "with grant would amount this year to £95 inclusive of house rent."

The Board made savings in salaries by appointing female teachers. Towards the end of 1878, they received 41 applications for such a post at Newtonmore. Miss Isabella Jeans was appointed with a salary of £57 per annum. Miss Jeans, who taught the younger pupils, was highly praised by the inspectors the following May: the lower department was then "taught with ability, vivacity and geniality. Order very good. Children much improved in tidiness and intelligence… . too many are taught in small room, a fireguard should be provided and the dangerous stone kerb removed." Like many of her successors, she quickly moved on to a better post. When a teacher was appointed for the younger pupils, the Board dispensed with the services of the sewing mistress and a pupil teacher. Before that, the Board had awarded Widow Rose a small pay rise, perhaps because of an increase in school use for non-school activities.

During 1875, the School Board agreed to a request that Newtonmore School could be used on Saturdays monthly by the parochial board, for the payment of paupers' allowances. Also, in October that year, the newly established Reading Club in Kingussie agreed reciprocal use of their resources with the members of the Newtonmore Club who met in the school. In December 1878, the Newtonmore Reading Club hosted what was probably a most interesting talk in the school. The Rev. Mr. Mackenzie spoke about how to encourage economic growth in the district. His conclusion neatly tied in the subject with his enthusiasm for education: "in these unsettled times especially – when banks collapsed and houses of business failed – the safest investment they could make was an investment in their children's education." The school was used for the Gaelic service on Sunday evenings and, since there was no public hall, it was probably used by groups for election and other meetings. Did the group who instigated the court action to restore a right of access to St Bride's Churchyard (*Cladh Bhrìghde*) also meet there?

The earliest memorial inscription in St Bride's is to Andrew Macpherson of Banchor, who died in 1788. St Bride's Churchyard was regularly used for burials until the mid 19th century, when it ceased to be cared for. From then, as is shown by gravestone inscriptions, people from Newtonmore and district started to bury in the churchyard at Kingussie.

When *Donull Catanach* died on 30 Oct 1842, he was buried at St Bride's. The headstone with the lengthy Gaelic inscription marks his grave. By that time, Donald's three surviving sons had left Newtonmore and set up good businesses. His son William, a spirits dealer in Edinburgh, seems to have kept strong connections with the land of his birth. He is said to have built a house for his parents on a tenement in Newtonmore leased for them in 1829. When Donald's widow, *Catrìona*, died

in June 1865, family and friends arrived to accompany the cortege to St Bride's. At the approach to *Cladh Bhrìghde* they were shocked to find that the farmer had ploughed over the road (then east of Banchor farmhouse) to the graveyard. That road had been a 12ft-wide pass through a grass field which had been used by many generations of local families. TSM reported that William: "found it necessary to break down the adjoining fence and take the cortege through the standing corn."[14]

Thus began a considerable Cattanach campaign for justice. The main player was William Cattanach, fence breaker and corn trampler. He had considerable status as noted in various editions of THE CALEDONIAN MERCURY. He was appointed 1st Baillie of Easter Portsburgh; secretary of the Edinburgh Highland Society, the Edinburgh Highland Rifle Volunteer Company and the Edinburgh Celtic Society. He was also a founding member of Edinburgh Camanachd, the earliest shinty club. Several years after the marred interment, William, aided by William Kennedy, *Dail a' Chaorainn* (Dalchaorinnmore); William Macintosh, crofter, Kingussie; Alexander Cattanach, Kingussie and Evan Cameron, gamekeeper, Kinloch Laggan, led a local reaction. Along with others whose relatives were buried in Banchor they set to work to improve the graveyard. They cut down 18 "fine old larch trees" growing on the margins of the plot and advertised them for sale in The Inverness Courier in December 1868. With the proceeds from the sale of the wood and their own funds, they erected a stone-and-lime wall round the graveyard and installed a lockable iron gate. At Whitsun 1874, a new tenant, James Farquharson, took on Banchor Farm. In April 1875 he began to construct a replacement farm steading over the original access to the graveyard and erected a barricade close to the graveyard's stone wall. Baillie Cattanach challenged both Belleville and his tenant, seeking a right of access to the graveyard. The problem was not resolved, so Baillie Cattanach and his four cohorts raised an action against Mr Farquharson and his landlord, Lt.-Col. David E Macpherson of Belleville. Lengthy Court of Session papers covering the period from August 1875 to July 1876 set out the background to the complaint and how it was resolved.

The five campaigners, who were represented in court by solicitor Robert Menzies, requested that the obstructions should be removed or an alternative access provided "from the turnpike road between Newtonmore and Fort William to the burying ground of St Bridget's." There were protracted negotiations over the route and specification for the road. In the spring of 1876, John Grant, Land Valuator, Grantown, reported that parts of the road needed to be made up to a higher standard: "it must be made even and smooth for the passage of vehicles"; hollows

which might collect water should be filled with soil, gravel or stones; the road should be 12 feet wide at all points; "marked out on each side with stones not less than 15 inches in height at intervals of 24 feet … the whole surface to be covered with gravel to a depth of two inches." The campaigners were delighted to be awarded a higher standard of guaranteed access than they had requested. TSM noted that the expenses had been paid partly from subscription but mainly (about £300) by Baillie William Cattanach whom he described as "a distinguished son of Newtonmore and an ardent Gael and patriot." William was also responsible for setting up the sign-post with the Gaelic inscription: "*An rathad daighnichte le lagh gu Cladh Bhrìghde*" signifying "The road affirmed by law to [St.] Bride's Churchyard."

Referring to the Court Case, the Rev. David Cattanach told The Cronies that his father, Edinburgh advocate Peter L Cattanach, had been "responsible for the institution of the Court of Session action." Peter's name did not appear in the court papers, (NRS/CS248/954), but "counsel for the complainers" was mentioned. Was that Peter? His father was Strone-born William Cattanach. Support from the Edinburgh-based Cattanachs would have delighted their Newtonmore compatriots, especially William Kennedy, who might have found it difficult to challenge their laird. Belleville had, in 1874, evicted William's family from

Dail a' Chaorainn. He then leased a tenement in Newtonmore (see Chapter Six).

The graveyard campaign was just one of a few signs in the 1870s that groups in Newtonmore were beginning to work on behalf of the community. The organisation of a public subscription for the new school, the reading group and the shinty group were some of the others. Newtonmore folk could also attend events managed by Badenoch groups including the Masonic Lodge "Spey" in Kingussie which was consecrated on 4 Dec 1872. Two of the founding members were Newtonmore tenant farmers. The Badenoch and Rothiemurchus Horticultural Society which held an annual show in Kingussie was also established that year. A long-standing annual meeting was the Badenoch and Rothiemurchus Farming Society show in Kingussie. A more recent event was the Badenoch and Rothiemurchus Highland Games which were held in 1878 in Kingussie "as an experiment, but so successful were they that it was resolved to hold them annually."

During the 1870s Newtonmore became recognised as a Post Office village. The Ordnance Survey map which was surveyed in 1870 showed a "PO" in one of a row of small cottages opposite Loch Imrich. It was described thus: "a small building used as a Sub Post Office. There is one delivery and one departure of Mails in the day, Namely, at 2.0 p.m. and 11 a.m. respectively." A Mr Cameron was the sub-postmaster, but

Fig 10 – Old wooden sign to graveyard. *(HFM)*

was not named as such in the census or the VRs, possibly because that job was combined with his main occupation. In Feb 1867 when Ewen Cameron, 16, enrolled in the Badenoch Volunteers, he gave his address as the Post Office, Newtonmore. Ewen lived with his parents, who by 1866, were merchants running a small shop at their home opposite the Loch. It therefore seems that the merchants also ran the PO, but, after Mr Cameron's death, the sub-postmaster's roll seems to have been taken on by a near neighbour, John Stewart. When John, an Alvie man, took over the lease of a building on the west corner of Glenbanchor Road, in 1872, his occupation was noted as "postmaster". By 1874, John and Barbara Stewart whose eight children were born in Newtonmore from 1862 to 1879 had moved themselves and the PO to their new building which is currently a restaurant: The Letter Box. Barbara's mother, Isabella Cattanach, widow of William Kennedy, lived in a small house on the opposite corner of Glen Road, currently Woodlea. By 1876 John and Barbara Stewart were proprietors of both buildings. They eventually bought the feus and made substantial improvements to the properties. They built up the PO business and in the early 1900s, especially in the summer, it was a very busy place employing several staff.

Because of Newtonmore's situation on the main road from Perth to Inverness and the North the inhabitants had occasional "treats" observing unusual comings and goings along that highway. In June 1873, THE GLASGOW HERALD reported that a group of four "veloci-pedists who left London ten days ago for an excursion to John o' Groat's, reached Blair Athol [sic] yesterday about half-past one o'clock. After a short halt, the party started for Kingussie, where, it is understood, they were to pass the night." Originally the group had numbered eight, but one-by-one four of them dropped out. They did not have the stamina to ride their velocipedes, also known as bone shakers, the whole way. Those bikes weighed about 60lbs and had wooden or metal rims but no suspension, gearing or pneumatic tyres.

Fig 11 – A bone shaker

In October 1879, a Mr Carlyle passed through Newtonmore. He had "undertaken to walk from London to John o' Groat's driving a wheelbarrow." He covered the distance from Kingussie to Inverness in a day.

The railway also brought folk to Newtonmore and not without incident. In February 1879, south of Newtonmore, the axle of one of two engines pulling a passenger train broke. "The damaged locomotive went over an embankment into the River Truim, and the other engine mounted the bank." No one was hurt as the passenger compartments stayed on the line. Part of the permanent way was torn up. The Highland Railway employed a big work force and because there was only a single line, many of them must have been deployed to repair and re-open the line. They managed to replace one engine on the line, but the engine which had been "thrown into the Truim burn, had to be taken to pieces and lifted onto wagons and taken to Inverness. The boiler, though the most important and cumbersome portion, was rolled up the bank on a road extemporised with sleepers, and lifted onto a wagon by means of a crane." That manoeuvre took place nine days after the accident. Road accidents also occurred. In January 1878 the mail-coach from Kingussie to Fort William overturned while travelling alongside Loch Laggan. No-one was killed but three passengers were injured.

Many of the folk who passed through Newtonmore would have been aristocratic or *nouveau-riche* shooting tenants and their entourages on their way to big sporting estates such as Ardverikie and Cluny which they would have rented for the season. For many years, the shooting tenant in Glen Banchor was Mr James T. Edge, who in 1870 was High Sheriff of Nottinghamshire. The shooting rental was £170 per year and he also rented the house which had been built for Forbes Macdonell at the road junction. Cluny Castle was the retreat for the Lord Chancellor and Lady Cairns during September and October 1878. During his stay, Hugh Cairns had to return to London for a Cabinet meeting but then came back to complete his sojourn in Laggan. Earlier in the decade, the Marquis of Bute was reported as travelling from Fort William to Kingussie on his way south. He had just enjoyed a few weeks of excellent sport at Dorlin House, Moidart.

The 1870s was the time when Newtonmore was put on the map, literally and metaphorically. The first OS map of the area, surveyed in 1870, was published in 1871. When undertaking that enormous task, the surveyors had to authenticate the names that were used for places and buildings. Those were noted in the OS name books which gave a short (sometimes very short) description and were verified by three trusted local people. Perusal of the name books gives a limited overview of Newtonmore around 1870. The brief description of Newtonmore was: "a small village consisting of a single row of houses chiefly of one storey; containing two Inns, Post Office, Free Church School and Shooting Lodges." The railway station details: "a small third-class station, built of wood, with a waiting room attached" were authenticated by Mr Sim, station-master; Mr J Grant, porter, and Mr J Macpherson, Newtonmore. Paul's Inn was described as: "a medium-sized building used as a public Inn, of two storeys, slated and in good repair." The proprietors of the building west of the Inn were then the MacBarnett sisters, who had inherited it from Forbes Macdonell. Sadly the description is limited to: "a large building used as a shooting lodge." Heath Cottage was: "neat with a garden." The market stance was: "an enclosed piece of heathy land on which was held two markets during the year on the 25th April and 26th October."

By the end of the 1870s things were looking up a bit in Newtonmore. There was evidence of an emerging community spirit. Did this happen because many of the 20 to 50 year olds of the 1870s had been born in the village, and had a greater sense of belonging there than the previous generation who had come into Newtonmore from elsewhere? Also, Newtonmore probably looked slightly better than when Queen Victoria had visited since Lachlan and Alexander Rose had renovated their house at the west end next to the inn rented by the Grants; the row of houses just east of where the Braeriach Hotel is now had been slightly improved and Dr MacRae's two-storey house had increased a little in value. Also, further east, John Macdonald's house, Rose Cottage, currently *Druim Alban*, rose in value from £4 in 1855 to £6 in 1871 and £8 in 1878. Furthermore, Ewen Cameron was rebuilding his property east of the Balavil Brae and there was some infill building on plots east of that. A few more visitors were coming to the area because of the easier access by rail. Also, road access had been slightly improved and the roads were a lot safer than in the previous century when travellers had feared for their lives at the hands of highway robbers including one of the Borlum family who lived at Raitts.

Selected further sources used in this chapter:

[1] Duff, 170

[2] IC, 23/2/1865

[3] CMM, panel 37

[4] Forres, Elgin and Nairn Gazette, 31/1/1877

[5] IC, 14/2/1838

[6] NRS GD44/27/10/132

[7] Cowper

[8] Sinton, 1906, 139

[9] TSM Archive

[10] NRS GD95/9/4, 241. NRS GD95/9/5, 245

[11] IA, 8/4/1851

[12] GB0232 CI/5/4/14/1, 93

[13] GB0232 CI/7/15/1a

[14] TSM Archive

							AGE		WHERE BORN	NOTES	windows	POSSIBLE HOUSE ID IN 2020
	67	2	X	Gordon	Isabella	Widow	76		Croftdhuac	widow of Alex.	6	Bruachville/Marlow Cott
	66	4		McGregor	Alexander	Married	60	Gamekeeper	Perthshire	MacBarnett lodge	13	Mains House
	65	6	X	Grant	Paul	Married	44	Innkeeper	Alvie		10	Craigellachie
	61	4	X	Rose	Lachlan	Married	79	Ret. Labourer	Killiehuntly		3	Dalchurn
	60	1		McKay	Elspet	Single	70	Ret. Laundress	Kingussie Parish	pauper	1	
	59	3	X	Macpherson	Catherine	Widow	58	Late Farmer's Wife	Laggan	widow of Finlay	2	Inveravon
				Old Glen Rd								
SS	64	4		Bain	Jane	Married	50	Unemployed	Strathpeffer	Toll house	2	Demolished
SS	63	3	X	Grant	Jessie	Married	65	Farm Servant's Wife	Alvie	Pauls's mother	2	Monarch Apartments
SS	62	1		Robertson	Jane	Widow	59	Farmer of 32 acres	grew up at Biallid	widow of John	9	Monarch Apartments
	58	1		Davidson	Amelia	Unmar	57	Annuitant	Kingussie Parish		1	
	57	1	X	Forbes	Robert	Unmar	58	Labourer	Raits, Alvie		1	Inverglen
	56	1		Crawford	Margaret	Widow	77	Ret. Hawker	unknown		1	
	55	2	X	Macdonald	Isabella	Widow	65		Laggan	widow of Alexander	2	Braeriach
	54	6	X	MacFadyen	Helen	Married	37	Shepherd's wife	Nuide	wife of Duncan	5	Craigdhu Cottage
	53	1		Macpherson	Margaret	Widow	62	Grocer	Laggan Parish	widow of James	2	following include -
	52	2		McCook	Elizabeth	Widow	66	Blacksmith's Widow	Kingussie Parish	widow of George	2	[but who lived in which?]
	50	2		Douglas	Emily	Unmarr	56	Annuitant	Urry, Rossshire		2	?Truim Cottage
	49	4		Macpherson	Margaret	Unmarr.	61	Annuitant	Kingussie Parish		2	?Tarlee
	48	5		Kennedy	Angus	Married	57	Labourer	Inverness-shire	*Aonghas Ruadh*	2	?Birch Cottage
	47	3		Macpherson	Andrew	Widower	73	Ret. Gamekeeper	Kingussie Parish		3	?Speedwell
	46	2		Halliday	Catherine	Widow	65	Ret. Hawker	Ireland		1	?Achuan
	45	3		McIntosh	Mary	Widow	54	Late Tailor's Wife	Kingussie Parish	widow of Finlay	1	?Glenthrone
	44	3	X	Macpherson	Angus	Married	63	Ret. Gamekeeper	Laggan Parish	meal dealer	2	?Moyle
	40	10	X	Cattanach	Malcolm	Married	49	Slater	Milton of Banchor		3	Seann Dachaidh/Sunnyside
	39	9	X	Kennedy	Christina	Widow	69	Merchant	Glenbanchor	old school	8	The Beehive
	31	2	X	Davidson	Alexander	Widower	66	Weaver	Insh		2	Dunruadh
	30	7	X	Rose	Jessie	Widow	42	Annuitant	Balgowan, Laggan	widow of Alexander	3	Rosemeade
	29	4		Macdonald	Ann	Widow	71	Annuitant	Kingussie Parish	widow of Alexander	2	
	28	2		Thomson	Peter	Widower	33	Merchant	Errol, Perth		6	restaurants
	27	9		Gordon	Duncan	Married	39	Master Shoemaker	Strone		3	Rowandell
	26	3		Macdonald	Daniel	Married	30	Joiner	Auldearn, Nairn		2	Rowandell
	25	6		Chisholm	Donald	Married	40	Baker & Grocer	Strathglass	Inverness-shire	4	Letterbox
				Glenbanchor Road								
SS	51	3	X	Macpherson	Alexander	Married	67	Merchant	Kingussie Parish		6	?Ardblair
SS	43	5	X	Stewart	William	Widower	57	Shoemaker	Killiehuntly	*Uilleam Mòr*	3	Caman House
SS	42	11	X	Cattanach	Donald	Widower	57	Master Slater	Milton of Banchor	employed 4 men	3	Craigbhuie
SS	41	2	X	Grant	Duncan	Married	65	Carpenter	Elgin		3	Clan Chattan
SS	38	5	X	Macpherson	James	Married	33	Tailor & Clothier	Newtonmore	son of Ranald		?Tir nan Og
SS	37	5		Cameron	John	Married	30	Shoemaker Master	probably Strone		3	?Cruachan
SS	36	2		Gibson	Thomas	Married	30	Foreman Platelayer	Ireland		2	?Craigview
SS	35			uninhabited	on census			the proprietor was Widow Jane Cattanach, Strone.					
SS	34	9		Macdonald	Alexander	Married	34	Quarryman	Newtonmore	*Alaidh laochan*	2	?Meadowbank
SS	33	7		Kennedy	Donald	Married	29	Shoemaker	Newtonmore	*Dòmhnall Ruadh*	2	?Meadowbank
SS	32	2		Cattanach	William	Widower	70	Slater	Alvie	probably born Raitts	2	?Tairis

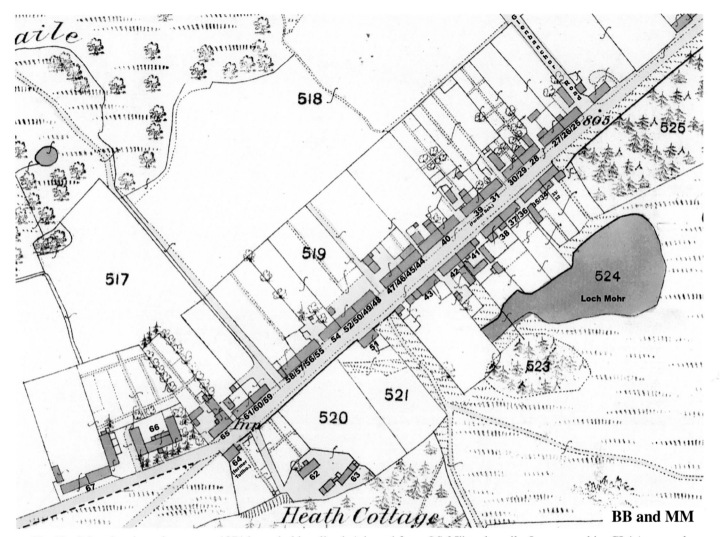

BB and MM

Fig 13 – Map showing where some 1871 householders lived. Adapted from OS 25" to the mile, Inverness-shire CI.4 (surveyed 1870, published 1871). The adapted map is not to scale. Original courtesy of National Library of Scotland.

Fig 12 – (Opposite) Heads of households in the 1871 census entries, from Bruachville eastwards to Glen Road.

SS is south side of Main Street.
Column 2 shows the number of each house as listed on the 1871 census.
Column 3 shows the number of people living in each house on the 1871 census.
An 'X' in column 4 indicates that the family owned the lease of the building they were living in.
The enumerator zig-zagged about making it difficult to work out in which house some of the people lived.

Chapter 6

Back to Borlum/Forward to Forbes   1880s

Mackintosh of Borlum: a name that was both revered and feared in Badenoch and beyond. The family held Benchar and Raitts from the mid-seventeenth century for about 100 years. Benchar then passed to the Macphersons of Benchar. The Borlums retained Raitts until 1787.

The most famous Borlum was Brigadier William Mackintosh, b.c. 1660. William's career took him to Oxfordshire where he married Mary Reade who had been brought up by her grand aunt, Mrs Anne Winwood. The Brigadier, a fervent Jacobite, gave outstanding service to the cause in the unsuccessful uprising of 1715. He was captured but made a daring escape, spending some time at Raitts where he was known as an agricultural improver. Eventually he was re-captured and spent his final years imprisoned in Edinburgh Castle. Two of his children were named Shaw and Winwood. Shaw's son, Edward, was the most infamous Borlum: "one of the most daring robbers that ever lived in the Highlands."[1] Ted and his gang were feared by travellers on the Highland Road. He lived at Raitts and used the cave as a "secure lurking place, from which to sally forth to rob travellers of their purses, and sometimes of their lives."[1]

Edward's sister married in 1763: "John Forbes in Raits and Winewood [sic] McIntosh daughter to Borlum free of scandal were matrimonially contracted and married." They had a granddaughter named Winwood, born in 1799 at Raits to their son, James, a carpenter, who became one of the first leaseholders in Newtonmore. In 1863, the London Gazette advertised for known descendants of Mary Reade to lodge their claims. Robert and Duncan Forbes (sons of James) were "awarded what remained of Mary Reade's property."

Duncan's son, James Forbes (b.c.1846), was one of the first to build a house to the west of the emerging village of Newtonmore. It was listed on the VRs from 1877. At that time, some leases for tenements in Newtonmore started to appear on the Register of Sasines where James's was recorded in 1881. It mentioned that in 1873, the late Lt.-Col. Macpherson of Belleville, Heir of Entail, had let those two roods of ground to James Forbes, plasterer, on a 99-year lease. The plot had been "lined off for a Building Let by the late Peter MacBey Land Surveyor in Elgin." It was bounded by two roads and on two sides by plantations. The house was named Forbes's Cottage, then

Viewfield, later The Bell Cottage. By 1920, the Forbes family had a row of adjacent houses: Viewfield, Eagle View and Sunny Brae. They also owned the house (currently Inverglen) on the original 1820 lease awarded to the earlier James Forbes.

The 1881 lease awarded by C J B Macpherson of Belleville whose estate was "now disentailed and held in fee simple" had interesting conditions. James and his foresaids had to "furnish a fit and proper person to attend at all public fairs and markets held on the said Estate … to assist in preserving the public peace" or "pay the Proprietor at least one shilling and six pence for each and every failure" so to do. He was also required "to furnish a man three days in each year to assist in making or repairing moss roads and cleaning or repairing other roads or doing other work that may be for the benefit of the village of Newtonmore or to pay four shillings and six pence as commutation for the said manual labour." James was prohibited from selling alcohol and "harbouring poachers or bad characters", the penalty being £10 for each offence. James was allowed to cast peats at the local moss beyond Craggan. His feu duty was £1. Several people built houses near the western periphery of the village pre-1890: their leases had similar conditions. Widow Jane Robertson, formerly of Banchor Farm, who had rented Heath Cottage since 1867, obtained a lease to

build Spey Cottage, now Speyville, in 1874. It was valued at roughly three times that of James's property.

In 1873 James's sister, Mary, married Badenoch-born plasterer John Anderson in Forfarshire. They moved back to Badenoch to bring up their family and in 1881 were living in the original Forbes house. When their next-door neighbour, Isabella Macdonald, aged 96, died in 1883, John bought the lease of her tenement for £20. It was purchased with the consent of widow Annie Macdonald, Windsor Castle, and Victoria Alberta Macdonald, then living at Balmoral, daughter of the deceased John Macdonald sometime residing at Balmoral, son of the deceased Isabella. That dwelling, which was still thatched, had become very run down, as had several of the original group of houses. Damage to some of those by a strong, gusting, north-easterly wind was reported in 1883: "In Newtonmore several houses have had the thatch stripped off."[2]

The multi-talented John Anderson set to and rebuilt the house. Around 1890, he became a grocer working from a shop within his house. When the west inn was vacated, John rented out his property. He took on the lease of the inn, renovated it and by July 1893 was running it as the Temperance Hotel. With a view to expanding his business, John bought the feu for his house in 1900. He immediately borrowed £840 from a building society and once again began building. He transformed his village house into Anderson's Temperance Hotel which included a shop and bake house. The value of the property rose from £6 to £36. That was not the final enhancement. In 1907, the Temperance Hotel (currently OYO Braeriach), was substantially improved by the next owner, John Simpson. John Anderson's early days in the building had been fraught by a problem over joint access with his neighbours in Ivy Cottage (currently Craigdhu Cottage). Helen MacFadyen, daughter of the original tene-menter, John Macpherson, was a widow with dependant children. She renovated her house in 1880 with help from her cousin, Edmond Grant, who had prospered in Australia after emigrating with his parents on the St George in 1838. In 2015, when the house was being refurbished an 1878 Australian newspaper was found packed-in around the dormer window for insulation. The MacFadyens in Ivy Cottage regularly erected a gate to stop the Andersons having access. The Andersons then removed it. In 1886 the dispute resulted in a court case in Inverness. "Mrs MacFadyen and her son [Neil] were digging a hole to erect another gate … altercation ensued … which ended in the young man Macfadyen throwing Mrs Anderson into the hole." The MacFadyens were found guilty.[3]

On the opposite side of the road, Donald Cattanach, who had previously been a shepherd, a carpenter and a merchant, leased a tenement in 1879. Donald and his brother William built a house which included a shop which sold "many things" from "an anchor to a needle."[4] Their site was well-placed at the intersection of the Highland road with the road to the West. Subsequently it has been used for different retail business the latest being The Harris Tweed Highland Shop.

The Cattanachs' shop was almost opposite the '*Tigh-Seinnse*' of *Alasdair Mòr* (Alexander Robertson), who had been renting the inn from Paul Grant since 1873. *Tigh-Seinnse* was the name for a change house, usually an inn, where coach horses were swapped for fresh ones. "It was ideally sited for that purpose in olden days as the old toll house was immediately opposite."[5]

Only patchy information is available about the toll system in Newtonmore. At the Inverness County meeting in August 1827, it was determined to erect toll gates on the Highland Road in places considered suitable by Mr Mitchell (of railway fame). When Janet, daughter of Finlay McIntosh and his wife, Mary Cameron, was born in September 1840, Finlay was the Newtonmore tollman. However, in the census of 6 June 1841, Finlay was listed as a tailor and Ewen Wilson, mason, and family were living in the area of the toll house. At an annual roup people bid to rent a toll bar for a year. In November 1846 John Macpherson paid £95, £9 higher than the previous year, to rent the Newtonmore Toll Bar. In 1848 Alvie-born Ewen Wilson paid £97, in 12 monthly instalments, to rent the Newtonmore Toll Bar. His brother Lachlan rented the Aviemore and Belleville Toll Bars for many years. Their brother Alexander, a carpenter, ran another type of bar. Since 1841 and perhaps as early as 1831, he had been the inn-keeper in what is now the Balavil Hotel. In 1851, Donald McKenzie was the toll keeper in the toll house on the south side of the Military Road (the name given to the Highland Road in that census). He was the son of Widow Margaret McKenzie, the keeper of the inn opposite. In 1856, Jane Bain was born at the "Tollbar, Newtonmore": her father was the toll keeper. The rentals achieved for the toll bar decreased over the years and by May 1867, the toll bar at Newtonmore had been removed. In 1871, Donald Bain's wife, Jane Macdonald, was living at the toll house and was listed as an unemployed toll keeper.

Perhaps McKenzie was the most flamboyant of the various toll keepers. In 1852, Donald and his counterpart at Dalwhinnie were taken to court by "George Fitzwilliam Ball, a fancy-bazaar keeper in London, who, it would appear, also drives a peripatetic business in the provinces." They were accused of "overcharging him [Ball] in respect of toll-dues upon the four-wheeled spring cart in which he conveys his goods." The toll should have been 3d, but he was charged 9d.[6] A bizarre story: one of

several involving Donald and the law. In May 1854 after his application for a licence to sell spirits at the Newtonmore Toll Bar was refused he appealed to the Court of Quarter Sessions which reversed the judgment in August. So, the toll keeper could provide access to the road and 'one for the road'.

Across the road at the inn, after the Robertsons emigrated, a new host had moved in. Samuel Macdonald was born in Newtonmore around 1845. His father's people had a long association with west Glen Banchor and Cluny. Sam was working in Kingussie as a groom when he married Margaret Mitchell at Maryculter in 1879. In 1880 Margaret and Sam were living in Kingussie when their eldest son, Alexander, was born. Their second son, John, was born in Newtonmore in July 1882.

Next door to Sam, the house erected for Forbes Macdonell was let out, for probably the first time, to a local tradesman. It was vacant for several years until William Cattanach Macpherson, tailor, moved there with his family and business in 1883. William, uncle of TSM, was born in in Strone. At age 25 in 1881 he was running his business in Newtonmore and employing two tailor's assistants. The following review of other local business people and some residents of the 1880s includes some quotes from The Cronies.

In 1875, John Cameron, bootmaker, had purchased the lease of a large tenement containing old buildings adjacent to Heath Cottage. John and his sons, Donald and John, built up a very reliable business within their homes now known as Ardblair (previously Rockview) and Fearn Cottage. The Camerons' shop became a focal point for dispensing information and generating discussion on anything from recent shinty matches to the progress of the Boer War. Geordie Macpherson, who lived most of his long life in New Zealand, recalled that some of the older men who could not read English gathered in the boot shop where Mr Cameron or his apprentice, Geordie (NZ), would read aloud from the newspapers.

Another newcomer to the west end was Lydia Brewster Macpherson, widow of Lt.-Col. Macpherson of Belleville. Lydia's red-harled house, *Baile a'Bhadain*, Balvattan,

Fig 14 – Veranda "at the end of the old Post Office and nearer the centre of the village". The tree outside the old village hall can be seen on the left foreground. *(Y Richmond.)*

(currently The Dower House), was built for her towards the end of 1887. Before that, she lived in her son's Newtonmore Lodge, Laggan Road, for at least two years. At Belleville in 1863, she had befriended railway poet, John Taylor. He recalled: "I had the honour of this gentlewoman's acquaintance … she invited me to her house… she gave me as many books as I could read; and years after I had left Badenoch … she sent me by post several very valuable presents of books." John described her as a Christian lady who was very concerned for the navvies and their spiritual welfare. Lydia was often mentioned by folk who wrote about early Newtonmore; the consensus being that she was a great benefactor to its people, not only with gifts of money and in kind, but also the time she gave to the children, the elderly and the sick. She loved the children and "devised amusements for them. She had annual treats to gladden them, and frequent prizes to stimulate them." She had classes for them: "giving instruction in Bible truth, in moral purpose, and in social service." In April 1891: "The children attending Mrs Brewster Macpherson's Sabbath School had a pleasant drive to Loch Laggan … in three brakes." In fine weather, they played games and "were liberally supplied with refreshments." The following evening she: "kindly entertained her scholars to dinner, and presented each with a gift."[7]

Lydia was very involved with the temperance movement and set up a junior group in Newtonmore: The White Well. The members ranged in age from 7 to 20. They were organised into companies of 14 with a director, "the leader", for the two female groups and a "captain" for the two male groups.[8] Lydia had her house designed to further her work with the children and she kept up with them when they left home. When Sir Thomas Stewart Macpherson (TSM) died in 1949, his son, Niall, later, Lord Drumalbyn of Whitesands, KBE, PC, spoke of the encouragement given by Lydia to his father. Tom was born in Strone in 1876. After gaining academic excellence at Edinburgh and Oxford Universities he became a High Court Judge in India. Niall Macpherson, M.P. continued: "His early recollections were of herding cattle with a school-book in his hand. It was not very long before he attracted the attention of Mrs Brewster-Macpherson … who at that time lived in the Red House at the top of the Station Road. She gathered the children of the village round her and in her regular classes introduced them in vivid fashion to the masters of literature and the great events of history. To her inspiration and culture he owed much of his future success." Lydia also added to a scholarship won by TSM. That helped him attend George Watson's College in Edinburgh from the age of 14.

Lydia brought new ideas to Newtonmore and played a leading role in their implementation. "At the beginning of last winter … Mrs Brewster Macpherson … set about collecting money for procuring and maintaining" street lamps for the village. "On Saturday evening [29 Jan 1887], in the presence of a large number of the inhabitants, she had the pleasure of lighting one of the lamps for the first time. The villagers conveyed their thanks to Mrs Macpherson "for her many and unwearied acts of kindness to them."[9] Lydia was accompanied by members of her 1st Company of The White Well: Leader Margaret Macdonald, Banchor Farm (aged about 16), Eva Guthrie (18), May Gordon (14), Jessie Logan (14), Katie Macdonald, School House (9), Mary Smith (11), Gracie Macdonald (12), Jessie Kennedy (9), Barbara Sellar (12), Bella Fyfe (7), Annie Rose (8), Jenny Dan (10), Alexina Middlemas (14), Bella Davidson (13) and Teenie Middlemas (16).

Lydia's thoughtfulness was recalled in The Badenoch Record of 11 Dec 1943. "Among her numerous gifts to the village, the late revered Mrs Macpherson caused two small wooden verandas or shelters to be erected for temporary shelter from rain or snow storms and to provide, for payment, light refreshments – biscuits, lemonade etc. – to anyone desirous of them. One shelter was built at the gable-end of the cottage belonging to the late Donald Cameron, railway servant. For many years this shelter – carefully looked after by Mrs Cameron – served a public need and was much appreciated. The second shelter, erected at the end of the old Post Office and nearer the centre of the village (see Fig 14), was the more popular, and as this particular spot has always been and still is the favourite 'howff' of men, lads and boys, I regret to say that the shelter got 'worn out' long before its time, and disappeared long before its twin at the East End."

Lydia lived in Newtonmore for about 15 years but spent part of the year away from Scotland. In May 1890, Balvattan, which was "very comfortably furnished" and had 13 apartments and bathroom, was advertised for let for six weeks at £16 per month. According to many commentators, she was the catalyst which brought forth the steady improvement of conditions in and the prosperity of Newtonmore. When she sold *Baile a'Bhadain* (for around £1600) in May 1899, Lydia was living in London. She later moved to Babbacombe, Torquay.

As the 1880s progressed, there gathered at the west end of the village a group of people who were well endowed with energy, foresight and determination. Such qualities complemented Lydia's altruism. Four of those families had young and able children who must have benefitted from growing up in that dynamic atmosphere.

Fig 15 – The Cattanachs, one of the west-end families, c 1892. Back row – William (Teela) and Ann Cattanach. Isabella, William, Donald (Donlan) and (Dr) Johnnie Cattanach. *(I Green.)*

The talented west-end group contributed much to community efforts in the village in the 1880s. Only a limited view of that is available because there appear to be no records of clubs and there was no local paper. Newspapers in Elgin and Inverness infrequently ran brief reports on Badenoch. Only six new plots were developed in the 1880s: the four at the west end plus two in the area of the village hall. Elsewhere in the village, new residents with new skills arrived from near and far. They were accommodated in 'in-fill' housing built on existing tenements.

Several families settled in various houses in the row opposite Loch Imrich. Catherine Macdonald and family had arrived from Westerton in Glenbanchor in 1876 and by the 1880s her young sons, John and Donald, were beginning to establish themselves as skilful masons. Another talented mason who arrived in the 70s was *Alaidh Bàn* (Alexander Macpherson), an Alvie lad, who settled in the village after his marriage to Hannah McCook. John Cameron described him thus: "a very shrewd man, long-headed and a great organiser." Joining them in the east end in the 1880s came Gregor Fyfe and merchant, Robert Sellar. Gregor, a native of Rothiemurchus, married Jane Cattanach from Croftbeg, Strone, in 1879. They and their young family lived at Gordonhall, moving to Newtonmore in the mid 1880s. Moray-born Robert Sellar married Barbara Riach in 1866. They had nine children born in Towie, Aberdeenshire, before moving to Badenoch.

The Sellars lived very near *Seumas Mòr* (James Macpherson), who, with his family, moved from Strone in 1882. James had grown up in Strone House, his wife Ann Stewart at Croftdhu, Strone. They and their children, Tom (TSM), Ian (James Ian), who became Lord Strathcarron and Katie, born before 1880, lived at Croftdhu. John Donald (JD), born in Newtonmore in 1883, completed the family.

Auldearn carpenter, Daniel Macdonald, had arrived earlier to the central area of the village. Daniel who had married Malcolm Cattanach's daughter, Anne, in 1870, became an enthusiastic shinty fan of his adopted village. His poems recorded for posterity the events of some of the early games. His family was easily distinguished by their byname: "The Dans". Their son, Malcolm, who had bardic ancestry on both sides of his family, became the voice of shinty for Newtonmore for many years. Their Ross grandsons were stalwarts of the village's all-conquering teams of the late 1920s and early 1930s.

The families mentioned above, along with many others, made important contributions to the later development of Newtonmore. Perhaps the seeds of that development were sown in the early 1880s but descriptions portray a still forlorn village.

In 1906, at an event to celebrate the extension of the golf course to 18 holes, one of the speakers, Cameron Macleod (who grew up in the Laggan Manse), said that he had first occupied Ralia in 1881 and had annually spent two summer months in the district ever since: "when he came to Newtonmore 25 years ago there were no houses to let, no hotels, no churches, and certainly no golf course." "Mr Gregor Fyfe, the club's very capable greenkeeper" was congratulated on his presentation of the course. The club captain that day was Robert Sellar, who had been in post since 1898. In THE PEOPLE'S JOURNAL in July 1931, Mr Sellar recalled that when they arrived in Newtonmore in 1883: "A straggling place it was, with little else than thatched roofs."

Those statements gave a retrospective view and contemporary sources have suggested that parts of Newtonmore in the early 1880s were fairly run-down. This was the decade when, from VRs and sasine records, there was the greatest amount of evidence of re-building of original properties. However, THE ABERDEEN WEEKLY JOURNAL of 14 Feb 1880 said that Newtonmore had three hotels: but the VR shows two small inns. In July 1883, the same paper said that demand for summer quarters was increasing in Badenoch because the area was becoming more accessible to city-based business and professional men: "Already the district is most popular with Dundee and Edinburgh people, and a tolerably sure sign that its health-giving properties are appreciated is that seldom a summer passes during which it is not invaded by medical men from both towns." Rental charges were dearer than those of the previous year because of demand. The following six properties were being advertised for tourism in the mid-1880s: Forbes Cottage; Heath Cottage; the west inn; the schoolmaster's house; Aultlarie Farm House and the inn managed by the Bentick family which was described by The Cronies as "small, comfortable, but with scant tourist accommodation."

Many Newtonmore businesses changed and developed in the 1880s. Newcomers to the west end have been noted. Some of them became long-term residents at their places of business but the MacBarnetts' house had two occupiers during the decade. When William C. Macpherson's lease finished in 1888, Samuel Macdonald moved from the west inn and bought the lease from the MacBarnetts for £300. Heath Cottage, was rented for long-term or holiday lets. East of that was John Cameron's shoemaker's building.

In 1883, a grocery opened within the house of Isabella Kinnaird on the west corner of what is now Curley's Lane. She was also the agent for the newspaper, THE NORTHERN CHRONICLE. Isabella, the eldest daughter of Donald Cattanach and Catherine MacMaster, had been widowed two years after her marriage to mason, Alexander Kinnaird. When Isabella died, the shop passed to her sister, Annie, who The Cronies said kept "a clean, tidy and well-stocked grocery shop." A bell summoned her when customers came in. She was always kindly and gave them a cheery welcome. The shops in the village at that time would have looked like private houses and did not have shop windows. A later proprietor of Annie's shop was her brother-in-law John Gordon who had been a gamekeeper on various estates in Badenoch including Glen Feshie. As was often the case, the Gordons named their house after a place which was special to them – Carnchuine.

Across the track (later Curley's Lane), at the eastern part of a largish plot stood the family home of *Uilleam Mòr Stiùbhart* (William Stewart), bootmaker. The Stewarts had purchased Donald Macpherson's 1835 lease when the Macphersons emigrated to Australia in 1852. Duncan Stewart, Inverness, renounced the lease in 1902 and feued the ground from Balavil. Two months later, Duncan sold the feu, including the old Stewart home, to J S Macpherson, his second cousin. Strone-born J S Macpherson, a Kingussie builder, erected a substantial building and shops on the the land adjacent to the Stewart home.

Across the passage from William Stewart was the home and workplace of Donald Cattanach, slater and catechist. Donald had leased his tenement from Belleville Estate in 1835 and the house, Craigbhuie, remained in that Cattanach family for about 145 years.

Donald's sister Ann and her husband, master joiner, Duncan Grant, lived in the adjoining house. Those attached houses were originally single storey, but in the early 1900s, Duncan's lease was converted to a feu by Mrs Marjory Duffes, who had previously been married to Duncan's deceased nephew, Ewen Cattanach. She had the house rebuilt with two storeys. Craigbhuie remained single-storey until after the feu was purchased by John Cattanach (Nelson) in 1926. A glance at the west gable shows the original roof line.

A passage way leading to Loch Mohr separated Duncan's building from a row of four single-storey houses. Donald Cattanach, mason, Strone, had leased the tenement in 1834. Part of it passed to James Macpherson, tailor, in 1862 and by 1887 Donald Kennedy, mason, had purchased the lease of the four properties from Francis Robertson Reid, farmer, Biallid, for £130 (see p. 224). They became known as Kennedy Cottages. Several rotations of tenants lived there in the 1880s. At least one of them ran his business from his small rented cottage. Flesher, *Alaidh Dòmhnallach*, (Alexander Macdonald) paid £4.10s in rent per annum. Tenants who paid less than £4 were usually not named in the VRs. For that reason we lose track of the

Macdonald family in 1887 until they reappear in 1890 renting from Alexander Cattanach, mason, who had a row of small houses in the area east of the Balavil Brae. *Alaidh* by then was a stone cutter. *Dòmhnall Ruadh* (Donald Kennedy) shoemaker was another small tradesman who was hard to trace because he lived in low-valued cottages. From census information it would seem that he lived in the central area of the village in the 1880s.

Donald Cattanach, mason, Strone, had leased the next tenement east in 1830. Around 1859, he sold part of that lease to John Kennedy, Moor of Strone, who later sold to Donald Cattanach, merchant. When the merchant became bankrupt, the lease was acquired in 1870 by the Cameron family, Kingussie. In 1887, Jessie Cameron sold the lease to Elsie Macdonald for £35. The low adjoining cottage also had a series of proprietors including, from 1862 to 1879, Archieston-based thatcher, John Buie. The lease then passed to William Kennedy, who had moved from *Dail a' Chaorainn* in Glen Banchor. William's siblings, *Ceit Dail a' Chaorainn* and *Seumas Dail a' Chaorainn,* lived with him at the house which was known for many years as Dalchurn, but is currently *Tairis*. The tales of *Ceit* and especially *Seumas* were legendary in Newtonmore.[10] They lived next door to a foreigner who probably had some interesting stories to tell.

For most of the 1880s, Jessie Cameron's house was let to a pedlar from Switzerland, William Schung, who had married Alvie lass, Ann Macdonald. When their son Charles, aged six, was enrolled at Newtonmore School in June 1880, they used the name Snug. Charlie Snug, along with Ackie Dan, later trained as tailors with young Malcolm Cattanach. Charlie's dad died in 1886 and his mum in 1890. Those semi-detached cottages were adjacent to the site of the current Village Hall.

Two new plots were developed near the Snugs in 1889. William Ross, master joiner, obtained a lease beside "Larch Hillock"and erected a home and workshop. William was the principal undertaker in Newtonmore. Geordie (NZ) wrote that his friend Donally, William's son, had taken Geordie into the workshop and pointed out a large key which hung on the wall. Donally described how when the key mysteriously gave a few knocks, his father knew that meant a death and started to prepare a coffin. "The villagers maintained it was infallible." In October 1890, death knocked on the door of the Ross family. Their infant daughter wandered off and drowned in Loch Mohr despite the gallant efforts of *Am Bèicear Bàn* who swam to the 15 ft deep centre of the loch to try to rescue her.[11]

The other new building was the first public hall, necessitated by the growth of the village and associated clubs and public functions. By that time, the Newtonmore area had a small number of regular annual visitors who also desired a hall for community events. In the 1880s the school was used for public meetings. The schoolmaster's son wrote: "When the public demand for a Village Hall became clamant, a meeting to consider ways and means was convened and met in the schoolroom. I well remember that meeting – a densely packed building and an exciting and, at times, uproarious meeting." That meeting probably took place towards the end of 1888 after embryonic plans for a hall had been discussed by the committee of the reading room with Mrs Brewster Macpherson, their president, and her son, Belleville. He offered a free lease of the land and a donation of £30. Contributions were also received from several shooting tenants: Mr Barclay, Glen Banchor, £25; Mr Clarke, Dalwhinnie, £5; Baron Schröder, Loch Ericht, £5; Mr Armitstead, Kinlochlaggan, and Mr Unwin, Phones £2. "So much being promised, collection sheets were sent round" the villagers and fund-raising functions arranged.

On 17 Jan 1889, "a very successful concert was given in the Public School, Newtonmore, by the Kingussie Free Church Choir, in aid of the Newtonmore Public Hall and Reading Room. Mr MacGillivray, farmer, Ballachroan, presided and there was a large audience present… a handsome sum was realised in aid of the funds for the new hall." Following

that report in THE NORTHERN CHRONICLE, a series of letters appeared in THE SCOTTISH HIGHLANDER. The letters raised concerns from a minority of the villagers who were opposed to the proposals to build a hall because of concerns that access to it might be restricted.

The majority, nevertheless, were comfortable with the proposals and the foundation stone was laid in the spring. Those trusted with the contract were: Alexander Macpherson, designer and mason; John Middlemas, carpenter; James Forbes, plasterer; and John Cattanach, slater. The villagers were enthused and TSM remembered helping the community effort when he was a teenager. A very attractive smallish hall built of stone and lime, and slated, emerged "on the rising ground near the main road – opposite the Post Office and about the centre of the village – a well-chosen site." That original hall sat across the site and farther back from the Main Street than the present hall. It was 40 ft long by 20 ft wide and 15 ft high. One document mentions a 10 ft by 7 ft entrance porch, but that may have been a later addition. "The west end is set apart for the library and reading room, and a moveable partition enables the apartment to be added to the hall proper when occasion requires."

"Last week a new Public Hall and Reading Room for the village of Newtonmore, Badenoch, was formally opened by a concert of vocal and instrumental music." That concert, in early Oct 1889, was preceded by a torch-light procession along the Main Street and back to "the hall where a bonfire was made of the torches amid loud cheers." The celebrations were attended by most of the inhabitants of Newtonmore, some from Kingussie and several guests. Mr Stewart, sub-postmaster, called on Belleville to preside. In his brief speech Belleville expressed his pleasure at being present, wished the project well and declared the hall open. Newtonmoracks Duncan Macdonald and Paul Grant sang Gaelic songs and Tom Grant played a Highland selection on the pipes. Kingussie folk contributed songs and recitals on a piano loaned by Mr Barclay. At the end of that momentous evening Mr Barclay proposed a "hearty vote of thanks to the performers… Rev. Dr Mackenzie, Kingussie, proposed a vote of thanks to Mr Barclay" acknowledging the help he had given the project. Mrs Macpherson, Balvattan, was thanked "for her numerous acts of kindness." The funds gained £9 from the opening concert.[12]

Belleville was president of the committee; the vice-president being Mr Barclay. The working members were: joint secretaries, Robert Sellar and Alexander Macpherson; the joint treasurers being Paul Grant and *Seumas Mòr*. A fee of 2s 6d was charged for membership. John Stewart was the next secretary of the hall, followed by *Seumas Mòr* at the end

of the century. Those named, along with other energetic villagers, were the men who drove forward the progress of Newtonmore.

"Well wishers – principally that old patroness and good friend of the village, Mrs Brewster Macpherson of Balavil, gifted papers, magazines, etc." and also "a bagatelle board." A donation of £50 from Andrew Carnegie enabled the purchase of more books. The millionaire, who, annually for ten years from 1888, rented the shootings at Cluny, gave generously to support the building of libraries in many parts of Scotland. The Carnegies liked to join in local activities and also to give treats for the local people.

That first big community venture must have given a great boost of confidence to the villagers. They had long struggled, in very difficult circumstances, to build a worthwhile and prosperous neighbourhood for themselves and their children. Their hard work would need to continue so that the hall was skilfully managed to pay for its upkeep.

The only other building on the south side of the street in the 1880s was the new school. However, the north side had an array of small businesses, including those already mentioned at the west end.

Opposite William Stewart's building was the small shop of *Aonghas Bàn*, meal dealer. Retired gamekeeper Angus Macpherson gained the lease of his row of houses by a process conducted by the Queen's Remembrancer. Drover Allan McDonald, the original lessee, died intestate with no obvious heirs in 1862. Several folk laid claim to Allan's estate and eventually, in 1866 it was "gifted to" two of them who had to pay the costs of the process.[13] The lease passed to Angus who died in 1886. His will listed the rental of his properties, which were in bad repair, for the half-year to Whitsunday 1886: Margaret Cattanach – £1.8s; Margaret Mackintosh – £1.5s; Widow Halliday – £1 and John Middlemas, master joiner – £2.

East of that was Malcolm Cattanach's double tenement containing two houses, each with a small shop. Malcolm purchased them from the original leaseholders, perhaps when he married Jane McLauchlan in 1845. In 1859, slater, Malcolm, set up a bakery which his son John, *Am Bèicear Bàn*, ran for many years. Another son, Malcolm, used the second shop for his tailor's business. Malcolm, senior, was a crofter at heart. He rented land, whenever and wherever he could, and built a barn and byre near the bakehouse in his backyard. At least 8 of the Cattanach children attended the adjacent, original Newtonmore School. The youngest children, Ewen and Tom, would have been educated at the new school.

Christina Macpherson, widow of Alexander Kennedy, Gergask, took on the lease of the school and schoolhouse. It remained in the Kennedy family until 1916. Christina and, from 1887, her daughter Jessie ran a shop which sold: "Drapery, napery, groceries, ironmongery, paraffin, vegetables and something of everything then in production, packed in the ill-ventilated shop, creating an aroma once endured, ever remembered."

That "high building", the former school, was adjacent to a "small, low-set house", the home and workshop of Insh-born, Sandy Davidson, hand-loom woollen weaver. Sandy and his wife, Catherine Kennedy, brought up their family there from 1841. The business ceased when Sandy died in 1888. His home was described as a half-house which shared the front door with the adjoining half-house: Sandy's feu duty was 5s. The half-houses were replaced by a "modern" building, comprising a shop and the house called *Dun Ruadh* in the late 1920s.

Moving east along the street, the next house was occupied by the Rose family. William, eldest son of cobbler Alexander Rose, ran a small grocery there for about five years until his premature death in 1886. William's family continued to live there until 1895 when the house was described as "ruinous". William's son, Alexander, who died in 1917 in New Zealand, bought the feu in 1905. The renovated house (currently Rosemeade) was sold to William Cockburn, tailor, in 1909. Conveniently, William Cockburn was able to rent part of the largish establishment next door for his business. Tailors had rented it from Dr John MacRae since 1872. Dr John sold the lease in 1891 to William C. Macpherson, who purchased the feu in 1904.

The Post Office was on the western corner of Glenbanchor Road. The Hallidays, stoneware merchants, were the leaseholders in 1849. Under their tenure, the property became ruinous but was rebuilt in 1869 by Donald Chisholm, baker. The next lessee was John Stewart, sub-post-master and mason. Perhaps his wife, Barbara Kennedy, manned the office while bringing up their young family of high achievers. Barbara might have had help with child-minding from her widowed mother, Isabella Cattanach, who had lived on the opposite corner of Glenbanchor Road from about 1851.

Next to Isabella there was a largish field beside the house that is currently Strathspey Hostel. Those were the workplace and home of James Maclean. Two of his sons, John and Sandy, worked with him as carters. (Jimmy Maclean, B.E.M. a descendant, had a lovely garden in the area where the carters' three horses were stabled.) They did general carting such as taking oats to the mill, returning with the meal. Goods and foods were transported to and from the station. Building materials were delivered from the quarry at Craggan. In early summer they carted home peats. Sandy was an expert ploughman and in great demand at the crofts and small-holdings on the periphery of

the village. The Cronies recalled that John's dun-coloured stallion was sometimes left overly-long outside the west inn, where he became aggressive.

John Macdonald and Margaret Davidson, next door to the Macleans, had strong attachments to the land having grown up on agricultural holdings at Croftdrealon and Banchor respectively. John, who leased his tenement (currently *Druim Alban*) in 1834, was a trusted farm-worker who sometimes had to live away from home. Margaret was at home on all the census returns. The Cronies remembered that: "Bàillidh Beag's wife for a time dealt in some commodities as well as keeping pigs." Their son, Donald Macdonald, became a crofter in Craggan in the early 1900s. Their younger son, Samuel, transformed the MacBarnett property into The Hotel. He also developed a horse-hiring business.

Donald and Isabella Cameron were long-term neighbours of the Macdonalds. Isabella's father, Laggan-born James Mackenzie, had sold the 1833 lease to them in 1862 for £4. Around 1882, Donald's son, James, built a dwelling house of stone and lime with a slated roof in place of the original house which had become ruinous. Donald, a railway worker, and Isabella continued to live in the house. After the children left home, Isabella took in lodgers in her 'Temperance House' which was sometimes called The

Coffee Rooms. She was a caring, hospitable Highlander, which is perhaps why Mrs Brewster Macpherson had the above mentioned veranda built onto the gable-end of Isabella's house.

The tenement to the east of The Coffee Rooms was leased to John Gray, weaver, who lived there until at least 1841. By 1851, John and family were domiciled in Craggan and tenants lived in his semi-detached houses. About 1878, John sold the western-most part of his lease to John Cattanach, slater, son of the catechist. John immediately renovated the building (currently Elm and Cluny Cottages). In the early 1880s, William Ross, carpenter, worked from one of those rebuilt houses. In 1886, John Cattanach sold his lease to *Seumas Mòr*, carter, for £125. Working from his new home *Seumas*, with an abundance of toil and sound perception, built up his enterprise. By the end of the decade it included the sale of coal which he delivered, by cart, from the station or sold, in small quantities, from his house. He made few improvements to the house, but in the backyard he spent about £150 on building stables, a byre and a store with a hay loft above. The Macphersons lived in part of their small property and let two parts to tenants. By 1896, with his business flourishing, *Seumas* was able to purchase Spey Cottage (currently Speyville) for £542. He was advertising it for holiday lets by June 1897.

The next business to the east was that of the Kennedy brothers: John, Ewen, Sandy and Donald (proprietor of Kennedy Cottages) who were talented masons and hewers. Ewen acquired the lease in 1884. Their father Donald had died in 1866, shortly after taking over Unie Macdonald's lease at Easterton, Glenbanchor. The Kennedys farmed there until they quit in 1875, when the estate demanded a higher rent. The Cronies commented: "like other families there [Glenbanchor] at that period, they had to make their way and seek a living elsewhere. The brothers undertook contracts as a firm and, also, assisted, individually, other firms when necessary." They were not at home in 1891 which was a quiet time for builders in Newtonmore. Many masons found work on the construction of the Aviemore to Inverness railway line. There were three Kennedy masons living between Avielochan and Kinveachy along with 10 other Newtonmoracks (three masons and seven labourers) in 1891. The art of the hewer fascinated the Cronies: "The old hewer with his wooden mallet, his selection of chisels, and the leather protection around his fingers was a real specialist … Ewen was recognised as a specially expert hewer of whin and granite." The Cronies' verdict: "Two cottages of character in the village, west of the Balavil Hotel, bear testimony of their ability as designers, hewers and builders."

Their neighbouring business was that licensed inn which had had a variety of names. In 1880, the proprietor was Flora Bentick, daughter of Alexander Wilson the original 1831 lessee. THE ELGIN COURANT in 1845 referred to it as "Mr Wilson's Hotel." The energetic and well-loved Alex Wilson, a Church elder and member of the Parochial Board, was admired for his individuality and praised by the Rev. Dr Mackenzie as "a man remarkable for his upright independence of character." He was possibly one of the community leaders who helped the village through hard times in the early days. After Mr Wilson's death in 1868, Flora and her husband continued the business, naming it "McPherson Arms Hotel" in 1871 and "Belleville Hotel" in 1881. Flora's support of shinty was highlighted after a match on 29 Dec 1888 on the Island of Banchor. For post-match sustenance: "Mrs Bentick, The Hotel, Newtonmore, sent her usual supply of refreshments, which consisted of a hamper of whisky, temperance drinks etc. Lengthy toasts by the captains and others were given, all of which spoke in high terms of Mrs Bentick. The captains, Alexander Cattanach [*Alaidh an Tàilleir*] and Donald Kennedy [*Dòmhnall Ruadh*] have received a challenge from the Braes of Lochaber, which they are prepared to take up, but the date has not been fixed."[14] That memorable match was played on Wed 16 Jan 1889: a month later Flora died. The lease of

the inn was bought for £409 by Robert Forbes, plasterer, at a public roup in the Star Hotel, Kingussie on 22 Mar 1889. It was transferred with the consent of the Rev. Charles Bentick, Flora's son. An obituary for Charles noted that the inn had been run by the Wilson family for over 50 years. Angus Macpherson, champion piper, remembered visiting the inn with friends on their way home from Highland Games at Kingussie. They walked to the "Balavil Inn, which was not then the majestic hotel it is today [1954]. Mr Robert Forbes was the genial proprietor, and ungrudgingly and at a price to meet our meagre purse, he himself with a slow-going white horse and dog-cart of rather antiquated appearance" drove them home to Catlodge.

Across the side road from the hotel, Ewen Cameron, Loch Laggan Hotel, had a series of tenants in his property during the 1880s. David Watson, road contractor, the original lessee did not tarry long and by 1841 Ewen's father, Donald, was living there. In 1879, Ewen rebuilt and extended the house. Robert Sellar, merchant, rented the property from 1887. Mrs Sellar continued running the shop after Robert became ground officer to Belleville. When the Sellars first came to Newtonmore, they had opened their shop a few doors away in one of the properties of mason, Alexander Cattanach, *Alaidh an Tàilleir.*

Alaidh, whose father, John, a tailor in Strone, was awarded the lease in 1835, had several small houses on that tenement. Early in the '80s, he rented one of them to his brother-in-law, William C Macpherson, tailor. In 1899, *Alaidh* assigned part of the tenement to John Cuthbert, another brother-in-law, who, having purchased the eastern part of the tenement from Angus Macdonald, Foregin, Carrbridge, renovated the original buildings to those which are currently known as Clune House and Granite House. Those were sold in 1911 to Widow Isabella Macbean, a daughter of John Cattanach, tailor; and to James Tytler, merchant, respectively.

The house of the plasterers was two doors farther east. Ranald Macpherson, (*Rao'll a' Phleastarair),* obtained the original lease in 1831. His eldest son, Angus, a plasterer, transferred the lease in the mid 1880s to his game-keeper brother-in-law, Charles MacIntosh. Charles, who lived and worked at Ralia, let his houses out to various folk including James Macpherson, tailor.

The neighbouring tenement was leased by Widow Catherine Macdonald. Her sons, John and Donald, became highly skilled masons after the family was evicted from Glenbanchor. During the 1880s, those sons continued to build and improve their row of family homes. Joseph Fullerton remembered his uncles working from their backyard, where they stored "their reserves stocks of sand and all that sort of thing." Catherine Fullerton remembered them

building Clune House.[15] They also built the house currently known as Enich in 1899 and sold it for about £550 to Alexander Waugh Young, who named it Dunedin. One might guess whence this scholar of the Classics escaped for his holidays to the fresh, bracing air of Newtonmore. The workmanship of the Macdonald brothers can be admired over 100 years later in large buildings such as *Talla nan Ròs,* which was built as the United Free Church in Kingussie; Ralia Shooting Lodge and Coig na shee (see Fig 40) , to name a few. The Cronies remembered the brothers thus: "As building contractors, their upright character and conscientious dealings marked them out for a fair share of the building programme." Catherine originally rented a house from Ewen Cameron. In 1879, Catherine, and family, moved farther east to become the proprietrix of a house which had been leased by Mary Cameron, widow of Angus Cameron. Mary's father, James Davidson, had obtained the original lease in 1833. The two smaller houses (Cairnsmore and Craigmore Cottage) at the east end of the Macdonald's row were probably built on the site of Mary's house.

The last row of houses at the east end of Moor of Clune was leased to John McIntosh, brother of Finlay McIntosh, tailor, in 1831. It seems that John, a mason, firstly built two small houses on the east end of his wide tenement. In 1887, after John's death, Annie

Cattanach, daughter of the catechist, bought the lease of the eastern part of the plot for £140. The remaining half of the lease passed to John Guthrie, husband of Margaret Young, niece of John McIntosh. Those various landlords had a variety of tenants including a mason and a slater.

To help sustain themselves, the tradesmen and residents cultivated the meagre plots on their tenements but many needed more land. Some of them had access to the now degraded Newtonmore Grazings let out by the estate. A resident complained: "Newtonmore grazings are about the poorest in Scotland."[16] A villagers' petition the previous year, 1885, asking Belleville for a reduction on the rent, had been ignored. At the New Year shinty match, some locals refused the free drams on offer from Belleville. One was overheard saying: "I won't sell my birthright for twopence worth of whisky."[16] Even those who managed to rent small amounts of land in various places felt that more should be available at reasonable rates. Jobs were frequently hard to obtain in the cold months of what was often a long, and sometimes severe, winter. Many people lived from hand to mouth and dreaded the possibility of a long winter lay-off. There was no social security to help tide them over and they feared the shame of being sent to the poor house. Folk did manage to find some short-term work clearing blocked routes which often required

many men for short periods. A report in January 1884 said that 150 men were needed to clear snow on the railway line south of Dalwhinnie. Some got work repairing embankments after winter flooding on the Spey. The laird made work space available in sheds at Belleville to shelter masons and hewers preparing pernickety work.[17]

Highland lairds, because of the structure of society at that time, were looked upon as leaders in many fields. Two of them contested the Inverness-shire seat in the General Election of 1880. Donald Cameron of Lochiel, the sitting Conservative MP had twice been returned unopposed. Inverness reporters enjoyed the prospect of a contest. Their newspapers widely covered the campaign. Eligibility to vote had recently been extended to give the franchise to approximately one third of the male population including rate-paying householders. The election of 1880 would have been the first time many men in Newtonmore were able to vote. In February 1880, a long list of Lochiel supporters including Donald Cattanach; John Stewart; C.F. Gwyer, tenant of Biallid; John Wood, shooting tenant of Glen Banchor and Dr Orchard was published. The opposing party was the Liberals who were known as Whigs. Their candidate was Sir Kenneth Mackenzie of Gairloch. From occasional newspaper reports during the 1880s it is apparent that *Uilleam Mòr Stiùbhart*, Malcolm

Cattanach, W C Macpherson, Duncan Forbes and young Neil MacFadyen were staunch Liberals. Dr Neil MacFadyen worked with Dr Orchard despite their opposing political views. Mrs MacFadyen sadly saw her only son predecease her in 1896.

Both the 1880 candidates held meetings in Kingussie in mid-March. Sir Kenneth was greeted by a large audience in the Drill Hall. After his speech, he was questioned by Mr Gwyer in a series of exchanges, with Sir Kenneth being applauded by his supporters. It was pointed out that: "Sir Kenneth did not throw himself upon us; he came forward at the requisition of the farmers, crofters, and labouring men of Badenoch." The following week Lochiel addressed a packed meeting at the Court House in Kingussie. It was a noisy meeting with the Liberals in full voice.

On the polling day, 156 Badenoch men (167 were eligible to vote) travelled to Kingussie School to use the only polling place in Badenoch. Lochiel won the closely fought contest by 29 votes. Throughout the constituency his victory was celebrated on Sat 10 Apr 1880. Col. Macpherson of Glentruim had come from Jersey to vote and Kenneth Logan, the oldest worker on that estate, lit the huge fire near Glentruim House. Cluny organised six bonfires in Laggan. Mr Gywer lit a large bonfire at Biallid. It illuminated many toasts including one by " 'The Bailie' a well-known character in the village, who was no doubt fired by the excellent Clynelish, made a very eloquent speech in Gaelic, which brought forth loud cheers and laughter."

"The Bailie", John Macdonald, was often asked to speak at public occasions, not only because he was the eldest at the event but also because he was an eloquent Gaelic orator. He spoke little English. John, born at Croftdrealon in 1808, was the son of Donald Macdonald and Catherine Macrae. The by-name was used for earlier and later generations of his family. But why "The Bailie"? The explanation can be constructed with snippets from THE KINGUSSIE RECORD. John and his sister, Margaret, died within seven weeks of each other in 1903. The registrar noted the great age they had attained and wrote: "Their progenitors … occupied a croft in Glenbanchor, and there is an old saying in the district that no 'Baillie' would be buried without Cluny sending his piper to do duty at their interment, 'Baillie' (*Bàillidh*) being the name that this family, Macdonald, were known locally by." When John's daughter, Jane Duncan, died in 1909, her obituary included: "Mrs Duncan's great-grandfather was the person who, with rare devotion, on innumerable occasions risked his life while bringing the necessaries of life to his outlawed chief while in hiding during the time that he was pursued by English soldiers. It is said that the chief's gratitude was such that he expressed a wish that the Cluny of the day should send his piper to play at the funeral of any of the direct descendants of this brave man. Mrs Duncan … was buried in the old graveyard at Cluny." Other members of that Macdonald family were buried at Cluny including Jane's uncle, Donald, who died in 1859 at Croftdrealon, and his siblings, Margaret and John. Their ancestor's loyalty and unstinting service to Cluny had made him the chief's right-hand man justifying his nickname. "The Bailie" worked on various local farms having picked up jobs at feeing markets.

A report about the George Fair Feeing Market held in Grantown a month after the 1880 General Election hinted at the state of things in the Highlands. Twice a year, farm workers would come to those markets seeking work for the following six months. The Feeing Market was a great social event for workers and masters. The half-yearly rates on offer were depressed: "first horsemen commanded from £12 to £13.10s; second men, £9 to £11.10s; halflins, for orrawork, £5 to £7; women, £4.4s to £5.5s." Wages were down due to "the depression of trade in great commercial centres." (Wages obtained at the Kingussie Feeing were usually less than at Grantown.) The Rev. Mr. Mackenzie had discussed that situation when speaking at the Newtonmore Reading Club in late 1878. That depression was partly due to the collapse of the City of Glasgow Bank in 1878 which wrought repercussions throughout

Scotland, destroying many firms. Such crises were fairly frequent, with smaller ones having occurred in 1825, 1847, 1857 and 1866. Agricultural prices were also depressed from 1873 to 1896. When reporting the George Fair, THE ABERDEEN WEEKLY JOURNAL, noted: "Temperance refreshments were supplied in the Public Hall." The Temperance movement had been gaining popularity for some time with the Countess of Seafield heading it in Grantown and Mrs Brewster Macpherson of Belleville championing it in Badenoch.

At that stage, the Macphersons owned Phones, Ettridge, Invernahaven and Belleville which included Newtonmore and the surrounding farmlands. The exception was the site of the school which had been feued. They appear to have been good to their tenants with regular gifts to the poor and prizes and treats for the children. They supported the reading club in Newtonmore and sponsored shinty games. Their shooting tenants were also generous to the villagers. One, an Indian Prince, was remembered for many years. His visit was described in THE SCOTSMAN in August 1887, "His Highness the Rao of Cutch, G.C.I.E. along with his brother" paid £800 for the lease of Phones grouse moor for the season. They arrived from their Indian princely state with "a retinue of black servants." One source said that the Rao had been born 25 Aug 1866, in which case he would have been celebrating his

21st birthday in Badenoch. He was a fascinating character with numerous emeralds on his apparel and turban. He spoke excellent English and had a good rapport with the villagers who referred to him as the Black Prince. On 23 August he "entertained the inhabitants of the village of Newtonmore and the people of Upper Badenoch generally to a 'banquet,' in honour of his visit to the Highlands." The gathering was in a marquee near Newtonmore Lodge, which was erected in 1877 and was known earlier this century as The Lodge Hotel. "Refreshments of all kinds were served to all … Games of various kinds were engaged in, the Prince watching the proceedings with great interest, especially the dancing, running and bagpipe competitions." He was particularly interested in the "Houlachans" (reels) and the sword-dances. At the end he presented handsome prizes to the winners. The Rao left a few days later to tour Scotland and to visit the Queen at Balmoral. He is said to have "enjoyed excellent sport among the grouse", where, no doubt, many local people gained seasonal employment. The boys received between 3s and 4s.6d a day's beating depending on the length of the drive. The Maharajah of Alwar, a Prince from a different area of India, rented the shooting at Ardverikie in 1929. He got on so well with Finlay McIntosh, the head keeper, that he entertained Finlay at Alwar, India, for a fairly lengthy holiday. The grouse moors

attracted many interesting and well-to-do lessees. They were a good money earner for the lairds, including Belleville.

The Macphersons of Belleville supported many organisations in Badenoch. The 1880s saw a burgeoning of clubs and associations, both there and in the wider Highlands. As well as those already mentioned, clan associations, shinty, curling, golf and tennis clubs were being formed or continuing to flourish. The many Liberal supporters in Newtonmore tried several times to form an association. Malcolm Cattanach chaired a well-attended meeting in the Public School in October 1888. THE ELGIN COURANT reported that Neil MacFadyen's proposal to form an Association was seconded by William C Macpherson "and adopted." THE SCOTTISH HIGHLANDER concluded their report of the meeting thus: "We believe the Association formed … will not see the New Year." Most clubs needed to raise funds.

There are several reports in the late 1880s of fundraising concerts in aid of the reading rooms. That held on Mon 19 Sept 1887 attracted audiences and artists from throughout Upper Badenoch. The Newtonmore schoolroom was packed. The star performer was holiday-maker Miss Caroline Lowthian, a celebrated composer. Local performers included Robert Forbes, Donald Macdonald, Malcolm Cattanach, jnr, and Miss MacArthur, Ettridge. The concert organised by Mrs

Robertson, Spey Cottage, raised between £5 and £6, roughly what was needed to run the Reading Room for a year. As usual the evening ended with the company singing "God save the Queen". Mrs Brewster Macpherson paid the rent of the apartment which housed the reading rooms. The choice of mid-September for the event meant that the shooting parties and the last of the summer visitors were still in the area and could contribute, in cash or performance, to the event. A concert "in aid of funds for lighting the street" took place on Fri 5 Apr 1889 in the school.[18] The large audience were treated to performances from locals: the Misses Cameron, Maggie Grant, Sarah Stewart, C Middlemas; and Messer D Mackintosh, P Grant, John Forbes, T Grant, P T Kennedy, D Ferguson, M Cattanach and L Logan. John Stewart, sub-postmaster, presided. Mrs Brewster Macpherson would have been delighted with the response.

The Belleville Macphersons and other landed proprietors diligently supported the local Volunteer Brigade. In Sept 1881, "the leading ladies of the district" organised a bazaar in Kingussie to try to raise £400 for "defraying the expense of the new uniform of the Badenoch Company of Rifle Volunteers."[19] The Volunteers had gone from strength to strength after their inauguration in 1861. Despite some of their members having to travel long distances, they trained regularly; turned-out at many local events; travelled widely to rifle competitions; entertained other companies to contests and looked forward to their annual camp. In Aug 1881 they attended the Royal Review, a huge event in Edinburgh. It was watched by Queen Victoria and later referred to as the "Wet Review". The parade, which included 39,473 volunteers, attracted around 400,000 spectators on the hills of Arthur's Seat and along the road leading into Queen's Park. Lt.-Col. Cluny Macpherson, aged 76, "stayed at the head of his Regiment in spite of the fearful weather, disregarding even the use of a plaid as protection. Riding along Princes Street at the head of the Inverness [shire] Volunteers, the brave old Chief, with his courtly and soldierly bearing, was a conspicuous figure in the procession, and was singled out for repeated rounds of enthusiastic cheering."[20]

Some of the Volunteers would not have had an opportunity to vote in a General Election until the middle of the decade. The Third Reform Act of 1884-85 gave the franchise to many more men. About 60% of adult males were then entitled to vote. Women were still barred from voting. In the 1885 General Election, 568 men in Badenoch were eligible to vote.

The new voters included crofters and farm labourers. There had been much unrest among the crofters during the early years of the decade and Charles Fraser-Mackintosh, a Highland lawyer and MP, had championed their cause. Fraser-Mackintosh had been one of the commissioners of the Royal Commission (Highlands and Islands), 1883. Commonly known as the Napier Commission, it had investigated the conditions of crofters and cottars. Belleville had given evidence and had received criticism at that commission because of recent clearances at Glenbanchor made by his father. The young laird, who often offered support to the people of Newtonmore, did not seem to understand the villagers' need for land. On several occasions, it was only after sustained lobbying that he offered to rent them additional fields. That was the case in 1886 when he made just over 12 acres of land in 11 lots on the Spey side of the railway station available for rent by Newtonmore residents. The agricultural depression of that time made it difficult to rent out farms and Belleville was farming Banchor Mains. The villagers benefitted by gaining access to a peripheral part of that farm. Fraser-Mackintosh might have received support from local soldiers as he had been a captain in the Inverness-shire Volunteers.

This time round there were three candidates: Reginald Macleod of Macleod, Conservative; Sir Kenneth Mackenzie, Liberal (Whigs); and Charles Fraser-Mackintosh, Independent Crofter. The latter two had similar liberal views and both, in different ways, supported land reform. In the lead-up to the election, a landless resident wrote to THE ELGIN COURANT, outlining the need for land of the people in Badenoch. "Cottar" pointed out that much good land was given over to sheep and deer and asserted that more should be available to the people. It is very likely that "Cottar" was Malcolm Cattanach, slater, who for many years campaigned on the land question. With the extended franchise, the crofters' Highland Land Wars and a new mix of contenders, the election was shaping up to be quite different from that in 1880.

Candidates busily toured the large constituency. They were well-received in some places and booed in others. Macleod and Fraser-Mackintosh each held meetings in Newtonmore. The result was declared on Sat 5 Dec 1885 at Inverness. The pro-Mackintosh crofters had prevailed with Macleod and Mackenzie rejected. Unable to hide his disappointment, Mr Macleod blamed illiterate voters and "they [the new electors] were therefore most easily misled by the wretched falsehoods of the Liberal Party."

Some new voters were baffled by the system, the terminology and how the candidates derided their opponents. When asked about Sir Kenneth, one West-coast voter reportedly replied: "We are informed that Sir Kenneth is a gentleman, but when one of the others was here he told us that Sir Kenneth was a Wig! But I confess I could not see it myself, as I thought he had as good a crop of hair as myself! Sir Kenneth had not a wig on when he was here." [21]

The Liberals won the election but remained in power for a short time only. In the following election of July 1886, Fraser-Mackintosh was unopposed and continued as MP for Inverness-shire until 1892. That time round he had stood as a Liberal Unionist while retaining the support of the Highland Land League.

A meeting concerning the Land League was one of the final events of the decade in Newtonmore. On the evening of 21 Dec 1889, the new hall was packed to welcome Donald MacRae, Balallan, secretary of the Highland Land League and Alexander Mackenzie, editor and publisher of THE SCOTTISH HIGHLANDER newspaper and THE CELTIC MAGAZINE. Mr MacRae "addressed the meeting in English, and then, on repeated calls, in Gaelic." He talked in general about extending the Crofters' Act and then about the particular land access problems of Newtonmore. Those arose because any lands used by the tenementers were small holdings separate from their houses. They had no security of tenure, one of the most important gains achieved by the agitation of the crofters. The Newtonmore land was let on annual leases and if, by hard work, they improved the land from a worth of 2s per acre to 30 and 35s per acre there was no guarantee

that they would continue to hold that land. He urged them to join the Land League and fight their case. The Land Leaguers wanted funds "for re-building the houses in the glens and straths from which the landlords had evicted their forefathers … Donald Campbell, merchant, Kingussie, delivered a speech in which he pointed out that Scotland would never get justice in the Imperial Parliament until she got Home Rule." Alexander Mackenzie "delivered a rousing speech on the importance of the people going in for a popular candidate for the County Council": nominations for this new system were imminent. The hall committee was thanked for giving the use of the building rent free. In reply, a committee member said that the next time Mr Macrae visited the district they would be delighted to renew their action, and "he wished to state in the most public manner that the hall was a public building and not a private one."[22] That lively meeting was chaired by long-term land agitator, Malcolm Cattanach.

The objectives of the Land League were important to many of the old-timers in Newtonmore. Alternative leagues about to be initiated were to become vitally important to the status of the village. The formation of the Camanachd Association in 1893 would lead to the development of shinty leagues.

Selected further sources used in this chapter:

[1] MacLean, 32

[2] DA, 13/12/1883

[3] SH, 30/9/1886

[4] BR, 25/7/1959

[5] BR, 13/2/60

[6] EC, 10/12/1852

[7] IC, 28/4/1891

[8] TSM Archive

[9] NC, 2/2/1887

[10] HFM, box 24g

[11] SH, 16/10/1890

[12] IC, 8/10/1889

[13] NRS E851/3

[14] SH, 3/1/1889

[15] HFM, BOHP

[16] SH, 8/1/1886

[17] Jimmy Sellar

[18] SH, 11/4/1889

[19] AJ, 10/9/1881

[20] CMM, panel 50

[21] DA, 11/12/1885

[22] SH, 26/12/89

Chapter 7

How stick skill stuck – village shinty families

Newtonmore is famous for its long association with *camanachd* and the success it has achieved in the game. Many of the contributions made to shinty by Newtonmore players have been logged in several publications over the years. Culturally and instinctively, *camanachd* was very important to the pioneer Newtonmore families and several of them produced shinty dynasties.

It is easy to imagine 18th century Glen Banchor as a nursery of *camanachd*. The ancestors of many of the 19th century players lived there. Cattanach, Kennedy, Macdonald, McIntosh and Macpherson families were numerous in the Glen around the start of the 19th century. Many descendants became outstanding players. Before 1890 few matches were reported and Newtonmore team members were not listed. For a few years from early 1893, shinty in Newtonmore seemed to be going through a sticky patch both on and off the field. That would have caused considerable concern among the elders of the village and the club, although some very good young players were clashing camans. Perhaps all that incited an inspirational song (noted below), '*Cluidh-bhall an t-Slèibh*', by *Calum Dòmhnallach* (Malcolm Macdonald)

who himself belonged to one of those Glen Banchor families. In that Banchor *brosnachadh* (encouragement to conflict) was he taking his lead from bards of the past, many renowned for rallying calls to battle? The gist of the song is that the bard encourages the audience to hear and heed the shinty news. He reminds them that many a hard (shinty) battle was played in the snow by their ancestors (*sinnsireachd*). There follows a list of the outstanding players of the early 1890s and those who had been prominent in the previous decade. The players and families listed or indicated in the song had ancestral connections to Glen Banchor. Towards the end of the song the bard recognises the contributions which will be made by future generations. The final two lines of the chorus suggest that there then were still players in Newtonmore as good as those who had ever played on 'the island'.

The island of Banchor, or nowadays 'The Eilan', was first reported in the press as a venue for shinty in 1820. On New Year's Day [OS] 1823, a team from Banchor played one from Kingussie at Ballachroan, the home of Capt. Forbes James Macdonell, RVB, "a zealous patron of the ancient Highland game of Camack [sic], whose health was afterwards cordially drank."[1] His relative, Capt. Gillies Macpherson, a visiting half-pay officer of the 11th Regiment of Foot, "liberally contributed" to the refreshments. The following January, Banchor was the location for a match between Kingussie and a team of "young Highlanders of Glentruim". It has to be remembered that Newtonmore, at that time, consisted only a handful of houses. The Banchor and Glentruim teams must have included players who later settled in the growing village of Newtonmore. In his article about the school at Ralia, TSM wrote: "The Eilean of Banchor, just north of the Spey Bridge, was but a short distance from the school… It had been the communal shinty ground from time immemorial, and there the pupils played the national game before and after school hours." TSM must be referring to pre-1829 when the new school in Newtonmore opened.

The song and notes were contributed to THE BADENOCH RECORD by TSM in October 1937. Two versions of the song with translations are available.[2] Some of the verses are printed below. A few notes and TSM's identification of the players have been added beside the song:

CLUIDH-BHALL AN T-SLÈIBH.

Eisdibh gus an cluinn sibh naidheachd,
'S an mu dheidhinn na Camanachd.
'S iom' baiteal cruaidh chaidh chluidh 's an t-sneachd
O shoan le 'ur sinnsireachd.

Sios e! Suas e! a mhàn 's an àird e!
Thuirlich e is thadhail e!
Tha cluidheadairean fhathast anns an t-Sliabh
Cho math 's chaidh riamh air Eilean.

"thuirlich e" – it's a bye; *"thadhail e"* – it's a hail
(*"anns an t-Sliabh"* – in the village)
(As good as ever went on an Eilean.)

fine boys of the crofts

John Macpherson, Duncan Kennedy,
John Macdonald, all Strone

Ranald, Allan Maclean, Ewen and Malcolm Cattanach
Duncan Mcdonald , Lachlan McPherson, Alex Falconer
Andrew Cattanach, Angus, Donald & John McDonald
Cattanachs, Charley & Robert Kennedy-sons of Don Ruadh.

Bha gillean gasda feadh nan croitean
De dhaion' a b'àbhaist ar comhnadh,
Macphearsan luath is Ceanadaidh cruaidh
'Us Seonaidh Mòr 's an t-Sròine.

Radhal is Ailean, Eoghann is Calum,
Donncha 's Lachlann 's Alasdair luath,
Aindrea, Aonghas, Domhnull is Iain,
Clann nan Catan 's mic Dhomhnuill Ruaidh.

An entry in the Kingussie Parish Register reads: "Donald McIntosh, Milntown of Banchor & Elspeth Macpherson were married January 1793." Donald and Elspeth were the great-grandparents of **Duncan, Robert and Charley Kennedy** of the song. The descendants of Donald and Elspeth, who include Paul McIntosh, b. 1868, have played shinty for Newtonmore in every decade since players' names were published. At least four great, great, great, great-grandsons have played in 21st century Newtonmore teams.

Four of the Macdonalds mentioned in the song were grandsons of John Macdonald and Isabella Stewart who farmed at *Torman*, Westerton of Glenbanchor. The three brothers **Angus, Donald and John** were sons of Duncan Macdonald and Catherine Rose. *Seonaidh Mòr* (**John Macdonald**, Strone) also known as *Seonaidh Dhòmhnaill Mhòir*, as his name suggests, was the son of Donald. Donald and Duncan were brothers. May Kennedy, wife of John Macdonald, descended from Donald McIntosh, Milntown of Banchor, and Elspeth Macpherson. Their six (Macdonald) sons were very good shinty players. The quietest of the brothers, Robbie, did not progress beyond the second team as he stayed at home to attend to the croft. The Macdonald boys, Donally, Johnian, Duncan, Alister, Robbie and Angie, were encouraged by both sides of the family. Their sister, Betty, related that their uncle,

Johnnie Kennedy, tailor, brother of Duncan of the song, regularly gave a New Year game, on his croft, between the eastend and the westend boys. The Highlander Hotel now stands on the field where those games were played. Afterwards they were treated to tea and a big Christmas pudding made by Johnnie's sister Katie. All the Macdonald boys looked forward to that event, as did Aeneas Mackintosh and his brother Alistair, father of Jackie Mackintosh, and the three sons of George Sellar, who lived in Croftbeg from 1910. **Duncan Kennedy**, known as 'Duncan Tidy', also encouraged the *"gillean gasda"* to play on his field in front of Croftdhu, Strone.

The brothers Duncan and Donald Macdonald brought up their families at Westerton and nearby Easterton respectively. Those townships were east of the *Allt Fionndrigh*. Glenballoch is the house just west of the *Allt Fionndrigh*. For most of the 19th century, a family of Macdonalds lived in Croft Drealan, the ruins of which lie south of Glenballoch. The children of Donald Macdonald and Catherine MacRae were born at Croft Drealan from about 1802 to 1816. This family appeared to have survived the threatened evictions of the Belleville lairds – one of the Macdonald daughters, Margaret (*Mairead a' Bhàillidh*)[3], was still living there in 1891 when she was 86. Margaret and her brother John Macdonald were both said to have lived to be 100 years old.

Samuel Macdonald was a son of John the centenarian. The name Samuel is not usually associated in Badenoch with a Macdonald surname. He would have been named after his maternal grandfather, Samuel Davidson, who was living at Milton of Banchor when he married Janet McIntosh in 1803. Samuel Macdonald became well-known in Newtonmore as the go-ahead proprietor of "The Hotel" which for many years was known locally as 'Sam's'. It is now Mains House. That family, known as 'The Sams', made a huge contribution to shinty in Newtonmore in the late 19th and early 20th century. Father Sam was an enthusiastic committee member and sponsor. Three of his five shinty-playing sons were in the 1907 team, the first to bring the Camanachd Cup home to Newtonmore.

There were many families of Cattanachs in Upper Badenoch in the late 18th century. That surname was not in widespread use throughout Scotland and the majority of Cattanachs could be found in Glen Banchor, Clune and Strone, with some also in Brae Laggan. Across the Grampians there were quite a number of Cattanach families in Braemar, Upper Deeside and Strathdon. In the 1940s, TSM wrote "The Cattanachs on both sides of the *Monadh Ruadh* always maintained that they were related by blood, but even a century ago representative clansmen in Badenoch and Braemar had only tradition to rely on."[4]

In the early 19th century, there were Cattanach families in Glen Banchor (Milton), Croft of Clune, and Strone whose descendants featured prominently in the Newtonmore teams from the 1880s. Those Cattanachs were also ancestors of several well-known Kingussie players. Although there were many Cattanachs in Badenoch (see appendix 1) in the 19th century the name has almost disappeared from the area now. There were many good Cattanach shinty players locally but the name does not currently appear in local team lists.

Malcolm Cattanach and Alexander Falconer both descend from John Cattanach and Isabella McIntosh, who lived at Milton of Glen Banchor in the early 1800s. Their younger relatives: Teela (William), Donlan, Dr Johnnie and Nelson (John) would have been honing their shinty skills at the time of the song.

'Clann nan Catan' refers to many good players named **Cattanach**. The Cattanachs at Croftbeg, Strone, descend from a Gordon Highlander, Donald Cattanach and Ann McKay, who married in 1816. Some of their successors were stalwarts in Newtonmore and Kingussie teams into the 21st century. Private Donald, a hardy, "intelligent man", had served with the Duke of Gordon's 92nd Regiment for nearly 25 years including the Napoleonic Wars. Donald, who grew up in Glenbanchor, on discharge, was given the croft in Strone for a small rent by the Duke. He drew his army

pension of 1s.1½d. per day for nearly 40 years. When he died, aged 88, in Jan 1858, he merited an obituary in THE INVERNESS ADVERTISER. His silver Waterloo medal sold for £2,700 in Sept 2013.[5] Donald's eldest son, John, *an t-Oighre* (the heir), took over the croft, where he lived with his wife and family until his death in 1900. John's sons were praised as "stalwarts" in a shinty poem of the early 1900s. That poem was written by "DS" who was probably the "D Stewart" who wrote some nostalgic Gaelic and English prose for THE KINGUSSIE RECORD. "D Stewart" may be Duncan, son of William Stewart the shoemaker. Duncan, a mason, set up home in Inverness after his marriage in the 1880s. Croftbeg remained into the 21st century with the Sellar descendants of Private Donald.

Another Cattanach, who, according to military histories was a cousin of Donald's, was also awarded a small croft, in his native area, and lived at Strone House until early 1841. He was the flamboyant John Cattanach who, having reached the rank of Captain was retired on half-pay from the 92nd in 1814.[6] Captain John's name regularly appeared in the press in connection with shinty patronage, letter writing, bankruptcy, and a legal wrangle with Lachlan Macpherson of Biallid and others over a trust deed. He was also summonsed to the court of the church in 1817. The Kirk Session officially recognised him, "By his own Confession of Guilt & the Woman's oath as Father of a child brought forth by Marjory Cattanach in Strone." TSM, who claimed to share Cattanach consanguinity with Captain John, left a chart showing MacRae descendants of the captain, some of whom were prominent in the military. In 1840, when approaching the age of 70, the eccentric Captain John, after selling his Commission, paid off his long-standing debts and, within a year, emigrated to Ontario, Canada. In Simcoe, in 1843, he continued his patronage of shinty by giving a match, followed by an entertainment.[7] Captain Cattanach died near there in 1852. The croft was worked until the 1930s by relatives of TSM who continued to use the name Strone House which made it sound rather grand. Strone House and Croftbeg were small turf houses until the early 1890s when they, and some others, were replaced by attractive single-storey, slated, stone-built buildings. Strone Steading now occupies the site of Strone House.

In one of the many small crofts between Strone House and Croftbeg lived Alexander Cattanach and his wife, Anne McIntosh, a lass from Glen Banchor. Their eldest son, John, a tailor, born in 1805, brought up his family in Croft of Clune. His son, *Alaidh-an-Tàilleir*, (Alexander Cattanach) b. 1851, was said by The Two Cronies to be one of the best Newtonmore full backs. Descendants of Ally's youngest sister played for Kingussie. John's younger brother Donald trained as a mason and when he married Jane Cattanach from Craggan they lived with their children on the family croft in Strone. Donald's three boys became masons: **Ewen**, b. 1855 and **Andrew,** b. 1860 were celebrated in the song. Andrew's descendants played their part in bringing home the Camanachd Cup to Newtonmore in the 1940s and 50s. Their other brother Alexander moved to The Laurels, Kingussie, where he worked as a mason/architect, constructing many of the villas and public buildings in Kingussie and Newtonmore. Several of The Laurels boys were Kingussie stalwarts.

Marjory Cattanach (*Marsag*), who lived in Craggan from the end of the 1880s and through the 1890s, told the Oral History Project that she "liked to watch shinty". Some of her descendants were still displaying great shinty skill for Newtonmore and Kingussie in the 21st century. *Marsag* is another descendant of Donald McIntosh, Milntown of Banchor and Elspeth Macpherson.

The others mentioned in the song: **John Macpherson**; **Allan Maclean**; two cousins named **Ranald Macpherson**, grandsons of *Rao'll a' Phleastarair* who was also the grandfather of **Lachlan Macpherson**; and **Duncan Macdonald**, son of *Alaidh Dòmhnullach* all had a connection to Glen Banchor, some to a greater others to a lesser extent. The father of *Alaidh Dòmhnullach* was an agricultural worker who, before becoming resident with his family in Newtonmore around 1831, was a grass keeper at Westerton, Glenbanchor. He contributed an important role to the township. His job was to preserve the grass at the shielings by driving off any other animals before the township cattle went up there. He could impound straying cattle and levy fines on their owners. *Alaidh,* b. in 1836, had a variety of jobs, two of which were connected to the livestock industry: droving and later butchery. He was a keen shinty player and was remembered for two memorable exploits with his caman. The Two Cronies reported: "It was said about Allie that on one occasion, in an inter-parish match, he performed an amazing feat. The only player in his teens, he started a rush near his own goal and actually took the ball to the other end. During his mad rush he had put three tailors and a shoemaker into the ditch which guarded the pitch." More than 30 years later, at the famous Badenoch/Lochaber match of 1889, *Alaidh,* a spectator, rushed onto the pitch, in stocking soles, to replace an injured player. **Duncan Macdonald**, a mason, and his brothers left the area to get work. John Cameron noted that Duncan was a great shinty player and when working in Edinburgh, along with Alexander Kennedy, travelled back to play for Newtonmore.

Although there were several Macphersons playing in early Newtonmore teams, the name has become much less prominent in local shinty since then. It has made way for new blood which had been attracted to the area when it appeared to have the potential for greater prosperity.

A surname to show up in later team lists was first mentioned in Newtonmore in the spring of 1883 when William, Robert, Andrew and James Sellar were enrolled at the school. Andrew and James were just beginning their education. William and Robert had transferred from school in Kingussie where the Sellars with their nine children had lived since about 1880. Three more children, including John, born in Newtonmore later that decade, completed the family. Most of the children were born in rural Aberdeenshire, where there would have been no tradition of shinty. However, the young Sellars, being natural games players, took to the sport as they grew up in Newtonmore. Several of the Sellar boys were talented Newtonmore players, as were their sons, grandsons, great-grandsons and great, great-grandsons. Many have argued that shinty is born in you. That was obviously not the case with the original Sellars. Douglas Lowe, in SHINTY YEAR BOOK, 1988, made the point that if good games players are coached: "No longer can it be argued that great shinty teams are born not made." When their skill was spotted, the young Sellars would have received coaching from the shinty enthusiasts of their adopted village.

John Sellar remembered being coached on *Dail Dhubh*, the part of Moor of Clune where the Free Church and adjacent villas were built. That was where he: "learned to tackle and manoeuvre the ball and try some trickery."[8] Coaching and training in those days were quite different from the way teams prepare in the 21st century. The team captain seemed to have a role in preparing the teams: Sam Macdonald was reported as having "stopped his men and held counsel" to discuss match plans with the team when walking to Ballachroan for a 16 a-side match. The Cronies remember meeting in the old hall with their captain, Ian Macpherson, brother of TSM, to pick the team and "mull over the games". Retired experts also had their say with *Dòmhnall Ruadh* often being mentioned as a great mentor. There were no indoor facilities and no spotlit pitches. Many youngsters carried a home-made caman with them daily and took any opportunity to have a hit around and copy the skills of their adult heroes of the first and second teams. Because families were big and extended families lived locally, many of the boys would have had plenty of older relatives to hit about with and to learn from. Matches took place between the youths of the eastend and the westend where Robbie Gordon's triangular field (near Croftdhuac) was used. Many of the young men would have been fit because of the physical outdoor work they did. Those who worked indoors found other ways to keep fit and practice. The Cronies recalled playing "shinty all the road, to and from" school in Kingussie which they attended after they passed the qualifying exam. Ackie Dan, a tailor, ran from Newtonmore to work in Kingussie daily. Perhaps Jamie Macdonald who did his banking apprenticeship in Kingussie also trained on the way to work. Dr Johnnie warmed up for a game by starting at his house at the cross-roads with a keepie-uppy and running to the Eilan without dropping the ball. Geordie (NZ), a bootmaker, played shinty up and down the street with a mate at lunchtime. When he was younger and lived at Biallid, he used to hit long balls and sprint after them along the Laggan Road. He also hit a ball against side of house, no doubt aiming at a particular stone.

Annually, many of the young men had the opportunity to earn good money (and keep fit while doing so) at beating on the local estates. They earned £1 a week compared to Geordie's apprenticeship pay of 3s 6d per week. One season a cousin of his obtained an old bike and they took turns to ride to the beating and back: everyone else walked. Some of the players were in the Volunteers and did keep-fit to music in the Drill Hall in Kingussie. Route marches also kept them fit. Geordie, who played in three Camanachd Cup winning teams (1908 to 1910) remembered: "after 2 solid hours training in the cold we all went to a back room of the Hall, where we were given a big glass of real hot stout." He also described one of the tactics they had worked out for those games: "Guild pushed the ball from throw-up to Sammy who, with a powerful hit, landed the ball among the forwards, Johnnie Kennedy was always on the spot." The Rev. John Sellar described another set-piece when Jimmy Guild in the centre would direct the ball to John, the left wing centre, who slapped it down to Nelson in the forward line.[8] John Sellar and his brother, Andy, were in the first Camanachd Cup-winning Newtonmore team in 1907. John, who captained the winning team in 1908, also mentioned the variety in the quality of the surfaces they played on and the 'nasty dip' on the Eilan at the Laggan Road end which knocked you off your stride. The Eilan was part of a working farm and would have been used for grazing or crops from about April onwards. Those players were hardy fellows who had to cope with heavy, unsophisticated equipment and some badly prepared pitches. John studied in Edinburgh and when practising shinty there met Bill Turnbull from Falkirk. Bill played at full back in John's 1908 team and in later Newtonmore teams. Bill's gift of good hand and eye co-ordination enabled him to also excel in golf, rugby, football and cricket.

In the late 1880s Donald Kennedy and family relocated from Lochaber to Drumochter Lodge, where Donald had been appointed stalker. Another Kennedy shinty dynasty was formed when some of the family later settled in Newtonmore. Those Kennedys made a great contribution to the Newtonmore teams before and after WW2 and still do in the 21st century.

In the early 20th century, another two families who would contribute much to shinty arrived in Newtonmore. Alexander Fraser, born near Forres, and his wife, Christina Cumming, moved (1918) to Newtonmore from Kingussie. Of their two shinty playing sons, Ally and Gaby, Ally, who became the Newtonmore club bard, was often teased because he had played in Kingussie when a youngster. Their sister Bella married Alister MacKintosh. Alister's father was a Moy man, while his mother, Grace, had been born in Duthil, her father, Angus Macdonald, belonged to Newtonmore. It is not known if Angus or his son, John, played for Newtonmore but his nephew Donald Middlemas represented Newtonmore in the Camanachd Cup finals in 1905 and 1906

Fig 16 Seven descendants of Donald Cattanach and Ann McKay, Croftbeg. *(Rob Ritchie)*
Back Row – L-R. – Andrew Campbell, Jock Paul Mackintosh, Sandy Ralph, George Macpherson,
front – Geordie Ralph, Mickey Aitken, Johnny Campbell.

before emigrating to Canada. Several descendants of Alexander and Christina Fraser were Newtonmore stars, past and present.

Donald Campbell was a young lad when his family moved from the Beauly area to Kingussie. Donald married Barbara Ann Sellar in1928 and they brought up their family in Newtonmore. Several of their sons and grandsons gave diligent service to Newtonmore shinty: Johnny Campbell being an outstanding player. Their great-grandsons are Newtonmore stalwarts in the 21th century. Barbara's sisters, Catherine and Marjory, had earlier married Stewart Aitken and Charles Ralph respectively. The Ralph family, as well as having several male shinty stars, can also be proud of Megan Ralph who was in the first Badenoch Ladies Shinty team to win the prestigious Woman's Camanachd Association National Division Trophy in 2019. The Campbells, Ralphs and Aitkens, through several maternal generations, relate back to Mary, one of the Croftbeg Cattanachs (see Fig 16). Mary was a sister of Jane Cattanach whose daughter, Annie Fyfe, married Paul Mcintosh.

It would seem, from the above genealogies, that Donald McIntosh and Elspeth Macpherson, Milntown of Banchor and also, Donald Cattanach and Ann McKay, Croftbeg, could be considered to be the progenitors of the longest shinty-playing dynasties in Newtonmore. Members of each of those families have represented the village at shinty in every decade since 1880. It would be interesting to know if other families with Newtonmore connections have equally long dynasties.

Although many long-established Newtonmore families featured in the shinty world, at least two families with long Newtonmore connections were hardly mentioned. Stories of the Rose and Forbes families are related throughout this history of Newtonmore with James Forbes being one of the first lease holders in 1820. The Rose family, in diverse ways, made a very significant contribution to life in 19th and early 20th centuries Newtonmore.

Selected further sources used in this chapter:

1. IJ 24/1/1823
2. Gibson, 2015; Maclennan
3. Donnie Wilson – 22 March 2006
4. Macpherson of Dalchully, 187
5. www.dnw.co.uk/auction
6. Gardyne, p.479/480
7. IC, 9/8/1843
8. GB0232, D1101/7/31 – Archive collected by Jack Richmond.

Chapter 8
Unique Ùnag

"**D**o you remember Unie?", Bel Cameron, Cruachan, Newtonmore, then a sprightly 90 year-old, was asked. Bel's face lit up. She quietly and wistfully replied: "O-oh, *Ùnag*." Bel was delighted to be reminded of *Ùnag* and spoke fondly of her. She remembered a "little smart lady" dressed in black, our midwife, "an angel, who never lost a babe". Bel said that when her wee sister, Maggie, was born in 1906, *Ùnag*, delivered the baby; while attending to her midwifery duties, she also cooked rice pudding in a big black pot hung from a hook over the fire. That was a great help to the family, who then numbered nine. (They lived in the building now called Rowandell. In the revaluation it was two houses with each having a room and closet downstairs and two small rooms in the loft. There was no lath on the walls and no water or toilet in the house. It was a happy home of a well-respected family.) Bel recalled that, when *Ùnag* set off, with her black bag in hand, she was followed by villagers curious to know who was in childbirth.

Unie's birth was noted in the Parish Register thus: "Hynie & May, twin daughters to Donald Rose in Easterton & Ann Kennedy,

Fig 17 – Unie   *(Anne Job)*

his wife, were born 14 July & baptized 5 Aug 1830". The people who gave the information for the register were speaking in Gaelic and the scribe was writing in English. Very often a name appears in different forms in different records. Our midwife is shown in records as Hynie, Una, Unie and Unnie. She was known locally as '*Ùnag*' – the diminutive form of '*Ùna*' usually referring to a child or a small adult. Unie and her twin were the youngest in the large family of Donald Rose and Ann Kennedy, Easterton, Glenbanchor.

Donald Rose, tailor, Milntown of Noid and Ann Kennedy, daughter of William Kennedy, Glenbanchor, married on 16 Jan 1812. They set up home in Glenbanchor where at least 11 young Roses were born from 1813.

William Collie was the son-in-law of Donald Rose's brother, Lachlan. Collie, in his autobiography, gave a brief glimpse into the family life of Donald. "Donald, in fact, was believed by many to be a saint. He had a good farm in Glenbanchor. His wife was one of the worldly-wise, and she was often much irritated with Donald's long services, particularly after breakfast, when his lengthy prayers almost induced his listeners to go to sleep. It often happened that his wife would wake up from a nap with a start and say [in Collie's Gaelic] – "'Dhiol beannaich mi as Dhomhanil nash leig u dhieud a tha mis a cinteach gu-m-bheil a crodh ar snamh's choire.' [*A Dhiabhail beannaich mi,*

a Dhòmhnaill, nach leig thu dhìot e? Tha mise cinnteach gum bheil an crodh air snàmh sa choirce.] 'The devil bless me, Donald, won't you give it up? I am certain sure the cattle are swimming in the oats.'" Donald was an elder in the Established Church but, along with the majority of the population, moved to the Free Church after the Disruption of 1843. Unie's obituary describes him as "one of the Disruption Elders." Donald's Church affiliation was so important to him that, when he died in Glenbanchor in 1862, his death certificate described him as an elder of the Free Church. Several of the children of Donald Rose and Ann Kennedy died young. Survivors are featured below.

Their eldest daughter, Margaret, b. 1813, married Alexander Robertson, Achnabeachan, Alvie, in September 1841. Following that, it has not been possible to trace either Alex or Margaret. Perhaps they emigrated as the 1840s were a particularly hard time in Highlands of Scotland.

Isabella Rose, born in 1817, married John Cameron: they brought up their family at Croftroy, Newtonmore. The Cameron family tenanted Croft Roy into the 20th century.

Ann Rose, born in 1819, never married, was living in Kingussie 1891 and died in 1899.

William Rose, the eldest son of Donald and Ann, was born in 1822 and studied at Edinburgh University and Free Church College,

Glasgow. By 1871, William, a widower, was the Minister of Poolewe Free Church. His sister Ann assisted him at the manse. Visiting them were three well-educated young men who were perhaps being mentored by the preacher. Three servants also lived in the house which had 14 rooms with windows. However William's parishioners were soon to be stunned as the following report in THE DUNDEE COURIER of April 27, 1875 related.

SUDDEN DEATH OF THE REV. MR ROSE, OF POOLEWE.

On Sunday forenoon, the congregation worshipping in the M'Donald Free Church, Glasgow, were startled by the sudden illness of the minister while conducting the service… the Rev. Wm. Rose, of the Free Church, Poolewe, Ross-shire, was officiating… the last Psalm was being given out, when Mr Rose exclaimed 'The hand of the Lord is upon me; I can proceed no further.' … immediately afterwards he swooned away, falling into the pulpit seat… . He had suffered a shock of paralysis and died the same evening." Mr Rose, aged 52, had been in good health when he arrived in Glasgow the previous Tuesday and had addressed a meeting in the Free Gaelic Church on the Saturday.

Alexander Rose, born 1825, became one of several shoemakers in Newtonmore. By the age of 25, he was employing two apprentices, the younger of whom, Alex Macpherson, in 1855, aged 21, emigrated to Australia. The apprentices lived with Alexander and his new wife and baby son. The house, which was also his workshop, was rented from John Rusell. Alexander also rented land at Croftduach acres because the small amount of ground which was part of a tenement did not enable villagers to keep a cow or grow crops. In 1859, Alexander obtained a lease to a tenement previously held by a Donald Kennedy. The feu was purchased in 1905 and four years later, the title of Rosemeade was disponed to William Cockburn by Ewen Rose, Wine and Spirit Merchant, residing at 273 Parliamentary Road, Glasgow.

The original lease had been awarded in 1823. Nine Roses and an apprentice were living in that house in 1861. It had two rooms with windows. Alexander and his Laggan lass, Janet Macpherson, had two more children, but Alexander died, of consumption, in May 1867, the month after his ninth child was born. In June 1867, Janet Rose, 38, Alexander's widow, claimed poor relief for herself and eight children including Janet, aged two months. The Parochial Board expected that two of her older children, William, 16, and Ann, 12, would help the fatherless family. William earned £4 per half-year and Ann earned a six-monthly 30s. Janet was initially awarded 2s. and 8 stones of meal per calendar month. In 1869, she was awarded "28s. per calendar month to include everything except education for dependants". The following year, the aliment was 24s. per month plus clothes and shoes for her dependants. Janet was awarded less and less each year, presumably as the children were able to go out to work. In 1871, Janet was living in Newtonmore with six children. Donald, 13, the eldest still living at home, was a pupil teacher: his earnings would have helped the household budget. In 1874, he was being paid £20 per annum. It would appear from the VRs that, Donald Macdonald, Glenbanchor, and John Cameron, Croftroy, helped by taking responsibility for the rent for a few years. In 1875, Widow Rose was noted as being paid £1 per annum for attending to the cleaning of Newtonmore School. By 1877, she was being paid £3 for similar duties at the school (see p 82). In 1881, Janet and several of her children were living at 22 Abercorn Street, Glasgow. Janet's eldest son, William, a carpenter, and his family continued to live on the tenement in Newtonmore.

Catherine Rose, born 1829, married Duncan Macdonald, her next-door neighbour in Glenbanchor, in 1855. The ceremony was performed by the Rev. Dugald Shaw, the Laggan Free Church minister. The witnesses were Catherine's siblings, Alex and Unnie Rose. In 1861, Catherine, Duncan and their children, John and Donald, were living on the family croft at *Torman* (phonetically – Torroman), Westerton, Glenbanchor. Also living in the house, which had two rooms with windows, were Duncan's widowed mother, Isabella, and his cousin, Isabella Smith. Donald Smith, brother of Isabella, was visiting from Achnahatnich, home of the Smith family. Two more children (Angus and Ann) arrived in the early 1860s but sadly Duncan died of pleurisy on 18/1/1866, aged 40. Catherine was left with four children under the age of 10 but she continued to run the croft at Westerton with the help of a farm servant, Alexander Maclean. She was surrounded by family in Westerton and Easterton. Isabella Macdonald lived with her and Isabella Smith, by then married to Archibald McDonald, lived next door. Catherine's brother-in-law, Donald Macdonald, lived just down the road at Easterton with his wife and family.

An article headlined "Evictions in Badenoch" in THE DAILY FREE PRESS in April 1876 painted a word picture of life in Glenbanchor. It told how Catherine "*Bean an Tormain*" had been left a widow some years previously, but "By dint of perseverance she succeeded in paying her rent, then £20, pretty regularly, and thus kept possession of her ancestor's home." Her rent was raised to £23.6s. in 1874, but, with the help of her eldest son, she was "able to keep the place" and in 1875 managed to rebuild the barn and thatch the house. (see Fig 18)

After a hard struggle for years, things were beginning to look up for her, and the boys were able to give her more help. Sadly, in 1876, they were cleared (along with others) from their beloved glen, home of Catherine's ancestors "from time immemorial." Catherine managed to rent a house in the village and two of her sons, John and Donald, became excellent masons. By 1878/9, Catherine had leased a tenement and was proprietrix of her own house, valued at £6. Her boys wasted no time and by 1879/80 they had built the second house, the

houses being valued at £6 & £4.5s. In 1891/2 there were four houses on the tenement with John and Donald each occupying one of the bigger edificies. Family lore has it that the big houses were for each of the young masons with their growing families and the little houses to the east of the block were for the grannies. The skilful workmanship of John and Donald Macdonald, masons, can be admired on many of the fine villas built in Newtonmore during the building boom of the final few years of the 19th century and the first decade of the 20th. John and Donald were noted shinty players as well as Church elders and supporters of the local branch of *An Comunn*. Their sister,

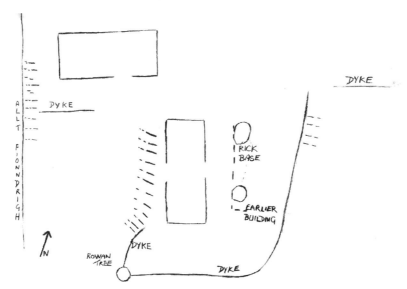

Fig 18 – In situ sketch of the ruins of Catherine Macdonald's home and workplace in Glenbanchor. The house, which is 11m long, is oriented to give protection from the strong west winds: the barn has opposing doors to assist threshing and winnowing. *(M Mackenzie).*

Ann, married John Morton and some of their family settled in Dundee. Their brother, Angus, became a shepherd and also helped his wife in their grocer's shop at Ingleside (currently Cor-arder). Thus they lived next door to *Ùnag*, aunt of Angus. Catherine died at Lochview in 1910 and was remembered thus: "Her kind sympathy and wise words of counsel were much appreciated." Her sons built the row of four houses – Lochview, Craigard, Cairnsmore and Craigmore Cottage.

Unie's vocation for nursing was apparent in 1851 when she was employed as nurse-maid to Elizabeth, 3, daughter of Duncan Macpherson, Bank Agent, Kingussie. Unie Rose, nurse, married Alexander Macdonald, farm servant, on 27/11/1856 in Kingussie and Duncan Macpherson was a witness at the wedding. Donald Rose transferred the lease of his small farm or croft to Alexander, known as Alister, and that became the home of the newly-weds. In the 1861 census, they were listed with their sons, John, 2, and Angus, 1, in Glenbanchor, where Alister farmed 7 acres. Visiting them were two Cameron siblings from Croftroy, children of Isabella Rose. Their house had three rooms with windows. Their close community included Alister's two brothers, Donald and Duncan; Unie's sister, Catherine, wife of Duncan; and also Isabella Stewart, widow of John Macdonald and mother of Donald, Duncan and Alexander. In 1851 John Macdonald was farming 16 acres at Westerton and employing three labourers. The family had moved to Westerton around 1842 when they had been evicted from *Beag Ghlean* near Loch Morlich.

Tragedy had struck the Macdonald family in February 1853. Across the Highlands there were many reports of a very severe snow storm which resulted in several deaths. John Macdonald was walking home to Glenbanchor from Kingussie when the snow storm struck. He never reached *Torman*. When the family searched for him in the morning, they found his body half a mile from his home. The wording on his gravestone – "Erected by his disconsolate widow and family" – strongly suggested the depth of the tragedy. Lightning, or in this case snow, did strike twice in the Macdonald family. Sadly, Unie's husband, Alister, died in a wild snow storm on 26/1/1862. His frozen body was found by Alexander Rose at the County March near Drumochter. He had been accompanying a relative who was travelling south; had parted company with him near the top of the pass, but did not manage to complete the return journey. Unie was left a pregnant widow with two small boys in Glenbanchor at the age of 32. Fortunately, she was surrounded by family. Her baby, Alexandrina, was born at Easterton on 2/6/1862. Lexi, alas, was hydrocephalic and died in 1867. Unie was listed in Newtonmore on the valuation roll of 1865 and in 1871 she was a 37-year-old widow and midwife living in Newtonmore with her young sons. In 1881, she was a sick nurse in the house of Archibald Cameron, merchant, Kingussie. In 1891 and 1901 Unie was working from home, Macdonald Cottage (currently Ordbhan), as a midwife.

Unie's adventurous sons decided to seek their fortune in the East but John drowned in Penang, Malaya, in 1883. Their eastern adventure also had sad consequences for his brother. Angus, who in 1881, was living in Newtonmore and working as a bank clerk in the Caledonian Bank, Kingussie, where he had served his time. His "business qualities and courteous demeanour" made him many friends. In early May, they gathered at the Belleville Hotel to wish Angus well and present him with a gold watch worth £17. He was off to take up an appointment on a sugar plantation in Penang but was struck by sun stroke on a voyage to India. John Cameron recalled how Angus saved a life in Newtonmore in the mid-1880s. "One day whilst in school we heard an awful howling coming from the small loch behind the village. That loch is now dried up and the small burn entering it has been diverted into the village sewage system … A strong frost set in and the loch was covered with ice." Much of the ice was four inches thick, but one strip cracked and refroze and was very thin. "Ally (*laochan*), [who, at that time, was a butcher], was going to

the Bank at Kingussie, and happened to cross the loch on his way to the railway station. Apparently he never thought the crack was weak, so he stepped on to it and went down through it. He stretched out his hands, and was hanging there howling when we heard him." When the schoolmaster and his pupils went to investigate, they joined a big crowd of people at Loch Mohr where "Ally was about 12 yards in, and the people were throwing in poles. The poles … did not reach as far as Sandy, but everybody seemed to be afraid to go over to him … But Sandy would soon drown if nothing could be done, when who came down but John Macdonald (Torroman) and Angus Macdonald, his cousin. It will be remembered that Angus was rather weak-minded – he was sun struck in the Red Sea whilst on a voyage to India … His cousin John was his attendant. Angus was a very powerful young man, and I remember seeing him standing in the crowd rubbing his two hands together between his knees, and keeping his eye on Sandy. Then, all of a sudden he walked in on the strong ice, and of course the people began to shout, 'There will be two deaths now!' However, Angus went out and placed one leg behind Sandy on the old strong ice. He took a hold of him between the shoulders, pulled him up, placed him on the strong ice, and said, 'Remember, Sandy, if you go in there again I won't take you out.' They both came out safely. What I always wondered at was, 'how was it that the most weak-minded man in the crowd grasped the situation, saw what could be done and did it?' It seems to me somewhat like a miracle." (See Chapter 9 for more on *Alaidh laochan*, Alexander Macdonald, who endeared himself so much to his fellow-villagers that they gave him the pet name of "*laochan*", meaning 'little hero' or 'good friend').

Ùnag died in 1907. Her obituary described how her strong Christian faith sustained her through a series of family tragedies. Evidence of the high esteem of her neighbours had been given practically. After her husband's death, a cottage, funded by public subscription, was built for her in Newtonmore. She had trained as a nurse in Edinburgh and her gentle sympathetic nature made her ideal for the job.

Unie's uncle Lachlan did not seem to share his brother Donald's zeal. Lachlan and his wife, Ann McKay, had ten children, one of whom, Ann, married William Collie. William related that "Lachlan Rose after his marriage bought an allotment in the township of Noid, but as he did not get on well with the McKays he subsequently bought a tenement in Newtonmoor (sic), and kept jobbing about, sometimes taking the position of a gamekeeper." Several of Lachlan's children worked at Blair Castle. Aeneas Rose, born 1832, was in fact pipe-major of the Atholl Highlanders. Before leaving Badenoch to join his brothers

in Atholl he was, aged 14, "appointed teacher in a school at the East End of Loch Errochd, near Dalwhinnie, and had 45 scholars under his charge. He remained there for a couple of years, then removed to Glentruim, where he taught for fully twelve months." Several of the children of Aeneas attended Kingussie Secondary School and his pipe tune, 'Lady Dorothea Stewart's Wedding March', is played in the 21st century by the Badenoch Fiddlers. Aeneas said of his ancestry that "some people in the district could trace it back to the Roses of Kilravock."

Lachlan's Newtonmore home was at the west end in the house now known as Dalchurn. William Collie, a gamekeeper at Monar, related that after Lachlan's wife died, "we brought the old gentleman to Monar, where after nine years, he died". The family took his remains to Kingussie and buried him with his wife in the churchyard at the east end. Living with the Roses in 1871 were their eldest son, Alexander, and his young daughter, Sarah. By 1891, Sarah was the only one of Lachlan's grandchildren resident in Newtonmore. In 1899, she bought the feu charter to the tenement in which Lachlan had lived. It was known then as Heather Cottage. Sarah's daughter, Annie Macdougall, lived there until the 1940s. Alexander, who died in 1897, was a contemporary of Malcolm Cattanach.

Chapter 9

Time of the Trowel

1890s

Malcolm Cattanach, after a busy and fulfilling year in 1889, would have been looking forward to more progress in the new decade.

Malcolm, then approaching his allotted span, and his wife, Jane, may have been anticipating the Christmas Day [OS] village shinty match on 6 January 1890. They had a least one son and grandson due to be playing. Ewen Macpherson Cattanach, shoemaker, aged 25, was their eleventh child. He had moved northeast for a while and married Marjory Taylor. Their son, Malcolm, was born in Nairn in 1886 at the home of Ewen's sister, Jane, known to later generations as 'Auntie Sinclair'. Ewen was in his nephew's, Alexander Falconer's, team. Sadly, Ewen collapsed near the beginning of the game and lay still on the ground. The Two Cronies take up the story: "Falconer, mounted on the 'Baikir Bhan's' [sic] well known mare galloped to Kingussie for a doctor." Dr Orchard returned on the mare which was "more speedy" than his horse, which Falconer rode back. Her speed was to no avail: Ewen was dead and the game was abandoned. Not so "the ample supplies" of food and drink provided by the sponsor. Those "were partaken of to the full,

after which fitting reference was made to the tragedy by the oldest man on the field – am Baillie Beg [sic] and by Dhonnuil Ruadh [sic] and Alistair Rose, an eloquent Gaelic orator." Perhaps the mourners then retired to "Sam's".

Fig 19 – Ewen Macpherson Cattanach. *(P Knapp)*

Sam's hostelry, The Hotel, had seen less sad days. After buying the lease to the property (currently Mains House), Sam had undertaken extensive renovations. His objective was to turn the building into Newtonmore's best hotel. A long advert in THE GLOBE, a London newspaper, on 22 May 1889, announced that "The Hotel, Newtonmore … replete with every Comfort" was now open. His efforts had seen the annual value of his hotel more than double in two years. After various extensions, it had almost doubled again by the end of the century. Sam had more plans to build up a successful and remunerative business. By 1891, he was employing shinty star Charley Kennedy to run his coach-hiring department. An early image

Fig 20 – The Hotel, letterhead.   *(Clan Macpherson Museum.)*

of Sam's fine establishment may be seen in a letterhead dated 1895.

From 1890, Sam and others, including Belleville, showed great commitment to the newly constituted Newtonmore Shinty Club. In early February 1891, the Newtonmore players were invited to Belleville to play a friendly game. The sides were drawn by 20 year olds, Duncan Cattanach, Croftbeg, and the above-mentioned Charley Kennedy. After-game refreshments were served to players and spectators by Belleville employees before the club captain, Sam, invited Malcolm Cattanach, "an old and well skilled player" on behalf of his successors in the team to present an ornate silver-mounted caman to the laird. Being born in the early 1820s, Malcolm probably played for Newtonmore during the difficult times of the 1840s and 1850s, perhaps in games sponsored by "Old Biallid" or Belleville's father. In an eloquent speech, Malcolm thanked the laird for his support of the club. Belleville was delighted with his presentation and voiced his appreciation (to the club and Malcolm).

Belleville supported his Newtonmore residents in other ways and their faith in him was evident the following year at the time of the second County Council elections. For health reasons, the Rev. N Dewar was not seeking re-election and a meeting was held in Newtonmore to discuss nominations for his successor. The observations of the large audience were extensively reported in THE INVERNESS COURIER of 22 Nov 1892. The candidates were Belleville and Donald Campbell, merchant, Kingussie, who often supported events in Newtonmore and was an ardent land reformer. Despite their opposing views, Mr Campbell "agreed with the opinion universally expressed that there was not a better landlord or more kind-hearted courteous gentleman to be found in the North of Scotland." William Ross endorsed that, pointing out that "Belleville was first landlord to make allotments, and that before there was an Act of Parliament." Newton Parks allotments have already been noted and in 1891, Belleville converted two good arable fields of 31 acres on Banchor Farm, between the Spey and the railway line, into 12 allotments. Donald Campbell fought the election partly on an anti-landlordism ticket. He contended that "the system of landlordism had in the past been draining the life-blood of the poorer classes" and that landlords elected to the council looked after their own needs. He also disparaged highly paid council officials who sat in their offices "drawing up elaborate reports and drawing their salaries. These officials were seldom seen in districts like Badenoch." Despite Donald's contentions, Belleville was elected and his delighted supporters built a bonfire which was lit by one of the oldest male tenants in the district, John Cattanach, Croftbeg.

In those days, the name Cattanach was

prominent in Newtonmore. Another highly respected man of that clan had died in May 1891. Donald Cattanach, catechist and slater, and elder brother of Malcolm was 77. His life had been devoted to his family and his church. At the tender age of 18, Donald "was called 'to speak to the question' at the Friday service of the Communion in Kingussie."[1] By his mid-twenties Donald was "frequently lecturing, and expounding the shorter Catechism to crowds of people" in Balgowan.[2] The catechist's duty was "to visit every family in their district … catechising the young, reading with and instructing the more advanced in the great truths of our holy religion, drawing their attention to the concerns of their immortal souls, and by a holy life and conversation setting an example to those among whom they are placed of the practical influence of that religion which it is their object to explain and enforce."[3] Donald's assiduous labour for his church and his strenuous occupation of slater had taken a toll. Several years earlier, deterioration in his health had prevented him continuing religious teaching in his beloved Free Church. His presence was greatly missed in many kirks in the Highlands where worshipers had thronged to hear him. Sadly, his church was in turmoil.

Since the mid-1860s some members had felt that the Free Church was moving away from its founding principles. Later, in several areas of Scotland, it was proposed that the Free Church should have instrumental music and sing hymns as well as the traditional psalms.[4] To help ease the problems, union with the United Presbyterian Church was suggested but was not supported by most Free Church people. However, in mid-1893, a small group including Duncan Fraser, Carrbridge, seceded to form the Free Presbyterian Church of Scotland. "The first meeting of the Free Church Secessionists in the Newtonmore district was held on Sunday

Fig 21 – Donald Cattanach. *(D Barr.)*

in the Public Hall, and was well attended, Mr Fraser, Carrbridge delivered an impressive address."[5] The Church of Scotland and the Free Church already had congregations in Newtonmore although neither had a church building in the village. Meetings were held in the main schoolroom on the Sabbath evening and attended by both denominations. The mother church for both was in Kingussie. The Newtonmore meetings were conducted once a month by Mr Dewar, the Free Church minister, and the following month by Mr Mackenzie, the Established Church minister. On the other Sundays, the services were led by The Men (*Na Daoine*) who included John Gray, Craggan; John Blair, Knock; and Ewen Macdonald, Ralia. Earlier leaders had been Alexander Cattanach, born in Strone, but later farmed at Auchmore and Donald Cattanach, Newtonmore. *Seonaidh a' Mhaighstir* observed that "there was no animosity between the two faiths when they met together." The Rev. Mackenzie spoke very highly of The Rev. Dewar, relating that "on our friendship there has never fallen a single shadow."[6] Those two churches served an area, in and around Newtonmore, populated by about 600 people. A third church might struggle to become established. For a few years, Mr Fraser continued to organise occasional Free Presbyterian meetings in Newtonmore and Kingussie.

It should be noted the Church of Scotland itself was not without internal tensions. An Act of 1874 had repealed patronage. Old habits died hard and established lairds often held entrenched views. It took many years, in some Established Churches, for the congregations to be given the freedom to use the powers of the Act. However, after working through that problem, the Church of Scotland started to gain members. Two churches in Newtonmore did survive and by 1896 each had managed to build an attractive place of worship. St Columba's Church of Scotland at the western approaches and the Free Church of Scotland on the site where St Bride's now stands, were built mainly by Newtonmore men, many of whom were skilled masons, carpenters, slaters and plasterers.

Earlier in the decade, some of those craftsmen were employed rebuilding and renovating houses. When thatched roofs were being prepared for slating, householders usually had the roof slightly heightened. As the village houses were upgraded plumbers began to be employed. William Grant, son of Paul, trained as a plumber in Inverness and worked on many local houses from the mid-1890s. Two decades later, around half of the buildings on the north-side of the Main Street had only an outside tap.[7] Tradesmen were also employed on business premises, such as the hotels being developed by Sam and by John Anderson, and public buildings. One public building which could have come to Newtonmore was a hospital. In 1893, Dr Ogilvy Grant, county medical officer, visited Newtonmore to see if there was a suitable site for a hospital, which needed to be "sufficiently isolated" but, also have ease of access. Those attributes were ultimately found three miles away and Dr de Watteville's sanatorium eventuated on the outskirts of Kingussie in 1901. Tuberculosis

was becoming a problem in Scotland. The settlements shared the Badenoch benefits of clean, fresh air: a particular boon to visitors from southern conurbations.

That unpolluted atmosphere drew a small annual increase in the number of visitors to Newtonmore throughout the 1890s. In May 1893, THE NORTHERN CHRONICLE reported that Newtonmore "is growing yearly in

High Street, Newtonmore. In Winter. P. T. K.

Fig 22 – Anderson's Hotel on right. Note single storey Rockview, now Ardblair, on left and the old toll house in the grounds of Heath Cottage *(S Macdonald.)*

popularity with summer visitors, surrounded as it is by some of the finest mountain scenery to be seen anywhere in the Highlands, while it lies in close proximity to excellent fishing streams." Often the hotels and every available letting house of the few on offer were full for the busy months of June through to September. Sam Macdonald and John Anderson anticipated the extra demand and expanded their hotels in 1893. Regular increases in visitor numbers were particularly noticeable after 1895 when villas began to be built in scenic areas away from the Main Street. Some of the earliest visitors to find Newtonmore were doctors and ministers, mainly from Dundee and Edinburgh. Word spread through them that Newtonmore was a healthy, scenic area in which to spend their holidays. Access from the South was becoming easier as trains became more comfortable and faster. The Highland Railway had introduced sleeping cars in 1878 and upgraded to Pullman cars in 1885.[8] In the 1890s, that company tried unsuccessfully to obtain land in Newtonmore on which to build a railway hotel.[9] The railway companies now recognised that Newtonmore was worth investing in and a service from the west was proposed.

In 1863, people from Fort William, being aware of the building of the new railway in Badenoch, realised the potential benefits of rail travel. They proposed building a railway line between Fort William and Newtonmore Station, engaging Thomas Bouch, CE to survey the line. Perhaps it was fortunate that the line did not materialise: Mr Bouch was the civil engineer who designed the ill-fated Tay Rail Bridge. An earlier survey in 1845 had been undertaken on a proposed line from Ballachullish Ferry to Badenoch. Fort William had to wait until 1894 to be served by a railway. During its construction, the West Highland Railway Company asked for Parliamentary powers to build a rail line from Spean Bridge to Badenoch. That project of late 1893 did not progress. A couple of years later, Badenoch folk took the initiative at a well-attended meeting in The Hotel, Newtonmore. That was chaired by Col Macpherson of Glentruim, whose family had shown much support of the railways. Cluny could not attend but sent his apologies:

Dear Glentruim, I am sorry I am unable to attend your meeting today, but I write to say that I am entirely in favour of the proposed railway extension from Inverlair to Kingussie, as I think it would be of great benefit to the country by opening it up and increasing the facilities of travelling, thereby bringing more people into the district, also of cheapening the cost of carriage of all sorts of produce. Yours sincerely, Cluny.[10]

Three railway companies were willing to bid for the line but William Cattanach urged the meeting not to consider a bid from the Highland Railway, suggesting that they were too slow. Newtonmore men: Alexander Cattanach; Malcolm Cattanach; William Cattanach; Sam Macdonald; Alexander Macpherson, builder; *Seumas Mòr,* coal merchant and Robert Sellar were appointed to the committee formed to promote the scheme. Team Badenoch had no more success than Team Lochaber. A year later, another meeting at The Hotel backed a scheme to build a light railway from Newtonmore to Drumgask on the south side of the Spey. The debate about a railway to the West chugged on. Even as late as 1919, a proposal for a rail link from Badenoch to Tulloch was being considered. By that time, the state of the roads had vastly improved, but in the 1890s a journey by road was still considered to be hazardous and many people preferred to travel by train.

Newtonmore Station hit the newspaper headlines in April 1893. The wooden station and the agent's stone-built house had been rapidly burned to the ground. The fire probably started from a spark in the grate of the office. It was unmanned as the railway servants were out attending to points and trains. The late-night blaze was noticed by Peter T Kennedy, the agent, who raised the alarm and rushed into the office to try to quell the fire. A number of residents from the village ran to help. By the end of July that year the Highland Railway Company had engaged Strone-born Alexander Cattanach, by then a builder in Kingussie, to erect a new station and station-master's house, plus two double houses to accommodate pointsmen and surfacemen.

The following summer, Newtonmore again featured widely in the British press when, a fatal train crash occurred there on Thurs 2 Aug 1894. At 3.10 pm, a north-bound passenger train ploughed headfirst into a goods train waiting on the station passing loop. The collision caused the engines and some carriages to be buckled and partially derailed. Professor John Dobie, a brilliant, energetic, adventurous young man was one of the many passengers. At Blair Atholl he had moved into the horsebox, the third carriage, to comfort his steed. On impact, the buffers of the second carriage had been pushed through into the horsebox and fatally crushed the Rev. Professor Dobie. It was the first fatal train crash on that line. Driver Adams of the goods train suffered a dislocated shoulder and his stoker had both legs broken. Some people with more serious injuries could not be moved from Newtonmore. Other casualties were shaken and less seriously hurt.

They owed thanks to David Adams who had put his stationary locomotive into reverse when he became aware of the impending crash. His prompt action probably prevented more trauma. Some of the wounded were prominent citizens. Col. Frederick Baillie from Edinburgh had critical spinal injuries. Mrs Jessie Taylor, wife of Prof. Malcolm Taylor of Edinburgh had a dislocated hip and other troubles. She was attended by Prof. Annandale from Edinburgh and lay in The Hotel, Newtonmore for many days after having the hip set. Her maid, Catherine Macrae, a native of Stromeferry, was also injured. Mr Robert Parker, an engineer in the Dundee area, was travelling in the first carriage and was badly shaken. The Parkers were regular visitors to Newtonmore. His wife had gone down to the station to meet him and witnessed him being pulled from the wreckage through a window. Their daughter, Bella, loved the area so much that she gave talks extolling the virtues of Badenoch to local groups near their home in Forfarshire. Mrs Parker was probably one of many who witnessed the carnage from the platform that day.

August was the busiest month at Newtonmore Station. As well as general holiday-makers, large groups came to the sporting estates. Most shooting tenants brought friends, families, dogs, an array of servants including grooms and lots of luggage. The village carters were kept extremely busy transporting folk and their paraphernalia to and from the station. Some of the visiting guns came on their own private trains and the Highland Railway often had to put on extra services at that time of the year. The railway squad succeeded in reopening one line at Newtonmore by seven that evening.

After the Board of Trade's initial inquiry on 4 August, the drivers of the two engines on the passenger train along with Peter T Kennedy, were arrested and examined "on a charge of criminal culpability." Peter, whose hours of duty were 07.30 until midnight, was the station-master. He also had to act as signalman at the south signal cabin, which was about 500 yards from the other cabin, manned by a pointsman. The inquiry reported at the end of August that: "The collision was due to the station-master's delay in attending to the signaling of the down train, to the signal not working properly, and to the drivers delaying the stoppage of the down train too long." It also highlighted the long working hours of railway servants: that had previously caused concern.[11] The three men were found not guilty after the trial on 16 Oct 1894. Peter T Kennedy who had the misfortune to be involved in both catastrophes at Newtonmore Station must have been relieved.

Following his arrival in Newtonmore, Peter was added to the "Roll of Communicants" of Kingussie Church of Scotland, "after examination", in June 1879.

From 1880 the School Board minutes listed Peter as one of the people who supplied coal to the school. Coal was delivered to local stations and often the station-master acted as the coal merchant. In 1881 & '91, Peter was listed as a railway agent. In 1900, he was mentioned as a Sunday School Teacher at St Columba's Church, Newtonmore. The 1899 VR lists him as "late station agent" paying £4 per annum to rent a bicycle store at the west end of Newtonmore. The station-masters from 1896, in quick succession, were Donald Macaulay, Alexander Duncan and James Aytoun. Alexander MacGregor was there by 1901 and stayed until at least 1911. The 1901 census saw Peter, a "cycle factory, coal and commission agent", visiting his mother at Inver, Perthshire. In 1911, Peter gave his occupation as a self-employed mechanic at his cycle factory. George A Hall, who wrote 'Leaves from a Rambler's Diary' left an interesting impression of Peter: "with whom I exchanged many happy hours in mutual pleasure on two subjects dear to both of us, cycles and photography ...What was the mystery behind this rare and interesting personality? Many times have I longed to probe beneath that gentlemanly bearing and find out what hid the gold from its proper circulation. But it was not to be." Peter produced several bonny postcards (Fig 22) of Newtonmore and also enjoyed music. He delighted in his gramophone which he played at his cycle factory. In the summer he opened the window and there are memories of the young girls dancing to it in the area between his premises and Sam's hotel.[12] He occasionally entertained on the violin at concerts and also in the band at local dances. He may have played at "the finishing assembly" of the two-month series of dancing classes held in Newtonmore by a Mr Wight in the spring of 1893.[13] The master of ceremonies, A Maclean, Banchor Mains, was assisted by Donald Cameron, Newtonmore; more than 30 couples were present. Dances were often held in the village hall after fund-raising events for local clubs, which increased in number throughout the 1890s.

Other physical recreations engaged the attention of Belleville. "Mr C B Macpherson of Belleville and a number of the villagers of Newtonmore played the first game on the new [golf] course on Saturday [20 May 1893]. The ground is very well adapted for the purpose, and the [nine-hole] course has been admirably laid out under Mr Macpherson's supervision. The youth of the village have been presented with a cricket set by Belleville; and it should also be mentioned that he is getting a commodious curling pond finished for the winter."[14] The laying out of the golf course and the building of the curling pond (near Glen Road) were organised by Robert Sellar, ground officer to Belleville. Tom Grant was the contractor for the curling pond and local men were offered much-needed employment. Belleville's efforts were applauded by Newtonmoracks. Accommodation providers recognised the importance of golf in attracting visitors. Sam was lauding the course in THE DUNDEE

ADVERTISER of 14 June 1893. Professional help was sought in 1897 when Tom Morris, St Andrews, was engaged to re-arrange the course.[15] Many of the shinty players became good golfers and supported both clubs in their fund-raising events.

Non-athletic societies functioning in the 1890s included the reading room, Newtonmore Burns Club and the (Grand) Lodge of the Good Templars. Many such temperance societies had sprung up in Scotland since about 1830. The Craigdhu Lodge of the Good Templars, Newtonmore opened in 1893 with 21 men and women enrolling.[16] It advocated total abstinence from all intoxicants.

The first half of the decade saw people in Newtonmore still agitating for more land. Two letters published in THE ABERDEEN PEOPLE'S JOURNAL in January 1894 were signed by Donald Cattanach, president, Newtonmore Land League. The extended Cattanach family had been prominent in their land quest for many years. Their fore-bears had lived, self-sufficiently, off the land, at Nuide, Ballachroan, Raitts and Milton of Banchor. Around 1835, their ancestor, widower John Cattanach, had been evicted from Milton. His children then obtained tenements in Newtonmore but were never happy about the diminutive area the tenement covered. They rented extra land wherever they could; mainly in unsecured, expensive tenancies. A "Mr Landless" wrote to

THE SCOTTISH HIGHLANDER in January 1890 detailing the lack of affordable land around Newtonmore. He asserted that crofters with secure tenancies paid about 10s per acre. Any short-term summer leases cost the villagers between 23s and 30s per acre. "Also they are paying £2 for every cow for summer pasturing, and their landlord is getting £10 for the wintering of this pasture." The land leaguers lobbied anyone who might have influence. In February 1893, THE NORTHERN CHRONICLE published a report entitled: "NEWTONMORE- The Allotments Movement." It said that some ratepayers in Newtonmore wanted extensions to land they already had; others just wanted some land. They had petitioned the Badenoch District of the county council. When their sub-committee, consisting mainly of big land-owners or factors, met in Newtonmore: "A number of ratepayers appeared and specified their requirements" for land around the village which was rented to Allan MacGillivray, farmer, Banchor. In May 1893, Dr MacGregor, Liberal MP for Inverness-shire, brought up the matter in the Commons. He pointed out that the county council had refused to put its powers under the Allotments (Scotland) Act into operation in Newtonmore and Portree, "owing to the heavy expense necessary to compel unwilling landlords to give the land asked for." The Act allowed for compulsory purchase of land by the council for allotments.

Dr MacGregor asked the Secretary of State for Scotland if the Government would "take steps to simplify and cheapen the procedure by which land may be obtained by the people on fair terms."

The years 1893/4 were an opportune time for the local group to pursue their cause for more land. The Royal Commission (Highlands and Islands), instigated by Gladstone's Liberal government in 1892, had been taking evidence at more than 60 venues throughout the Gaidhealtachd. It had been set up in response to pressure for more small areas to be made available to those needing land. In Kingussie, on 14 Aug 1894, the commissioners took statements from several landowners and factors who claimed that there was little suitable land available. They also heard contrary evidence from Donald Campbell, merchant, Kingussie, and several Newtonmore Cattanachs who each made a strong case for re-occupation of much Badenoch land given over to sheep farming or deer forests.

When Malcolm Cattanach, 74, stood up to give his evidence, the commissioners asked about his relationship to the previous witness: Donald Cattanach, 55, merchant. Malcolm explained that Donald was "the son of my half-brother." Did they suspect a Clan Chattan conspiracy? The relationship question was later addresses to Alexander Cattanach (*Alaidh an Tàilleir*), 43, mason

who said he was "a distant relative." That gave a link back to Milton. Malcolm's father, John, had a lease there through his wife's father – a McIntosh. Malcolm's connection to Alexander was probably through Alexander's paternal grandmother, a Milton McIntosh. The Cattanachs and McIntoshes were both part of the 1830s partial clearances at Milton with the McIntoshes having been previously

Fig 23 – Malcolm Cattanach. *(O'Reilly family.)*

threatened with removal between 1801 and 1806. Alexander's father, John Cattanach, had been menaced with eviction from Croft of Clune in 1874. Those persecutions gave them cause to resent the Macphersons of Belleville, who had instigated the evictions. Malcolm had travelled extensively in Badenoch for his work as a slater. He was therefore able to give a very comprehensive report on present and previous land use throughout the area. He also spoke knowledgeably about his grandparents and his parents, their lifestyles and their problems. His evidence gave a brief insight into Newtonmore and its environs in the 19th century. It is one of the few pieces of indigenous history we have from that time and place.

The report of the Royal Commission (Highlands and Islands, 1892) – also known as the Deer Forest Commission – was published at the beginning of April 1895. It scheduled many acres in Inverness-shire that would be suitable for crofting. However, the failing Liberal government introduced an insipid bill which did not advocate the creation of new holdings. Dr MacGregor, MP, was so disgusted that he resigned his seat. The Liberal government was replaced by a Conservative one which held office from mid-1895 to the end of 1905. James Baillie of Dochfour, superior of Kingussie, became the MP after he had battled through two election campaigns against two different Liberal candidates in the space of

two months following Dr MacGregor's resignation. His June opponent, Donald MacRae, Balallan, who was well-known locally, visited Newtonmore at the beginning of the month. He spoke mainly about the land question, pointing out that Mr Baillie was a proprietor and many landlords "had declared that there was no land in the Highlands which could profitably be converted into small holdings." He added that the "Deer Forest Commission had unanimously reported that there were two million acres which could be devoted to such a purpose, many of them on the properties of landlords who themselves insisted there was not."[17] William C Macpherson, clothier, chaired the meeting and Duncan Forbes, flesher, proposed the vote of thanks. Duncan and his son, Robert, innkeeper, had both signed the nomination papers for Balallan who was comprehensively defeated. The following month, Neil Kennedy, an Edinburgh advocate, was selected to stand against Mr Baillie. Mr Kennedy, having been brought up at Creich in the heart of the notorious Sutherland clearances country, was a strong supporter of the land lobby. This time, Mr Baillie won by only 100 votes, which says a lot for the reputation of Mr Kennedy. In 1912, as Lord Kennedy, he became the first chairman of the Land Court, which over the years has held several sessions in Newtonmore.

It did not need such a body to resolve the 1890s land issue there. According to

THE INVERNESS COURIER of 20 Dec 1895, "Balavil … has just allotted to the people of Newtonmore, one of his Badenoch estates, between 20 and 30 acres of the finest arable land on the farm of Banchor, contiguous to the village… skilled surveyors divided the ground into between 25 and 30 allotments, and in order to show the extreme fairness of Mr Macpherson regarding the division of the ground, he has decided that the respective plots shall be balloted for." The new allotments ran alongside the railway from the Spey bridge to Station Road. They were awarded to villagers who had not previously had lots. Balavil (formerly Belleville) had now put 72 acres of farmland, around half the arable area of Banchor Mains, into lots. Although those lots and the other rented, poorer-quality, land (about 74 acres) around the village did not have security of tenure, it became obvious, from each successive VR, that the same tenants rented the land each year. Balavil had also lost the rental income from the area which he gifted to the village for the golf course. If those allotments, on which they grew corn, potatoes, carrots, turnips and forage, had been available to the early villagers, life would have been much easier for them. The same article noted that the laird "had agreed to give a site for a Free Church on the same nominal terms as he had given for the recently erected Established Church."

There had been an Established Church in Kingussie serving the whole parish long before Newtonmore emerged. From 1843, Kingussie Free Church of Scotland drew much support throughout the parish. As the population of Newtonmore and the number of summer visitors increased, members of both churches felt the need to have, in their village, their own church and their own minister. Guest preachers, holidaying in the area, had offered their services in the summer. Layman Alexander Cameron was a missionary to the Newtonmore Free Church congregation in 1893/4. During the following summers, Professor Iverach, Free Church College, Aberdeen, led the services in Newtonmore. James Iverach was a keen golfer. He rented Aultlarie Farm House from Paul Grant, jnr, and built up friendships in Newtonmore. At his funeral in 1922, one of the pall bearers was the Minister of Pensions at Westminster, the Right Hon Ian Macpherson, (younger brother of TSM). Another on the cord was Aberdonian architect, Duncan McMillan, who shared his love of Aultlarie with the late professor. Duncan's grandfather, John Ross, had farmed there in the 1840s before moving to Gaskbeg Farm, Laggan.

In September 1894, Donald Cattanach, William Ross and two other Newtonmore residents appealed to the Church of Scotland authorities that, "the district was annually becoming more popular as a summer resort …

and that many of the older native population [who walked to Church] as well as visitors were unable on account of distance to attend any of the Sabbath Services in Kingussie."[18] They requested a missionary at Newtonmore and for regular mid-day services in Gaelic and English. Progress in that initiative was reported in THE KINGUSSIE PARISH MAGAZINE: the congregation did well to persist with their campaign. Their Newtonmore church was considered a mission station of the mother church in Kingussie and was given the same name, St Columba's. The attractive church was built at the west end of the village near Balvattan. Designed to house up to 600 people, it was opened on Thurs 7 Nov 1895 by the Rev. Dr Norman Macleod of Inverness, who preached in English and then in Gaelic. THE NORTHERN CHRONICLE reported that there had been a large attendance which included some who did not adhere to the Church of Scotland. The estimated cost for the church was £850. Of that, £500 had been obtained through church grants and £100 had been donated, half by Lachlan Macpherson of Corrimony, grandson of 'Old Biallid'. Lachlan, who grew up at Nuide, had a military career before emigrating to New Zealand where he prospered. He married Elizabeth Hussey an English heiress with Badenoch connections in 1885. Elizabeth was the great granddaughter of *Iain Bàn a' Gharbhath,* the well-loved tenant of Garvamore

earlier that century. Corrimony "was a man of great force of character, combined with great kindliness of disposition. He was held in the very highest esteem by everyone"[19] He was very fond of his ancestral area and gave many donations to organisations and people in Kingussie Parish as well as in Corrimony. Despite Lachlan's generosity, about £250 was still needed.

The kirk session praised Robert Sellar "for the amount of time and trouble he took in attending to all matters connected with the Newtonmore Church during the first few months, and before committees and officials were appointed." The Rev. John McKechnie, assistant, St Columba Parish Church, Glasgow became the minister of Newtonmore "mission station" in February 1896. Newtonmore was unfortunate: young teachers at the school didn't stay long. It was a similar story with the early ministers. Young Mr McKechnie moved on after two years. He was replaced by the Rev. Coll Macdonald, incumbent from May 1898 to September 1899 who was succeeded by the Rev. Norman D Mackay. The minister's stipend of £115/year was paid by 58 resident-worshippers and donations from Mrs Brewster Macpherson, Mrs Carnegie and others. Grants from church committees also helped. THE KINGUSSIE PARISH MAGAZINE of February 1897 reported: "The congregation have lately placed a heating apparatus in the building, and this has added much to their comfort. The idea was suggested to them by Mr Parker, Dundee, who, during a long series of years, has been a welcome visitor to Newtonmore."[20]

On 30 Dec 1896, Balavil awarded a feu charter, for the ground on which St Bride's Church now stands, to the "Trustees for the Mission Station of Newtonmore, Parish of Kingussie, belonging and adhering to the Free Church of Scotland … presently worshipping at Newtonmore under the pastoral oversight of Rev. N Dewar." The attractive building seated

around 250 and cost £640, of which £400 was raised by the congregation – a huge amount for that congregation at Newtonmore to find. They were to occupy that building in peace only until late 1900, when internal strife caused another secession.

The erection of the churches appeared to herald a building boom in Newtonmore. The policy for allocating building land seemed to alter about the mid-90s when Balavil's preferred option changed to offering feus. As the years went on, more and more plots became

E. End, Newtonmore, Inverness-Shire. D. A.

Fig 24 – Part of Pine Cottage and a glimpse of the newly rebuilt Balavil Hotel. *(S Macdonald.)*

available. By the time of the revaluation in the early 1910s, Balavil had land assigned for feus as far north on Craggan as the cattle grid on Strone Road.

The earliest feu charter (apart from that for the school) was awarded to Andrew *Clachair* (Andrew Cattanach) on 26 Nov 1895. Andrew, a mason, built Pine Cottage for himself and his new wife, Isabella Gordon. About a decade later, Andrew built, behind his house, the house currently known as Glenbrae. It was situated about the middle of the long strip of wood which then clung to the brae face, stretching between the two legs of the ∩-shaped Strone Road. The only break in those trees was a pass to accommodate the track which ran from Strone Road between Croftbeg and Croft of Clune and was used by crofters to take cattle and sheep to their grazings on the Dell. That right-of-way then ran between Pine Cottage and Birch Cottage, in which Angus Macpherson, his wife Margaret Sellar and their large family lived from 1896 to 1914. Having crossed the main road it continued past the east side of Loch Imrich. That access was written into the feu charters of several houses. It almost coincided with the old boundary between Clune Estate and the Duke of Gordon's land at Strone.

It was to springs above Strone that the district council went for a new water supply. By August 1896, William Grant, plumber, had installed a system costing just under £500. A new sewerage system was also needed, but was deferred because of cost. House plots were awarded that year in wooded areas.

Alexander Macpherson, a busy builder, erected Larch Cottage (currently Greenways) on land leased from Balavil. On part of the "old market stance plantation", Ronald Macpherson, tailor, had Craggan View built and John Middlemas built Willow Cottage (currently Cairngorm), his access being a track from the Main Street running by the west side of the school grounds. In the area near Loch Imrich, Robert Sellar had Bonanza (currently Ballytrim) erected and Newtonmore flesher, Duncan MacDonald, born at Lakefield Estate, Glen Urquhart, built a wooden house. By 1902, Duncan and his son, Alexander, a mason, had built the stone house on the Lakefield feu. At the west end, one of the holiday brigade, Rev. John Campbell, had Croftdhuac built. The Campbell family, who loved the Strath of the Spey, chose Newtonmore because the rail fare from Kirkcaldy, their hometown, was less than £1. The Rev. Mr Campbell was "the first Old Kirk minister to be appointed by the wishes of the congregation following the repeal of Patronage by the Act of 1874." The Campbells let out their house for part of the summer season. Outwith that time, they enjoyed using Croftdhuac for family holidays. Over many

	Name in 2020	1897 proprietor	Lease or feu	Water*
1	[Original] Pine Cottage	Andrew Cattanach	Feu, 1895	Y
2	Novaar	Angus Macpherson	Feu, 1896	N?
3	Greystones & Larchview	Miss Annie Cattanach	Lease, 1831	Cold water in both
4	Greenbank & Mo Dhachaidh	John Guthrie	Lease, 1831	Cold water in one
5	Craigard, Craigmore Cottage, Cairnsmore, Lochview	Widow Catherine Macdonald	Lease	Cold water
6	Rose Cottage	Charles McIntosh	Lease, 1831	N
7	Bhun-a-Mhonadh	Mrs Eliza Wallace	Lease, 1831	N?
8	Clune House & Granite House	Alexander Cattanach	Lease, 1831	N
9	Glenavon Ho. was Moy Cottage.	Donald McIntosh	No lease	N
10	Co-op Car Park [was Daisy Cottage/Rannoch Cottage]	Representatives of late Ewen Cameron	Lease, 1835	Cold water
11	Balavil Hotel	Robert Forbes	Lease, 1831	Hot & cold water
12	Lynbeg, Beryldene	Ewen Kennedy	Lease, 1834	?
13	Hawthorn Cottage	John Gray, Craggan	Lease, 1831	N?
14	Elm Cottage, Cluny Cottage	*Seumas Mòr,* James Macpherson	Lease, 1831	N?
15	Briar Cottage	Widow Isabella Cameron	Lease, 1833	N
16	Druim Alban	John Macdonald	Lease, 1834	N
17	Ordbhan	Widow Unie Macdonald	Lease, 1865	N
18	Strathspey Mountain Hostel	John Maclean	Lease, 1856	N?
19	Woodlea	Mrs Barbara Stewart	Lease, 1869	N
20	Greenways	Alexander Macpherson	Lease, 1894	Hot & cold water
21	Craggan View	Ronald Macpherson	Feu, 1896	Y?
22	Cairngorm	John Middlemas	Feu, 1896	Y?
23	Ballytrim	Robert Sellar	Feu, 1896	Y?
24	Larick House	Duncan Macdonald	Feu, 1896, wooden house at Lakefield	??

*Water in house in 1910 – not noted for some

Chart for 1897 map. Information from VRs, sasines and IR revaluation notes.

Plots 1 to 24 had been developed by 1897. Since then many more houses have been built.
Some of the original houses have since been rebuilt.

Fig 25 – Chart for 1897 map. *(M Mackenzie.)*

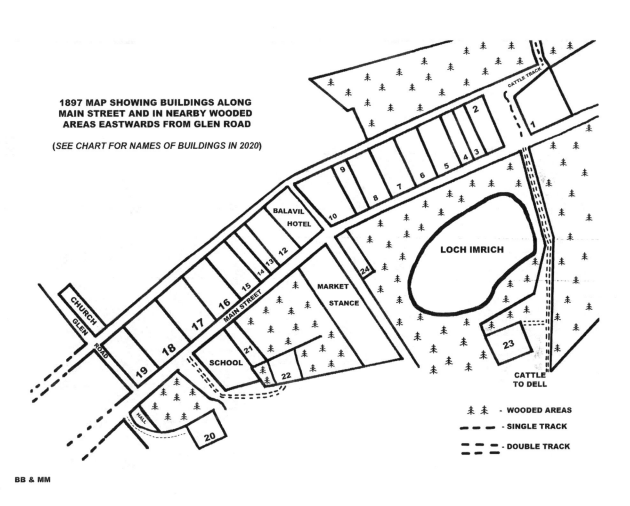

1897 MAP SHOWING BUILDINGS ALONG MAIN STREET AND IN NEARBY WOODED AREAS EASTWARDS FROM GLEN ROAD

(*SEE CHART FOR NAMES OF BUILDINGS IN 2020*)

CATTLE TRACK

2

1

9

8 7 6 5 4 3

BALAVIL HOTEL

10

14 13 12

LOCH IMRICH

CHURCH

GLEN ROAD

15

16

17

18

19

MAIN STREET

24

MARKET STANCE

21

SCHOOL

22

23

CATTLE TO DELL

HALL

20

⚘ ⚘ - WOODED AREAS

― ― ― - SINGLE TRACK

▬ ▬ ▬ - DOUBLE TRACK

BB & MM

Fig 26 – 1897 map. *(B Bielby, M Mackenzie.)*

years this talented family cheerfully contributed to clubs and ventures in the village.

Charles Grant Kennedy and his siblings missed Newtonmore. After the death of his father, Angus (*Aonghas Ruadh*), in 1873, most of the family moved to Edinburgh. Shinty supporters Charles and his brother Alexander (*Alaidh Ruadh*) gifted the Kennedy Caman for shinty competitions. In June 1897, Charles obtained a feu off Station Road, where he commissioned Victoria Villa. A former shinty mate of Charles, Ewen Cattanach (*Eòghann Clachair*), built his house, New Glen, sometimes known as *Druimbreac* (currently *Rhu Grianach*) at the east end of the village. Those houses were almost identical and were probably designed by Ewen's brother, Alexander, whose house, The Laurels, Kingussie, was similar in style. Those were the only new substantial stone-built houses listed on the VR of 1898. An article in THE ABERDEEN PEOPLE'S JOURNAL of 25 Sept 1897 extolled the attractions of Badenoch to visitors and explained the finances of building for letting: "Having acquired two or three hundred pounds by his own industry, our speculator borrows two or three hundreds more from the local banker or solicitor, and builds a comfortable villa." The feu, materials and labour were cheap and a handsome villa in Newtonmore could be erected for £600 as compared to Broughty Ferry where it might cost £1000.

"The furnishing probably costs another £200. Such a house, should the owner be fortunate, may be let for four months at from £20 to £30 a month." The owner had the use of it for the other months and summered in a garden hut. Ewen had recently sold a property in Kingussie for £365, so that gave him a good start towards his handsome house. Those figures seem to be accurate as Geordie (NZ) said that his sister built Ravenswood for £600 and the income was about £20 per month in July and £30 in August. Glenmore, at the east-end was built for the same amount according to the daughter of John Macdonald, the original feuar.

Ravenswood and Glenmore were built around 1900, but in the late 1890s wooden houses seemed to become popular. Thomas Williamson, china merchant, obtained a site in the wood, north of the school, beside the path that now leads to the swing park. In 1901, Thomas and his wife and seven children were living there and working from their house which has three rooms with windows. It was the first house in that wooded area.

Angus Macdonald, widower and half-brother of John Middlemas, also used wood for his house next to Birch Cottage. It first appeared on the 1898 VR, despite his feu charter being dated 20 Oct 1896. Ellen Stewart, wife of Angus, had died in 1877, soon after the birth of their son, John. Christina Macdonald, mother of the half-brothers, helped to bring up John and his sister, *Gracag*. John became a carpenter, perhaps with his uncle, John Middlemas. Angus was one of the first in Badenoch to build with railway sleepers. His circumstance made that feasible. Angus worked on the railway and his brother and son were both carpenters. When surplus sleepers became available, "employees of the railway were given priority and they also paid a reduced rate." In 1927, rail worker, Duncan Macdonald bought two hundred sleepers at one shilling and sixpence each to build his house in Kingussie. They were positioned vertically, "butted together and secured with massive nine inch nails driven through at an angle from one sleeper to the next… Outside, the vertical joints between the sleepers were sealed by timber cover strips."[21] In many cases chicken wire was nailed to the cover strips and a "layer of harling" was applied. Sleeper-built houses were more common in Newtonmore and Kingussie than elsewhere in the Highlands. The VRs indicate that a house was made of wood. However not all wooden houses from that period were built with sleepers and it is sometimes hard to tell if sleepers had been used. In 1905, Grace Macdonald, married Alister MacKintosh , a joiner from Moy who had come to work in Newtonmore. Their descendants lived in Angus's house for over 100 years.

The VR of 1899 listed seven new houses. Two were sizeable and stone-built, The Birches for Duncan Anderson and Broomfield (currently *Coire Cas*) for Donald Macdonald, brother of Sam. The houses were built, with borrowed money, to service the ever increasing tourist trade. Although a few building societies existed in Scotland, that did not seem to be the preferred option locally. Many people arranged private loans through solicitors, agents or friends. Should the lender call a loan in, more private funding had to be arranged very quickly. The Register of Sasines shows details of the loans, with those being recorded soon after the feu charter was registered. The value of the house was used as surety for the loan. Some householders and businesses in Newtonmore defaulted on loan payments and lost their homes or livelihoods. A smaller stone house appeared on the 1899 VR. John Smith purchased a site with building thereon where Grogarry now sits beside the Laggan Road. The two buildings shown on the 1870 OS map in that vicinity were probably farm workers' cottages. John's father, Duncan, was working in Glen Banchor about the time of John's birth around 1844. The family lived in several parts of Badenoch depending on where work was available, but John and two of his siblings ended up back near where they were born. The house had a public room, kitchen and a bedroom, without a fireplace. The ceiling height was 7ft 6in. The two attic bedrooms upstairs were 6ft 6in high. There was no lath on the internal stone walls. The water tap was outside, as was the earth closet in a portable wooden shed.[7] Four of the new houses were small and wooden. Two on the north side of Church Terrace belonged to Thomas Williamson and his neighbour, Donald Campbell, carter. Two well-loved village characters occupied the others, which were south of the Main Street.

The road to the golf course was the site for the wooden house of *Alaidh Dòmhnallach*, Alexander Macdonald. He was the energetic and "likeable" *Alaidh laochan,* who nearly drowned in Loch Mohr.[22] During his long life he had many occupations. He was a 19-year-old farm servant when he married Balgowan lass, Margaret Macdonald, in 1856. In 1861 he was a carter and a quarryman in 1871. Later in the 1870s, he worked on the rebuilding of Ardverikie Lodge along with other Newtonmore men including Malcolm Cattanach whose initials are on a chimney there. On a Saturday, after work, they walked home to Newtonmore, returning on the Sunday afternoon. On one homeward journey, as they were approaching Newtonmore, *Alaidh* found Cluny's gold watch at the side of the road. He turned around and walked back to Cluny. The delighted Macpherson chief rewarded *Alaidh* with a 5s silver coin.[12] That would have paid his rent for four months. *Alaidh* rented various small cottages and by 1881 the family, which included six youngsters, was living in one of

James Macpherson's cottages. It was described 30 years later as comprising a room and bed-closet downstairs with a bedroom in the low roof. The stone walls had no lath and there was no water in the house.[7] Like many others, it had a basic shed at the rear. In 1881, *Alaidh*, who worked from home, gave his occupation as a butcher. The shed must have been his business premises. There was very little regulation of the meat trade in those days. The Cronies remembered the "rather crude methods of slaughtering." *Alaidh* "depended upon local production for his supplies of meat with occasionally a supply from Kingussie sources." *Alaidh* had also been a drover.

Dòmhnall Ruadh, Donald Kennedy, shoemaker, was described as "a universal favourite."[23] Donald was the eldest brother of Charles, Victoria Villa, their grandfather and great grandfather belonged to one of several Kennedy families who lived in Glen Banchor. That particular family was distinguished from the other Kennedys by the appellation, "*ruadh*" (red): fittingly the Cronies noted Donald's "bushy red beard and whiskers." Donald had settled in Newtonmore with his wife, Ann McIntosh, also of Glen Banchor stock, and family, before his widowed mother with five offspring moved to Edinburgh. It would be hard to chart Donald's occupations chronologically – he had so many. Originally he was a shoemaker, but his business hit hard times and on 17 Mar 1871 he was an inmate in the debtor's prison in Inverness. Donald, 29, was not detained much longer as he was home on 2 April, with his wife and three eldest children, when the 1871 census was recorded. Their 1871 dwelling which had two rooms with windows, also housed lodgers: John Macdonald, the new head teacher, and George Harrower, the police constable. It is hard to imagine the free-spirited Donald and his equally uninhibited neighbour, *Alaidh Dòmhnallach,* minding their Ps and Qs, even with those lodgers around. Did they have a shared business interest? *Alaidh* was a flesher and *Dòmhnall Ruadh* was said to be the person sent for when a villager needed a cow dispatched.

Alaidh and *Dòmhnall* shared their life-long love of shinty from their playing days to supporting their talented sons and, in Donald's case, his various roles within the shinty club. He was an eloquent Gaelic orator but spoke English less fluently. *Dòmhnall* is praised by everyone who mentions him in written or spoken reminiscences. They wrote of him as a mole catcher and a fencer but in successive censuses he was noted as a labourer or a shoemaker. There were several cobblers' businesses in the village in the 1890s. *Dòmhnall* probably topped-up his income from his fiercely competitive trade with one or two of his other occupations. His wooden property, which ran at a right angles to and sat back from the Main Street to the east side of Craggan View, was remembered for the many unofficial shinty forums held there. His fellow enthusiasts gathered there to ruminate on last weeks' result and plot how to win the next game. No doubt Donald's hospitable wife kept them supplied with tea and scones – her great nieces in Strone were famous for their girdle scones. Perhaps *Dòmhnall* supplied them with something stronger to drink. He was a regular at the Belleville Hotel in the days of Robbie Forbes's stewardship. The Cronies remembered that *Dòmhnall* had a "perpetual hard cough, for which according to him there was only one cure – a good dram." Perhaps *Dòmhnall* fitted in his lamp lighting on his way to the Belleville. "In all weathers Donald could be seen hurrying along the street with his ladder and oil-can" wrote *Seonaidh a' Mhaighstir,* adding that *Dòmhnall* was "a faithful and capable public servant." John Forbes, brother of Robbie, was likewise a cobbler who lit the lamps. *Dòmhnall* was also called upon for grave digging. *Dòmhnall* died in October 1916, not long after his house had been valued at £112. (The Newtonmore house of his brother Charles was valued at £805, but he had to work in Edinburgh to buy it). That of *Dòmhnall* was of wood and plaster, with an 11 ft high corrugated-iron roof. It contained three rooms and a bed recess. The workshop, lean-to, measured 8 ft by 12 ft with a roof height of 8 ft.[7]

Dòmhnall Ruadh and *Alaidh Dòmhnallach* both had small, low-valued houses. Their intangible riches lay in their love of and enthusiasm for their culture; also their commitment to their native place and its residents.

Ann, wife of *Dòmhnall*, lived on until 1934. She was remembered by the Strone Macdonalds as *Antaidh Bean Dhòmhnaill Ruaidh* (*Bean*, means wife). She was, in fact, their great aunt, but looked after them well. When they attended the school near her house, she provided lunch for them, to save them hurrying back to Strone. There were eight Macdonalds, quite a commitment for Ann Kennedy.

Kennedy was one of the widespread surnames in Newtonmore in the 19th century, the most popular being Macpherson, followed by Cattanach and Macdonald. Most families continued the tradition of naming children after their grandparents and other family members. Christian names were therefore reused and sometimes caused confusion among cousins with the same forename. Popular Christian names included John, Alexander, Angus, Donald, Isabella, Elspeth, Janet and Margaret. The Gaelic-speaking inhabitants of Newtonmore used traditional ways of differentiating possible misunderstandings when referring to people. One way was to associate a person with his or her father or mother. Andrew and John were names used by a particular Strone Macpherson family, with one of them remembered as *Seonaidh Anndra* – John, son of Andrew. One of the McIntosh families used the names John and Robert. *Iain Robaidh* was John, son of Robbie. He lived at the larch trees in Craggan and the Strone Macdonalds called him *Uncail sa' Chreagan*. Ranald Macpherson, *Rao'll a' Phleastarair,* was distinguished by his occupation and founded a dynasty of plasterers which spanned four generations. Some names stuck with families even to this day. There was the group of Macdonalds who were and are called *Bàillidh* and other Macdonalds were the Tormans. Names in a mixture of Gaelic usage and English lingered on in Newtonmore into the second half of the 20th century. Did you ever hear of Peggy Tom? Yes, dear Peggy O'Reilly, grand-daughter of Malcolm Cattanach. Peggy's father was Thomas Cattanach, *Tòm Chaluim* (Tom, son of Malcolm). In 1891, of the 364 persons in Newtonmore, 265 were listed as being able to speak both Gaelic and English and more would have heard it at home as many did not list their children as Gaelic speakers. The gentry were often referred by the names of their estates. Examples were "Old Biallid" and "Old Cluny". Both survived to a grand old age. They lived locally and were fluent in Gaelic, which they used with their tenants. The Forbes family did not attract nicknames, perhaps because there were only a few of that surname around.

Duncan Forbes, flesher, was the Newtonmore agent for THE SCOTTISH HIGHLANDER. Small amounts of Newtonmore news appeared intermittently in several Inverness-based newspapers. It is not clear who contributed that news. Much of it concerned good deeds being done by various benefactors to the people of Newtonmore. The question of whether that was an early example of spin, on behalf of the gentry, begs to be asked. Certainly there were examples of bias in reporting. In the run-up to elections, THE NORTHERN CHRONICLE seemed to prefer the Conservatives and THE SCOTTISH HIGHLANDER favoured the candidate who supported land reform. Despite the possibility of spin and bias, those are the sources of the following information regarding the inhabitants of Newtonmore.

The vagaries of the weather were very important because the people of Newtonmore still grew much of their food, and also, fodder for any animals they could keep. The winters of 1892 and 1895 were particularly bad for snow: rail and road access was regularly blocked. Flooding after snow melt or torrential downpours caused havoc on roads, railway and pastures. Poor weather caused problems with the harvesting of peat and oats and the growth of crops. Dr Mackenzie, parish minister and chairman of the school board was, as always, concerned for the pupils. At the end of August 1895, when the area was at its busiest with visitors, he organised a concert in Kingussie, which, at that time, had many more annual visitors than Newtonmore. The proceeds of the event "were to augment the local fund for providing hot dinners for pupils coming long distances to attend the burgh school." He reminded the audience that "Not a few of their pupils in Kingussie School came [walked] distances of three to six miles. In winter they had to leave home before daylight, and were absent for nine hours … a basin of warm soup in the forenoon was … greatly relished by them and did much good. Last winter they had had, on more than one night, forty-six degrees of frost. They were snowed-up, some of their roads being blocked for two months." Locals, including Miss Macarthur, Etteridge, and visitors contributed to the high class programme. Many organisations held fund-raising concerts in the summer when visitors were in residence. Those included shinty, golf and curling clubs and also the Kingussie, Alvie and Insh Provident Nursing Association.

That organisation had commenced in August 1894 with one nurse covering all areas from Dalwhinnie to Alvie: another suitable person to be sent for training had to be found quickly. In their inaugural year, 1,770 day visits and 135 night visits were made. Two thirds of those visits were made to the poor and elderly. No charge was made to them and "suitable food and special nourishment" were given when funds allowed. The association was funded by members who subscribed 1s or 2s per annum and paid the same per week when a nurse was required. They had precedence over non-members who were charged a little more. There was no charge for the head of the house who was usually the breadwinner. Annual expenses were around £100 so donations from residents, visitors, shooting tenants and proprietors were gratefully received.

Landowners and sometimes the shooting tenants, like Andrew Carnegie, gave dinners or balls for local people. Newtonmore folk annually enjoyed their laird's dinner for his tenants and workers. A similar event was the estate ball at Glentruim. At such events there were often many toasts. Old people were highly respected and usually the eldest in the company was asked to do the honours. The same applied to the lighting of celebratory bonfires. Kenneth Logan, Glentruim; John Cattanach, Strone; Lachlan Grant, Glenbanchor; John Macdonald (*Bàillidh*), Newtonmore, were, among others, recorded in the Inverness press as performing such tasks. The Inverness papers occasionally reported on young men who had pursued illustrious careers away from Badenoch. TSM and his brother Ian received mentions as did the children of the PO family, the Stewarts. THE INVERNESS COURIER reported that the Rev. C Bentick, Kirkhill, preached in Gaelic at the Crown Court Church, London in December 1896. That church had many Highland worshippers and Alexander Macrae, whose father, Donald, was born in Glenbanchor was their resident minister for 17 years.

Charles Bentick was the grandson of Alexander Wilson, said to be the first inn keeper in Newtonmore. A few months before he died in 1868, Alex had led a celebration for the home-coming of Major Duncan Macpherson of Cluny and his bride. The young couple had received an overwhelming reception when they arrived at Kingussie Station. Their cavalcade heading to Cluny was led by Col Macpherson of Belleville. They were greeted at the east end of Newtonmore by a long procession of residents headed by 88 year old Mr Wilson who was "dressed in full Highland costume", as were most of the men. Following the practice of those days, the horses were unyoked and "the carriage was drawn by scores of brawny Highlanders" through the village and under a magnificent 36' high arch at the Laggan Road junction. Leading the procession, which included 150 school children, Mr Wilson, who carried a long pole with a showy banner, was flanked by Cluny's piper and Donald Macpherson, piper to the Volunteers. After the horses had been reunited with the carriage near the Calder, the young couple galloped off for Cluny being cheered by the numerous spectators. "Colonel Macpherson and the inhabitants then returned to the arch, where, by his orders, refreshments were served round" and the young pair were toasted. "The hundreds of spectators remained dancing at the arch for a couple of hours, when they retired to apply the torch to the bonfire erected near the village [east end] by Colonel Macpherson's tenants". The bonfire was one of several in prominent places around Badenoch that evening.[24]

Bonfires featured in two celebrations in June 1897 – the diamond jubilee of Queen Victoria and the marriage of another of the Cluny brothers. After singing the National Anthem, the jubilee procession was led from the village hall by the "tall figures of Mr A J Macpherson, Balabhadan, and Mr MacGillivray, Biallid, the one bearing the flag of the Royal Arms, the other the grand old Union Jack." The procession was piped along the flag-bedecked street by Tom Grant and passed through a beautiful arch erected at the east end by Robert Sellar. "On the golf course a stand was made on a picturesque hillock" where the crowd gathered for the festivities. After the singing of Psalm 100 and a speech by Balavil, his wife presented Jubilee medals to the children who later "engaged heartily in sports of all kinds." The celebrations were resumed at 10 pm: a bonfire was lit, "abundant refreshments were again served" and young and old danced to the pipes for many hours. The events were funded by public subscription and a donation from Balavil.

The wedding of Ewen Macpherson of Cluny took place in Cheltenham but the local members of the clan met to celebrate at Drumgask Hotel. That event was organised after an initial meeting in April 1897 of "members of the Badenoch Centre of the Clan Chattan Association" including Newtonmoracks, Alex Macpherson and Malcolm Cattanach.

After many years of supporting local efforts, Malcolm died in the autumn of 1899. His obituary in THE PEOPLE'S JOURNAL of 14 Oct 1899 told of his many years in business including his "most important and extensive contract" which lasted over several season – the slating of Ardverikie after the disastrous fire of 1873. In private, Malcolm, a staunch Free Churchman, was "of a genial, social, and most hospitable disposition." In politics "he was a sturdy Radical, holding very advanced views on the land … An extremely vigorous speaker in Gaelic, his appearance was always welcomed on the platform, and he seldom failed to give utterance to pungent sentences that stuck in the memory."

The newspapers of 14 Oct 1899 were dominated by reports of the outbreak of the Second South African War with which Newtonmore would have very tangible connections.

Selected further sources used in this chapter:

1 IC, 19/5/1891

2 GB0232, CH2/394/2, 81-86

3 GB0232, 01241/1/42, p. 16

4 Ansdell, p. 168

5 NC, 25/10/1893

6 GB0232, CH2/1419/5 1904

7 NRS/IRS68

8 Sinclair, 2013, p. 60

9 Sinclair, 2013, p. 95

10 IC, 15/11/1895

11 www.railwaysarchive.co.uk/documents/BoT_Newtonmore1894.pdf

12 Macdonald family

13 NC, 17/5/1893

14 NC, 24/5/1893

15 AJ, 16/7/1897

16 NC, 22/11/1893

17 GH, 6/6/1895

18 GB0232, CH2/1419/4 – p. 241/243

19 Otago Witness, 7/12/1904

20 GB0232, CH2/1419/5

21 Kerr, 16

22 BR, 18/4/59 [Cronies]

23 BR, 9/5/59 [Cronies]

24 IC, 19/3/1868

Chapter 10

Soldierly and Spiritual Strife

Early 1900s

By the beginning of 1900, Britain, supported by troops from its Empire, was deeply entrenched in major hostilities in South Africa: the Second South African (or Boer) War. There had been unrest and conflict in the various states in the southern region of Africa for many decades. The British government wanted to unify South Africa under Imperial British rule but two Boer republics wished to remain independent. The discovery of gold in the Transvaal concentrated the minds of those opponents: each desired to have control of, and benefit from, the lucrative mines. Britain was also negotiating for incomers to the Transvaal who were mainly British to be given the vote. Following the failure of talks to resolve those problems, hostilities against the South African Republic (Transvaal Republic) and the Orange Free State had started in October 1899. British troops, fighting an atypical war on strange territory, were struggling, especially around mid-December. The Boers achieved several impressive victories during the period termed "Black Week" in the British press. Private William Ritchie, Newtonmore, was in the 1st Battalion, Gordon Highlanders,[1] which suffered heavy

losses in the Battle of Magersfontein during that week. The conflict was widely reported in local and national newspapers and serving men wrote home about the severe difficulties they were experiencing. Badenoch people may have felt a closer connection to the war when the trains carrying successive Northern units being drafted to the front passed through Kingussie and Newtonmore en route for Southampton.

In its first edition of 1900, THE PEOPLE'S JOURNAL reported that at Kingussie: "A crowd assembled at the Railway Station on Tuesday to hail the detachment of Seaforths en route by special train to Southampton where they will embark on the Kildonan Castle for South Africa." The soldiers were in khaki uniform and seemed in good spirits. They were followed south in mid-February by 400 Cameron Highlanders Reservists. On 9 March, three trains connected with the recently formed Lovat Scouts passed through Badenoch on their journey south. The first carried 110 horses and equipment. Their riders, the 1st Company, followed on the second train. The 2nd Company, the dismounted section of 114 men, travelled later that day. In mid-April, Badenoch people bade an emotional farewell to some of their own. Crowds thronged the platforms at Kingussie, there to wish good luck to their male kith and kin. As the train pulled away "a thundering cheer swept along from end to end of the platform." The 1st Volunteer Battalion Queen's Own Cameron Highlanders (QOCH) which included F Company (Badenoch) was on its way to Southampton.

That company evolved from the original 6th Badenoch Company of the Inverness-shire Rifle Volunteers formed in 1861. The Rifle Volunteers had been raised for home defence and this was the first time they had been asked to serve overseas. Over the years, young men from many of the families previously mentioned had served with the Volunteers for long or short periods. That service would have broadened their horizons, enabling them to mix with a variety of folk outside their immediate area. As well as the challenges of the training and the adventure of the annual camps, military experience may have provided job opportunities and introductions to future spouses. The Volunteers had a high profile in the community. They supplied guards of honour at civic functions and at special celebrations of the gentry. Their annual ball was greatly enjoyed and their regular shooting competitions were fiercely contested. Many young Newtonmore men, aware of the unrest in South Africa, had joined F Company in 1899 and early 1900 and were not slow to volunteer

for service there when the call came.[2] After demanding tests and medical examinations, those selected were sworn in and undertook a short training course. Meanwhile our army was faring better. Newtonmore celebrated with the rest of the country when our besieged troops were relieved in places such as Ladysmith. Nine Grantown Volunteers, members of the 3rd Volunteer Battalion Seaforth Highlanders, had helped to lift that siege. THE PEOPLE'S JOURNAL of 10 March reported great excitement in Newtonmore when a flag hoisted at the Post Office alerted folk that "important news had arrived." Word about the relief of Ladysmith quickly spread. In the evening, the community gathered round a huge bonfire which was set ablaze by Robert Sellar at 8pm. "Refreshments having been served and several toasts drunk, with loud cheering, the company marched through the village to the stirring strains of the pipes, cheering enthusiastically, and illuminating the place with torch light."

The Badenoch communities enthusiastically raised funds for the troops. Large quantities of socks, clothing, toiletries, chocolate and cigarettes were sent to South Africa. A local fund was set up to assist soldiers invalided home. Gifts were also sent in the reverse direction. Two young men, Pte. R Smith, Spey Street, of the Argyll and Sutherland Highlanders, and Sgt. P Macdonald, Feshie Bridge, of Brabant's Light Horse, sent chocolates to spouse and mother respectively. The sweets had been a Christmas gift to the soldiers from Queen Victoria. Newspapers occasionally made mention of local soldiers serving in non-local units, but they gave many column inches to the local regiment. Out of the ten companies which made up the QOCH Volunteer Battalion, that of Badenoch supplied more soldiers (14) than any other except those of Inverness. The Volunteer Battalion drew to the Colours more men than other regiments: 75 served in the only Volunteer Service Company sent out to the Cameron Highlanders. Four Badenoch men fought with the newly formed Lovat Scouts. In early 1900, both the Scouts and the Service Company undertook several weeks

Fig 27 – News arrived at the post office (front right) by telegraph.
Thatch can be seen on some of the roofs. The foremost high building on the right belonged to William C Macpherson, tailor. The next high building was the original school. *(Peter Moore Collection.)*

of training; the former at Beaufort Castle; the latter at Cameron Barracks, Inverness. The Badenoch Company led by Lt John Campbell, Kingussie, included soldiers from Aviemore to Kinlochlaggan. Five Newtonmore men, aged between 31 and 20, had been selected: Sgt. George (Hannah) Macpherson and Ptes. William (Dan) Macdonald; John McIntosh; Alfred Macpherson and James (Jimsie) Sellar. L-Sgt. Donald Cameron, Loch Laggan Hotel, had strong links to Newtonmore through his father and his paternal grandparents.

Combat training included fitness, route marches, parade drill and rifle practice. In the days before their departure, trainees paraded in Inverness and were treated to farewell events with personal presentations and the usual toasts and speeches. Their communities gave the men various gifts: khaki-bound New Testaments, clothing, tobacco and insurance policies. In Newtonmore, the Band of Hope and the LOGT had presented George, John and Jimsie with "a handsome pocket-book and fountain pen". William had received a khaki-coloured bible and pocket knife from the Gaelic Bible Class. Inverness Town Council hosted a dinner in the Palace Hotel for all ranks. On Fri 13 Apr 1900, led by pipers and a military band, the soldiers marched from Cameron Barracks to catch the

Kingussie Section of the South African Field Service Company 1900-1901.

Fig 28 – The 14 Volunteers from F Company (Badenoch) selected to serve in South Africa.
(Book of Kingussie, HFM.)

15.30 train. Flags flew from buildings and the streets were lined by hundreds of well-wishers who gave them an unforgettable send-off.

The following day they embarked on the *Gaul*, which called at Tenerife and St Helena.

Despite the fact that only two of the Badenoch contingent had previously been at sea and many suffered when crossing the Bay of Biscay, they are reported to have found the passage quite enjoyable. Letters sent home from Tenerife and published in the Inverness press said that they were "excellently treated on board" and kept busy with rifle practice and fitness drills. They landed in Cape Town on 9 May and ten days later reached their base camp near Bloemfontein, the capital of the Orange Free State. On 28 May, they were "selected to take part in the ceremony of the proclamation, at Bloemfontein, of the annexation of the Free State." The celebrations must have been a pleasant break from the routine service. Letters published in the North press described that event. The troops often had to cover long distances in a sometimes inhospitable climate. Their sleep was regularly disturbed; for many days they were unable to wash body or clothes; food rations were meagre. It was winter and they were issued with blankets totally inadequate for bivouacking which, at one time, they did for three weeks. "The nights are beastly", one wrote. The badly-worn blankets were "Government stamp dated 1879." The war zone was huge and getting supplies through was a big problem. The Boers regularly sabotaged the railways, the main lines of communication. Simon Dallas, Inverness, wrote to his mother: "bridges and culverts have been blown up for miles." The Boers' superior knowledge of the landscape allowed them to mount quick and deadly attacks despite improved British scouting by the Lovat Scouts and the Cyclists Brigade. 'Alicky Hannah' (Alexander Macpherson) from Newtonmore served with the Cameron Highlanders Cycling Corps in South Africa, but his "efforts to push a bike round the veldt left him weak" and he was invalided home in 1902. Alick was able to return to work as an architect in the office of Alexander Mackenzie in Kingussie, where he was very highly esteemed. Sadly, on his way home from work on 29 May 1903, when taking a short cut from Newtonmore Station across the field called 'America', 25-year-old Alick collapsed and died. At his military funeral at Banchor, he was saluted by about 40 of the Badenoch Volunteer Company, some of whom, including his elder brother 'Geordie Hannah', had served in South Africa.

The various sections of the QOCH, in their letters home, were very keen to give news of fellow Camerons. The Volunteer Company, reinforced by 100 Cameron Highlanders Reservists, looked forward to joining the main contingent of the regiment. On 5 June

1900, under the command of Major Haig of the King's Own Scottish Borderers, they were involved in their first major incident, near Vredefort. Lt. John Campbell, Kingussie, and L-Sgt. Donald Cameron, Kinlochlaggan, were wounded in that engagement. Our Volunteers spent much of the next month helping to guard the railway line and bridges in the area. They were often on the move and during one day they covered "27 miles without food." On 2 July, having been part of an escort "to a large train of supplies" they reached Heilbron. After various duties there, they were on the move again on 13 July, that time helping to escort a supply convoy of over 400 wagons which "occupied ten miles of road." Their 87-mile march was not without incident but they arrived safely at Bethlehem with "the loss of only one vehicle." At Bethlehem, they were delighted to be welcomed by the 1st Battalion QOCH, their parent Battalion, with whom they were linked for the rest of their manoeuvres. Reports said that "Lt. Campbell and his men played a distinguished part in the engagements which led to the surrender of General Prinsloo's army in the Brandwater Basin, and that they shared in all the hardships of the strenuous campaign in Wittenbergen." They were also involved in the relief of Ladybrand in early September. Our Volunteers returned to Bloemfontein on garrison duty for the second half of their year-long engagement. While there, in January

1901, they would have mourned the death of Queen Victoria who regarded her Highland Brigade highly. The Highlanders were proud of that and showed great loyalty to her. By that time the Boers were losing the war and some of the British troops were being sent home. Unfortunately two privates of the 1st Volunteer Battalion QOCH lost their lives in the sub-continent. Most of the others embarked on the *Tagus* on 10 April 1901 and sailed into Southampton on 29 April. The following day they entrained for the journey home to the Highlands. Families and friends were able to greet them briefly when their train paused at Kingussie. It was noted that some of the soldiers had lost weight. On reaching Inverness they received "a truly magnificent welcome." They spent a busy afternoon and evening in Inverness working through the necessary paperwork and demobilisation procedures. Later, Lt. John Campbell and some of his men attended a Civic Reception in the Highland Capital.

Of the original 14 men from the Badenoch Company, ten had returned. The other four, Peter Stuart, Alfred Macpherson, John McIntosh and Sgt. George Macpherson had remained in South Africa. There they "received appointments at the theatre of war under the government". George's brother, Alick, went to South Africa with the Cyclist Corps later that summer. Two Newtonmore siblings in the Boer War: at least three of their younger brothers fought in WW1. Hannah's sons were both home by 10 Dec 1902, the day 33 year old Geordie married Ann Macpherson, daughter of James, the tailor. The best man was George's brother Alick who had returned from South Africa in the spring of 1902 on the troopship, the *Gascon*, along with another Newtonmore lad, James Macdonald. James, who had gone to South Africa after volunteering for service with the Fife Light Horse (20th Coy Imperial Yeomanry), was awarded the Queen's medal with five clasps. James related that, when a youth, he "was regularly commandeered by *Am Bèicear Bàn* to ride his horse to either of the fields 'America' or 'Australia'" when the horse had finished his daily round with the baker's cart. Those fields, named by the baker, lie between Station Road and Golf Course Road. The "rudiments of horsemanship" which he had acquired then helped when he rode "in subsequent adventures overseas and on many ceremonial occasions" including the Royal Review in 1935. *Am Bèicear Bàn* was so pleased to see another South African veteran return that, when Willie Ritchie of the Infantry Brigade walked home from Newtonmore Station, the baker placed two standing crossed rifles in the middle of the road as a sign of welcome.

The ten Badenoch Volunteers, including Jimsie Sellar and Willie MacDonald, received a tumultuous welcome from family and friends when they returned to Kingussie on 1 May. A public holiday had been declared. "Almost the entire population was present at the station" for the arrival of the afternoon train which brought them from Inverness. After family greetings had been exchanged, the Volunteers and followers were piped through the streets and eventually ended up at the Dell. The crowd made use of the grandstand associated with the Highland Games. A platform had been erected in front of it. The chairman, Provost Macpherson, welcomed the men and the invited guests. The latter included Cluny Macpherson; the Rev. Dr Mackenzie; Capt. Francis Robertson Reid, late of Biallid and formerly of the 6th Badenoch Company of the Inverness-shire Rifle Volunteers; Mr G Sellar and Mr P M Watson, Kingussie; and Mr Macpherson, Balvattan. The weather was fine and, after the formalities, there were games. Refreshments were provided by William Wolfenden, then of the Star Hotel, but, in 1881, coachman to Capt. Reid at Biallid. "The concert party of Frame, the well-known Scotch comedian, gave an entertainment in the town in the evening."

Newtonmore Templars arranged their welcome home for early May: "In connection with the homecoming of the Service Company of the Cameron Volunteers, a very successful social was given by the members of the Craigdhu Lodge of L.O.G.T... . Private

William Ritchie of the Gay Gordons Militia, and who was present at the battle of Paardeberg was amongst the guests."[1] Campaign medals were presented by Donald Cameron of Lochiel, Lord Lieutenant of Inverness-shire, on 17 Oct 1901 at Castle Hill, Inverness.

During the period of their engagement in South Africa, friends and families of the Volunteers had witnessed strife of a spiritual kind. About half of the population of Newtonmore was associated with the Free Church which, nationally and locally, went through difficult times in the early 1900s. As previously mentioned, its congregations had been beset by dissension during the 1890s. When no resolution could be found, the 1900 Free Church Assembly approved a union with the United Presbyterian Church of Scotland. Many ministers carried their congregations with them into the union, The United Free Church. Nationally, the UF and the Free Churches argued for years through the courts about which could rightfully occupy the buildings and use the assets. Locally, the Rev. Neil Dewar, long-term minister of the Free Church, supported the union and became minister of the new United Free (UF) Church. The Free Church congregation in Newtonmore lost its minister, its assets, many of its members and its lovely new church building. The congregation struggled to survive and reverted to using a public building. After a ruling by the House of Lords in 1904 in favour of the Frees, their numbers locally started to increase with some, including Newtonmore's Gregor Fyfe, leaving their recently adopted UF Church. When Mr Fyfe died in 1930, the Free Church congregation contributed to his gravestone in tribute of "esteem for his 25y faithful gratuitous service as Church Officer." Much later a youngster of the 1920s expressed her appreciation of Mr Fyfe's efforts in keeping the church cosy with the 'huge … old American stove'.[3] A report in July 1905 highlighted the difficulty faced by the Newtonmore UF Church: The Rev. Mr McAlpine, their short-term minister, had to preach in the larch wood adjoining the hall. Later that year, a Royal Commission was set-up "to secure the redistribution of church property." For several years, it travelled the country holding open meetings to decide how to allocate the assets. The image opposite shows the Free Church group outside Newtonmore Village Hall. The images, from February 1906, are from the KINGUSSIE RECORD.

Meanwhile the struggles over assets continued. In July 1905, the local Frees were fortunate to obtain the services of the Rev. Angus Mackay. The Mackays had to live in furnished apartments as the Rev. Alexander Bain, who had succeeded Mr Dewar in the UF Church, refused to leave the manse. Ironically, when Neil Dewar died in Jan 1906, his funeral service had to be conducted in the

Fig 29 – Free Church party outside the original Newtonmore Village Hall. (STRATHSPEY AND BADENOCH HERALD.)

Free Church Party at Newtonmore.–Names, L-R. – Mr Finney, Solicitor, Edinburgh; Mr Fyfe, Church Officer; Rev. Mr Mackay, Kingussie; Rev. K. Cameron, Edinburgh; Mr Simpson, S.S.C.; Mr Hodge, secretary to Sub-Commissioner; Provost Campbell, Kingussie; Mr Kennedy, Newtonmore; Mr Chisholm, Kingussie

Victoria Hall, Kingussie, as his church then had no building. Eventually the commission allocated the central church in Newtonmore to the UF Church, but in Kingussie, the church and the manse (currently McInnes House Hotel) were allocated to the Free Church. When the final decisions had been made, the churches were able to move forward and raise

U.F.C. party, led by Rev. Alex. Lee, making their way through the snow to Newtonmore Hall.

Fig 30 – United Free Church party making their way past Anderson's Temperance Hotel and Ivy Cottage to Newtonmore Village Hall. *(Strathspey and Badenoch Herald.)*

funds for the buildings they needed. The UF Church in Kingussie was opened in May 1909, eight months after the laying of its foundation stone. The architect was Alexander Cattanach, a native of Strone. Many of the contractors were former Newtonmore shinty players. Glenbanchor-born brothers, John and Donald Macdonald were the masons. Alexander Falconer did the slating and brothers Ranald and Lachlan Macpherson were trusted with the plaster work. Their fine workmanship can now be admired at *Talla nan Ròs*.

Newtonmore's new Free Church was opened on Friday 16 Aug 1912. It was located near the church they had previously built which had been awarded to the UF Church. It served the village well until declining numbers caused its closure in 2006. Among the last congregation to worship there was Gregor Fyfe's grand-daughter. Two Newtonmore trustees were named on the feu charter – Gregor Fyfe and merchant John Gordon, son-in-law of Donald Cattanach, catechist. John's wife, Catherine, and her siblings Annie and John were the only children of the catechist still alive in Newtonmore in 1912. Their brother Donald MacMaster Cattanach had worked away from home for many years and their remaining four siblings were dead. John Cattanach (Nelson) and his cousins, Katie and Jessie Cattanach, were probably the only grandchildren who continued to live in the area. Others, including

Seonaidh a' Mhaighstir, one of Newtonmore's best shinty players, and his brother Jamie, had left Newtonmore to pursue their careers.

Soldiering and spirituality were united when the Rev. Dr Mackenzie proposed the toast to the armed services at the Volunteers' homecoming celebrations at the above mentioned function on The Dell: "Whether it was a good or a bad sign in the martial history of their country that a clergyman should propose that toast he could not venture to decide." The crowd cheered his final thought: "It was now acknowledged that the Volunteers rendered as good service in the war as the most experienced troops in His Majesty's service."

Selected further sources used in this chapter:

1   PJ, 11/5/1901
2   HFM – muster roll
3   HFM, BOHP, Mackenzie Historical Records of the Queen's Own Cameron Highlanders, Vol 11

Chapter 11

Progression and Processions 1900–1911

The Volunteers returned to a different world. The country had a new monarch, two of the Presbyterian Churches were in turmoil and local employment was to become, at various times, increasingly difficult to find. On his return, William Macdonald found work labouring. He later worked as the village officer. Bel Cameron remembered seeing: "Willie Dan, the lamp lighter with a ladder for the paraffin lamps." Jimsie Sellar returned to his trade as a mason but moved briefly to the Central Belt for work. He continued serving with the Volunteers and was promoted to sergeant. In 1908, the Volunteer Force was merged with the Yeomanry in the new Territorial Force. Jimsie served with them in the artillery in WW1. Before that he had taken up keepering and after the war, despite receiving a bad wound on the hip, he was able to return to his job as gamekeeper at Etteridge. George Macpherson returned to his work as a mason in his father's business.

Geordie Hannah was remembered by the Two Cronies in an earlier role: that of herd laddie escorting the villagers' cows to and from *Dail an t-Slèibh*, the west dell. Some of the tenementers rented pasture for the summer and the herd laddie cared for their cattle as they roamed over that extensive area (now part of the golf course). Other herd laddies they recalled were Sam Macdonald at Banchor and "Drum-an-Staink" (sic) who walked along the Main Street collecting the cows shouting "*Mach Iad*", "*Mach Iad*" ("put them out"). Lassies also herded. Sarah Macpherson was known as "Umburella nam bò", (*bò* is cattle).[1] The umbrella sheltered her and helped with unruly cattle. Sarah's younger cousin John, b. 1873, worked as the village herd before leaving for Inverness and developing the well-known business, Macpherson's Sporting Stores. Herding on the west dell was a lonely job compared with that on the east dell, part of the Strone crofters' common grazings. The boundary ran from the high tee (3rd tee) to the Spey. Each crofter employed a youngster of about 11 years old to stop his cattle from straying across the Spey or onto the west dell. The following herded for the crofters in the 1880s: Angus Robertson ("Crask"); Lachie Campbell; Jean Macpherson; Bobby MacIntyre; George Maclean; Alexina Middlemas; Malcolm Macdonald; Duncan Cattanach and May Kennedy. Several were crofters' children. John Macdonald, elder brother of one of the Cronies, described the work. He was "fee'ed for 6 months from May to November 1885 with Seumas-an-Taillesr (sic), who occupied the, then, most easterly croft in Strone, near to the Strone burn." He lived in, and was paid 23s plus a fleece of wool for 6 months. The following year his employer was *Aonghas a' Phleastarair,* neighbour to *Seumas.* In 1888, Angus had the house now known as Strone Cottage built on his croft. His artistic plaster work survived in the 'good room' until 1986. John's pay for that half-year was 30s. He recalled being well fed on porridge, brose, broth, mutton and milk. They had happy times on the Dell. Geordie (NZ), and his pal, Donly Ross, were herd boys on the crofts in the mid-1890s. They amused themselves bird-nesting, swimming, running, long and high jumping. A 'bonus' was that they were allowed to miss Sunday School! Many of the crofters adhered to the Free Church which practised strict Sabbath Day observance. Preparations for Sunday meals would be done on Saturdays, keeping the work for such to an absolute minimum on Sundays. A similar scenario applied to feeding their animals but they still had to be herded. In winter the herd boys returned to the grind of school lessons. They tried hard to catch up but Geordie remembers them being ridiculed in front of their class mates. The School Master "alluded to us as 'cows' tails" [sic]. Although education became compulsory in 1872, there are numerous accounts in the school log books of pupils being absent on 'agricultural' duties. Attendance dropped when assistants were needed for peats, neeps, tatties and grouse beating. In 1890, the head teacher, John Macdonald, informed the school board that 12 pupils had gone herding. Occasionally the crofter was questioned by the School Board but mostly absences for agricultural work seemed to be tolerated. The Parish was aware that the extra income of the herds' pay was vitally important to some families who lived from hand to mouth.

Several of those herds were among the many young men and women who moved away from Newtonmore during the score of years before WW1. Some sought work in all the five continents while others departed to continue their education. Women often obtained employment in service in the Central Belt while others took training in nursing, dressmaking and millinery. Glasgow and Aberdeen attracted some of the youths but many of them congregated in Edinburgh where some played shinty for the University or Edinburgh Camanachd. An Edinburgh derby in 1904 saw John Sellar playing for the 'Varsity and his brother, Andy, playing for Camanachd. Others who turned out for Camanachd included *Alaidh Ruadh*; Robbie Kennedy who lived with *Alaidh* for a few years before his premature death in December 1901 and Duncan Macdonald, son of *Alaidh Dòmhnallach*. In Nov 1903, various men "who from time to time leave home for Edinburgh … banded themselves together with a view to maintaining in 'Auld Reekie' the shinty traditions of Newtonmore."[2] M Galbraith; J, A & J Sellar; D Douglas; J & A Macdonald; D & J Cattanach; D Mackintosh; D Maclean and J I Macpherson formed a team which "proposed to play friendly fixtures with the 'Varsity and Camanachd clubs."[2] Those young men, aged 18 to 29, were a mixture of students and tradesmen, including three masons, a labourer and a tailor. Ironically, that double decade of departure was when a major development of Newtonmore occurred. The start of that, in the late 1890s, has already been noted.

The pre-WW1 years of the 1900s saw approximately five new houses being built each year in the areas outwith the main street core of Newtonmore. Also some buildings were being renovated and some gained small extensions. The allocation of land for new houses was fairly haphazard. An exception to that was at *Dail Dhubh* the area around where St Bride's Church now stands. The following houses were built there about the same time, 1908-09: Sherwood, now Cherry Glen; Thelma, later The Manse and now *Dochas*; Glengarth; Hill View, now Bruiach; Montgreenan, now Creageiro. Thelma was built for Annie and Jessie Cattanach, the

daughters of *Alaidh an Tàilleir*, mason, but by the late 1920s, the name, although occupied by the same family, was Daldhu. Contractors were very busy from autumn 1906 and through 1907 with more houses than usual being erected and hotels and shops being extended. The locals were intrigued by the unusual Gaelic of the Lewismen who were necessary additions to the workforce.

Newtonmore was becoming progressively popular with holiday makers. They were attracted by the fresh clean air, good walking, golf, fishing, shooting, and the gentle pace of life in Badenoch where they received a warm Highland welcome. The mood of the villagers must have been very buoyant. They were able to earn a good income from the visitors; the village amenities were expanding and, in April 1907, their shinty team won the Camanachd Cup for the first time. The demand for holiday accommodation encouraged folk to obtain feus, take out loans and build appealing villas. The expansion of such can be inferred from letting lists which were regularly published in THE KINGUSSIE RECORD. It listed 28 houses being let in the summer of 1902. By 1904, there were 62 houses available but less than ten of those were new builds; the others new to the list were older houses whose proprietors had not previously let them. Availability rose to 82 houses in 1907, 90 in 1909 and 100 in 1911. The varied accommodation suited many tastes and purses. Some houses were offered with service by the owner. Others had servants' quarters for the occupiers' own staff. A few of the houses, including Woodlea, New Glen and Clune House had tennis greens and some had a piano. In 1904 the most basic cottage offered a public room, a bedroom with a three-quarter bed and a pantry. One of the best specified properties, Clan Chattan, had three public rooms, nine bedrooms, three WCs, a bathroom, hot and cold water and a kitchen. It also had a coachman's house with stable at the foot of the garden which became the house now called Broomlea. Clan Chattan, now Alvey, had been built in 1900 for Donald Cattanach, business partner of William.

Those brothers were closely related to Malcolm Cattanach, slater, and shared his knowledge and enthusiasm for their local cultural heritage. The Cronies commented: "a family conspicuously associated with the progressive spirit that" transformed Newtonmore "from a one street irregular collection of small dwellings, lacking conveniences and planning pretensions, to a modern suburban village, having renovated houses and attractive villas."

At various times William's wife, Ann Kennedy, "a quiet, gentle and kindly disposed lady" and their four children worked in W & D Cattanach, general merchants. The sons, William (the 'gentle Teela'), Donald (Donlan)

and Dr Johnnie, were keen shinty players and contributed much to the game over many years. Their father was one of the men who worked extremely hard, over several decades, to drive forward development of the village, his Free Church, and many of the village clubs.

Before 1908, the community had several committees and loosely-formed groups which contributed to the development of the village. There had also been a constituted, but short-lived, Village Council established in 1906. On 29 Apr 1908, after a "meeting of ratepayers convened by the promoters of the lighting scheme" who had held three fundraising concerts during the winter, a new committee was elected. That group then formed the Village Committee to oversee ways and means, lighting and cleansing. It later took responsibility for running the village hall. The members had a big portfolio, demanding a lot of time and work; all voluntary. The committee comprised Donald Cameron, shoemaker, convenor; James Tytler, clerk; William Cockburn, treasurer; James Macpherson, JP (*Seumas Mòr*); Peter M Watson, merchant; Thomas Grant; Robert Sellar; John Macdonald, mason; John Simpson; William Cattanach, merchant; R Allan, chemist; Angus Macpherson, fish-monger; D A Cattanach, mason; William Barnett, grocer and Thomas Cattanach, slater. Several of that group had served the community for years and would continue to contribute to the development of

Newtonmore. They were progressing the earlier input of *Alaidh Bàn* (Alexander Macpherson); *Alaidh Mòr* (Alexander Stewart); John Stewart of the PO and Malcolm Cattanach.

The 1908 village committee held regular monthly meetings. In a short time that hard-working group facilitated many improvements. They purchased and erected more street lights and outdoor seats, reorganised the running of the hall, and arranged the tuning of its piano. They addressed the chronic litter problem and purchased a cart to help with waste disposal. The committee organised a series of concerts and lectures to raise funds for their work. They even managed to appoint a village official, William Duffes, to oversee the working of that infrastructure. After consultation with the rate-payers, they persuaded the Badenoch District

The Hotel, Newtonmore.

Fig 31 – 'Allie Sam' is leading the two horses: 'Teela' and his father are standing by the roller. *(S Macdonald.)*

Committee of the County Council to take on the responsibility for lighting and cleansing.

An earlier problem with infrastructure was the rudimentary drainage system in Newtonmore. As the village began to expand after the mid-1890s the need for a sewerage system became urgent. A very basic system was introduced at the west end. A "pipe sewer" was "constructed at the south end of the village to drain the hotel and adjoining premises" in 1898.[3] It also drained the stream in Old Glen Road. The pipe, which passed "through mounds near the south end of golf course … discharged into the hollow near the railway."[4] The need for a modern drainage system was brought up at the Badenoch District Committee in early 1900. Decisions on it were postponed on several occasions because of the estimated installation costs of £1000. Pressure by Newtonmore councillors continued and eventually the work began in April 1902. Pipes were laid in the Main Street first, so that the work there would be completed before the tourist season. By late autumn the scheme which included a sewage farm on land 'beyond the then ninth hole of the golf course' was completed. Unfortunately, in January 1903 a fierce storm carried away water pipes in Strone: also the "new sewage banking gave way." The sewerage problem was resolved in 1906 when the golf club wished to extend the course to 18 holes over land where the sewage farm was situated. It was demolished after

Thomas Grant secured the contract for "the new tanks and extension of sewage." Newtonmore Golf Club agreed to pay the costs, which were estimated at £250.

Tom Grant's civil engineering expertise was much appreciated by local groups. In a letter to THE KINGUSSIE RECORD in October 1908 he wrote: "I believe the street in Newtonmore is among the worst bits between Perth and Inverness." He added that the side channels were useless and "consequently the water accumulates into stagnant pools, almost to the danger of the public health … I have no doubt that to a certain extent the motor car traffic injures the roads, but as a practical authority I may say that the motor car gets more than its own share of the blame." Although cars brought certain advantages to their owner, villagers complained of noise, dust, fumes and damage to roads caused by the automobiles. In mid-1907, they welcomed the local authority's reduction of speed limits on the main streets of Newtonmore to 10 mph.

The street had few pavements although the 1899 feu charter for Woodlea noted the need to construct and maintain the footpath in front of the house "with a sufficient kerb and gutter." The piping brothers John and Angus Macpherson appreciated the need for a substantial pavement at their fishmongers attached to Rosemeade. John had purchased the two-storey building from William C

Macpherson in October 1906. By June 1908 they had "made extensive alterations on their premises, which should greatly facilitate their business." It was also downsized to one and three-quarter storeys. Improvements included a concrete pavement in front. "It would be a great benefit to the village if other shop keepers would follow Messrs Macphersons' example in this respect."[5]

The brothers, sons of *Calum Pìobair*, Cluny's highly-talented piper, contributed much to the developing village. In those days many of the pipers, including the brothers, were also trained in Highland dancing. John Macpherson (*Jockan*) gave great support to the many fundraising concerts appearing on the list of performers at nearly every one. He was piper at village celebrations and for the shinty

Fig 32 – Angus Macpherson's shop at *Cor an easan*, c. 1909/10. *(S Macdonald.)*

team. Angus piped regularly, ran dancing classes in Newtonmore Hall and served on the Village Committee.

In 1909, Angus purchased a semi-detached building containing two small houses and shops on the south side of the Main Street for £830 from J S Macpherson, Kingussie. Angus named his property *Cor an easan* and opened a grocery business at the west-end of that building. His feu covered 1 rood, 5 ½ poles, the original plot having been 2 roods and 7 poles. In 1910, Margaret Borland bought the smaller part of that plot, which had a house and shop. Her husband, William, who had previously tenanted

a shop at Simpson's Hotel, opened a bakery there. It was probably the Edinburgh-born Borlands who named it Restalrig. In the 1920s, the whole building was bought in two stages by Christina Ferguson, wife of *Am Bèicear Bàn*. Restalrig was then renamed Achnafauld, after Christina's Perthshire birthplace.

Am Bèicear Bàn was very well known throughout Badenoch. John's father, Malcolm Cattanach, had started the bakery in 1859 to supplement his income from slating and provide employment for his children. From at least the 1880s John drove his horse-pulled baker's cart east to Insh or west to

Fig 33 – *Am Bèicear Bàn* with his horse and bakery cart inscribed "JC".   *(M Slaney.)*

Kinlochlaggan. His customers anticipated the sound of his bugle. Many Badenoch residents had stories to tell about the baker's exploits. He was a very strong, fearless man and in the long, cold winters of 1895 and 1912, he drove over the frozen Spey at Dalchully. Residents in out-lying areas greatly appreciated the strenuous efforts he made to reach them. John's four eldest sons served in the army during WW1, his namesake, John, being killed at Ypres. Another son was badly wounded. After the war each of the Cattanach boys became businessmen in the village.

An earlier itinerant merchant was Michael Macdonald, born in Moidart. "Mee-chall" toured the countryside with his "shaggy pony, Katie Beag" and dog cart. He announced his presence by calling, "*Sgadan Ùr, Sgadan Ùr, Sia air son Sgillinn*"(Fresh herring, fresh herring, six for a penny). The boys in the village teased Mee-chal, walking along near him calling "Sgadan Grod, Sgadan Grod, Sia air son Si'-Sgillinn" (Rotten herring, rotten herring, six for sixpence). Despite his age, Michael leapt off his cart and reprimanded them. Michael had become a fish merchant during his retirement. He, and his brother Roderick, had continued the family tradition of droving when they moved from the west to Laggan. Mee-chall's sister who kept house for him at Moor of Strone ran a small shop there. The steep brae at the bottom of Strone

Road was for many years known as "Sarah Mee-chall's Brae." In appreciation of Michael, who died in 1904, aged 79, THE KINGUSSIE RECORD published a lovely elegy written by Malcolm Cattanach, junior.

Malcolm's ancestors were bards and several of his generation, including his cousin, Malcolm Macdonald, continued that tradition. Malcolm Macdonald's eldest brother, Alexander, a mason, may also have been a bard. He was probably the A Macdonald, mason, reported as being elected secretary to the reconstituted Newtonmore Camanachd Club in January 1895, who appeared in several team lists about then. When Newtonmore played Kingussie on 9 Jan 1897 THE ELGIN COURANT praised the "three brothers Macdonald" (possibly Alex, Malcolm and William) who "upheld the fight well on behalf of Newtonmore." Their second cousin *Seonaidh a' Mhaighstir*, John Macdonald, was also lauded for his performance in the forward line. That first local derby in a Camanachd Cup competition attracted a large crowd and was extensively reported in the Courant and THE INVERNESS COURIER of 12 Jan 1897. Apart from John Macdonald, the Christian names of the players listed in both papers were not identified. One of the halves "J Macdonald" may well have been Jamie, the younger brother of *Seonaidh a' Mhaighstir*. Jamie played for Newtonmore before leaving, in May 1900, to work in Parr's Bank, Liverpool.

Alex, the mason, built Fjeldheim in Kingussie in 1900. His Norwegian wife, Mathilde, was a hotel cook in Kingussie. Did she have an influence on George Sellar when he named one of his hotels as Silverfjord? George had spent his childhood at Silverford in Aberdeenshire. In October 1904, THE KINGUSSIE RECORD reported that the building trades had been "practically at a stand still here" but things were improving. Masons had been having a tough time and some sought work in the cities. The Macdonalds advertised their house for holiday letting in 1904 and Alex started working as a carter. Eventually, Alexander, Mathilde, and their daughter decided to emigrate to Montreal. Alex rouped his carts, harnesses, agricultural tools and house contents in April 1908. Alex's brother William was strongly influenced by an organisation which was very active in Newtonmore and reputed to be one of the best in the Highlands, the Gaelic Bible Class.

That association had been run by James Forbes since the mid-1880s. The popular ecumenical group usually held its meetings in the Village Hall. The highlight of the year was its annual social and concert. "This function has been for many years one of the outstanding events of the village. Mr Forbes has experimented with different methods, but

always with success." As with many social events, the hall was painstakingly decorated for the evening. Each programme was varied but always included Gaelic Christian songs and recitations. Another staple was 'the baggies' containing 'goodies'; quite different from today's versions but very much appreciated in a village where many families had a lean Christmas. Sometimes they had a cinemato-graphic performance which, in 1907, included the Coronation of King Edward VII. Mr Forbes took a friendly interest in promoting the welfare of the youngsters. They returned his loyalty with presentations and letters. Jamie Macdonald, Liverpool and William Macdonald who was serving in South Africa both wrote in December 1900. They sent their best wishes and spoke of the benefits they had derived from their membership of his class. It was reported after the Dec 1915 event: "Mr Forbes hopes to be in a position to provide comforts for the troops from the proceeds." The following spring he received many letters of thanks. Excerpts from those from Duncan Cattanach, John Leslie and William Budge were quoted in THE BADENOCH RECORD. *Seonaidh a' Mhaighstir* finished his in Gaelic: "'*Guma fad bhios sibh beò 's ceò às ur tigh. Slàinte mhath agaibh airson ioma bliadhna fhahast.*" (A rough translation in Scots would be – lang may you live and may your lum reek. Guid health tae ye aw' the year). They were deeply grateful that Mr Forbes had taken the trouble to find out where they were.

In the 1890s James Forbes lived at the east inn, a small establishment with "scant tourist accommodation". In late 1900 his brother sold the inn:

> The old-established hotel ... the Balavil Arms, has just been disposed of by Mr Robert Forbes, the proprietor, to Mr George Sellar, general wine & spirit merchant, Kingussie, who contemplates ... the erection of a large new hotel suited to the growing popularity of the village and district as a summer resort, the fine golf course being a great attraction. Mr Sellar has also obtained ... a piece of the old market stance in front, which he intends to lay out as a pleasure and tennis ground.[6]

Although he was only the leaseholder, George began a programme that would transform the inn. He did not purchase the feu until the end of 1902 when he immediately set-up loans of £4250 from three different people. His security was three properties in Kingussie and the Balavil Hotel. By May 1902, the rebuilt hotel was open for business. It included three large public rooms, a smoking room and 20 bedrooms and was leased to John Simpson. Mr Simpson, previously the postmaster in Kirkcaldy, came to the "old 'Balavil' a year ago."[7] Under Robert's governance (and

that of Flora Bentick), the annual value of the hotel was £18, but by 1906 it was £175. The rebuilt Balavil Hotel "is a large and handsome edifice, and should prove very popular with Kirkcaldy holiday makers who patronise Newtonmore, which is considered one of the finest health resorts in Scotland."[7] In 1907, 15 apartments, a motor garage and stabling were added to the Balavil Hotel and John Simpson had bought the Temperance Hotel. John Anderson, its previous proprietor, had commissioned and moved to a new private temperance hotel, later the Badenoch Hotel, on the wooded knoll overlooking the station.

In 1908, George Sellar moved to his Glasgow office to run his business, Dew of Ben Alder Scotch Whisky. Sam Macdonald jnr became the manager of what was "the oldest licensed house in the district" in 1910.[8] In June 1911, the feu of the Balavil was transferred to Robert Adam Stevenson for £2300. The accommodation in the hotel at the time of the revaluation was: ground floor – private parlour; smoke room; kitchen; coffee room; bar; staff room; 6 bedrooms; and a beer cellar in basement: first floor – 2 bathrooms & WCs; drawing room; 15 bedrooms: second floor, bathroom & WC; 8 bedrooms. By July 1913, the optimistic Mr Stevenson had added a large dining room and 10 bedrooms. The hotel now looked very similar to what we see today with a three-bay frontage.

In 1895, Newtonmore had one main hotel which Sam named 'The Hotel'. By 1910, in response to the growing popularity of the village as a tourist resort, six well-appointed hotels were offering accommodation – Rowanlea, Craigmhor, Anderson's, Simpson's, Mains and Balavil. They were very busy in the summer and from 1906, they may have had some winter trade as skiing was developing locally.

Inverness-born carpenter Alexander McGregor began building a house and shop on his feu at the west end around 1899. During the following decade, extensions

Fig 34 – Two-bay Balavil Hotel and gardens. *(J Robertson.)*

including a furniture showroom were added to Rowanlea which became a small hotel. Along with John Anderson, he may have been one of the first to build a dedicated shop window. Others at the west end, including William Cattanach and Benjamin Grant, followed their lead around 1908. The pre-1900 image below (Fig 35) shows their properties without shop frontages.

Although Paul Grant, Benjamin's father, used Heath Cottage almost exclusively for letting, it was Paul's son, Tom, who recognised the potential for a hotel in the extensive grounds. THE KINGUSSIE RECORD of 3 Nov 1906 reported:

> Newtonmore is having its fair share in the building boom … in the Badenoch district, and the village is rapidly increasing in size … Considerable additions are at present being put to Mr Tom Grant's large and handsome villa, Heathfield, which he contemplates converting into a first-class temperance hotel.

Fig 35 – Two shops without shop frontages, Cattanachs' on right and Grant's on left, Pre-1900. *(S Macdonald)*

Earlier in 1906, Heathfield (originally Heath Cottage) had two public rooms; seven bedrooms; a kitchen and a bathroom. For several years Tom and his resourceful sister Maggie had been taking in guests. The Grant siblings moved towards their ambition for the hotel in two stages. Alexander Cattanach, their architect, asked for tenders for the final stage in October 1909. Heathfield would be demolished and an extension added to the west of the 1906 additions. The widened edifice would contain 38 bedrooms, several public rooms "a smoking room, servants' hall, entrance hall, a kitchen and the usual modern conveniences. The acetylene gas, with which the building will be illuminated, will also be a great advantage."

64317　　　CRAIG MHOR HOTEL, NEWTONMORE　　　VALENTINES SERIES

Fig 36 – This 1908/09 image shows retail developments at the West End.
McGregor's furniture shop is attached to the Rowanlea Hotel. W & D Cattanach has a new shop frontage: beyond the car is the new shop of J M Kidd, jeweller. Newtonmore Hiring Establishment's sign is beside the old Toll House. Behind that is the first part of the new Craig Mhor Hotel beside the soon to be demolished Heathfield. *(R Brown.)*

The only Newtonmore contractors selected were the masons, J & D Macdonald, although the plasterers, R & L Macpherson, Kingussie, were Newtonmore men. The hotel had land-scaped grounds; tennis courts and a "commodious" garage and pit. The Craig Mhor was valued at £1,763 in the revaluation. The high Craig Mhor was an excellent vantage point for photographers who took interesting images of the Simpson's Temperance Hotel across the road. The postcard below dates to 1908.

The industrious and talented Simpson family was active in the village, in business and in sport. By 1911 the annual value for the hotel including its shop had risen to £60 from £36 in 1906. John advertised in March 1907 for tradesmen to carryout additions to the hotel. He was obviously optimistic about the trade. In contrast, the following week a roup of Sam's hotel was advertised. The upset price had been reduced from £6,000 to £5,000.

Samuel Macdonald had taken chances when developing his business. Sam had purchased the lease but never owned his hotel. He spent lots of money on improvements, taking out loans to cover the cost.

Fig 37 – Group outside Simpson's Temperance Hotel.   *(Y Richmond)*

Perhaps that is why, in April 1898, to protect his family, he set up a fairly complicated Trust Settlement of his affairs in case of his death. The trustees were instructed to pay his debts and funeral expenses, give his spouse a yearly income from what remained, and to maintain and educate his children.[9] Sam's neighbour across the road, William Cattanach, set up a similar Trust. The Cronies remembered Sam as "heavily built – under average height", alert, inventive, "genial and knowledgeable." He was ably supported by Mrs Macdonald who was very popular and "a wise and careful business woman." Sam was a great sponser of shinty. To celebrate the opening of his hotel, he had organised a grand ball in early 1889, combining it with "an entertainment" to the "Badenoch Shinty Club, of which he is the captain." The large hall adjoining the hotel was festooned with evergreens and other decorations.

The Macdonalds built up the business and simultaneously sent their talented sons off to Edinburgh for further education. Sam sustained his drive for development. In November 1903 he engaged Alexander Mackenzie to prepare plans for another extension to The Hotel. It is not clear if the plans were implemented as the VRs showed no increase in value. He did have The Pines in Station Road built, the cost being over £1,000. Construction started in early 1904 but Sam had heart problems and died in July 1904, aged 59. He may not have inhabited the house but his wife was the proprietor there until she pined away in December 1906. In 1908, the house was sold to London-born Walter Ralph Herring, Chief Engineer of the Edinburgh and Leith Gas works. During the first decade of 1900, his annual salary rose from £900 to £1,500. (The primary school teacher in Newtonmore earned about £70 per annum.) Was the sale an early example of local people being priced out of the housing market? The sale of the house was complicated by the terms of Sam's Trust Settlement.

Sam's Trustees purchased the hotel feu from Balavil in December 1904. After the death of Mrs Macdonald, it was eventually sold to young Sam in March 1907 for £5,000. The locals were delighted but, by 1910, Sam was employed at the Balavil Hotel. A notice of 3 Dec 1909 had asked all parties who had "Claims against the late Mr. Samuel Macdonald, The Hotel, Newtonmore, his Widow, his son, Mr. Samuel Macdonald, junior, or any member of the family …" to lodge their claims with the solicitor in Kingussie. That demand would have been in preparation for the sale of The Hotel to George Main, Bonar Bridge for £3200. The complicated sale eventually ensued after the agreement was signed by the Macdonald brothers in different parts of the world: in early May 1909, George and James Macdonald had emigrated to

Australia. Financial difficulties, possibly due to over expansion, hit several business men in pre-WW1 Newtonmore including hard-working mason, Alexander Macpherson; two John Cattanachs, baker and crofter; P M Watson and William Duffes, plasterer.

William had married Marjory, widow of Ewen Cattanach, shoemaker. In 1901, they were resident in Cromdale with their daughter and her son, Malcolm Cattanach, but soon moved to Newtonmore. William Duffes took an active part in village life. They lived at Holmfield after Marjory purchased the feu. Homefield was dilapidated and underwent a significant rebuild during 1903/4. After Tom Cattanach (Tee Tee) bought that house, he changed its name to Clan Chattan – "always loyal to his clan". Jimmy MacLean then claimed the name Holmfield for his house opposite the school.

House names changed a lot. The original Clan Chattan had gained a new name, having been transferred in 1923 to Mrs Jessie Anderson whose husband had been the minister at Alvey (now Alvie). A name which appeared only in the 1901 census was Daisy Cottage. Jimmy Sellar knew where that was as his father, Jimsie, had donned his kilt and Cameron Highlanders uniform there before going off to the Boer War. The cottage was renamed Rannoch Cottage, by the Campbell family whose father was from Rannoch. That site is now the Co-op carpark.

Another short-lived house name was Kilvey, one of the houses in the new block built by J S Macpherson. The house was occupied by his sister, Christina (Teenie), and her husband, Cromdale-born, Alexander Mitchell. When newly-wed they set up home in a suburb of Swansea at the foot of Kilvey Hill. In 1902, they moved to Newtonmore with their young son, James. Alex ran a grocery from the shop attached to their house and also produced some postcards of Newtonmore. In 1905 the Mitchells moved again when Alex took over a shop in Kingussie. In 1910, the family emigrated to Manitoba where Teenie died in 1960. When youngsters, Teenie and her sister Edith who lived at Croftdhu, Strone, were seriously ill. Despite medical attention Edith died of scarlet fever. Their neighbour at Croftbeg, Ann Martin, wife of John Cattanach, known locally as a healer, offered to help when Teenie began to deteriorate. Ann's granddaughter, Mrs Innes, recalled that Ann used a cotton sheet soaked in a mixture of locally-sourced herbs to make a healing poultice she called scarrich. "Granny applied the scarrich to the baba's neck … just like a collar … and the scarrich wasn't on she said ten minutes when she could see the relief it was to the child." Ann tended Teenie with the scarrich until she was better. It also worked for leg ulcers, chest infections and other ailments. Geordie, NZ, remembered Ann using a pin with circular movements above the eye to cure a stye.

Several houses built in the double decade before WW1 were named after local place names. Clune House was the home of *Alaidh an Tàilleir;* Mrs Sinclair, daughter of Malcolm Cattanach had Milton Cottage (currently An Dunan) built; Craggan View was the home of shinty stalwart Ranald Macpherson, tailor, and, Knockview was built for Malcolm Macdonald's wife, Margaret Leslie. William Leslie's wife, Marjory Cameron, was responsible for the name, *Dochanasaidh*: their home, built in 1908, at the junction of the Main Street and Laggan Road. It now houses the very interesting Clan Macpherson Museum where the story of the house is fully documented. Another Cameron, Margaret, whose father, Donald, came from Camghouran on the southside of Loch Rannoch, was the mother of John Macdonald. John and his wife, May Kennedy, built their house, on the hill, adjacent to the Kennedy croft at Moor of Strone. Their house name, Glenmore, held poignant memories for the Macdonald family. John's grandfather and his wife, Isabella Stewart latterly lived at *Torman* in Glenbanchor. They had been forced to move there from *Beag Ghleann* in Glenmore where John had been the Duke of Gordon's deer forester. The story of the family's evictions from there and from Glenbanchor can be found on plaques in Glenmore forest and in Strone, north of the croft where John and May brought up their family.

Both May and John had numerous relatives in Newtonmore and the surrounding area. "They are cousins of ourselves" was a common expression used then. It encompassed second, third and fourth cousins etc. Isabella Macdonald, Ralia, John's second cousin, devoted her life to others, both family and the community. Many of her relatives were Free Churchers and she started their Sabbath School around 1890. Glowing reports of its annual outing and winter soirée are mentioned in various newspapers. That Ralia family followed their minister, Mr Dewar, into the United Free Church. Later, Miss Macdonald organised ladies work-parties at Ralia to assist with raising the funds to build a UF Church and manse in Kingussie. In 1908, 20 ladies were involved. Isabella's father, Ewen, was one of The Men along with Johnnie Blair.

The Blair family arrived in Laggan from Argyll around 1828. *Iain Blàr* (Johnnie) and his siblings including Duncan Black Blair received a good education from John Finlayson at Sherramore Assembly School. Duncan became a Free Church minister in Nova Scotia where his many eloquent Gaelic manuscripts in poetry and prose are still preserved. In two beautiful elegies he praised local schoolmasters – John MacMaster and John Finlayson. Johnnie contributed to the Free Church through his teaching and lay preaching. At his Crubenmore school there was much emphasis on the teaching of the Bible and Shorter Catechism. TSM was told that Johnnie "was popular with his pupils for many reasons, among them, doubtless, that his kindly disposition made him a gentle disciplinarian compared with the relentless rulers" of some other schools. In his church work Johnnie was remembered as "the gentle little elder with the happy smile, grey whiskers and bright eyes, whom all held in great respect." Today, he is remembered as the creator of Johnnie Blair's garden in Glen Banchor. In his retirement, Johnnie lived with his sister Mary and her husband, *Dòmhnall a' Chnuic* (Donald Macpherson) who was a Gaelic bard and crofter at Knock, one of the nearest crofts to where Johnnie laboured with his garden. He fenced in the flat ground on the top of the *Sìthean Mòr* (big fairy hill), a high gravel mound which, a long time ago, had been made into a double palisaded fort to give some protection to the inhabitants of Glen Banchor. To clean the ground he encouraged the local crofters to plant a potato and see which one would produce the best crop. Some of the keen crofters made the mistake of going to tend to their potato on the Sabbath. Johnnie did not approve: the story goes, to stop that happening, he took down part of the fence and let in the sheep. Johnnie did continue his experiment with the garden and "for twenty years or more it bloomed under the gardener's loving care."[10]

From the top of the knoll named *Sìdhean Mòr Dail a' Chaorainn* on OS maps, the low walls of the deserted township of *Dail a' Chaorainn* (dell of the rowans) can clearly be seen. Of the many families who had lived there, one family of Kennedys were at Dalchaorinnmor for about 100 years. Maddy Kennedy, her children, *Uilleam*, *Seumas*, *Ceit* and Kate's son, Andrew, were evicted in 1874. They moved to central Newtonmore to a small house called Dalchurn. The Kennedys were fiercely protective of their property and their heritage. *Uilleam* (William) was the local leader in the campaign to protect the right of access to St Bride's Churchyard. *Ceit* was feared by the local youths since she threatened them with a shotgun as they 'eyed up' her apple tree. *Seumas* (James), a drover and cattle dealer, was well known to the local boys. One of The Cronies remembered being: "in his peat-moss squad at the 'Aourdhan Bheag' (3d a day if passed as proficient)" and joining up "with the rear guard of a strong company of Newtonmore demonstrators who, led by *Seumas* and other Newtonmore stalwarts, armed with hatchets and hammers, marched up the 'Glenbanchor' Road to Dalchurn Bridge in their determination to secure for posterity the [then disputed] freedom of the road to Seumas's birthplace." That piper-led protest took place in late August 1904. Mr Schofield, the tenant of Glenbanchor shootings, assumed he had exclusive use of the Glen and erected notices to try and exclude locals and holiday visitors. The flag-waving campaigners did not want to see their access to rights of way, favourite haunts or ancestral places being barred. THE KINGUSSIE RECORD reported: "When a halt had been called, the crowd was addressed by some of the oldest inhabitants, who described the different landmarks in the vicinity, and urged upon the younger generation to do all in their power to preserve intact, as far as possible, the freedom of the district as a noted resort for summer visitors."

That was an inauspicious start to 36 year old George Schofield's long tenure of the Glenbanchor shootings. Mr Schofield came from a family who, based in the South Pennines, had made their money in cotton spinning. He had young children, many servants, and was one of the early owners of an eye-catching, yellow-wheeled, 6hp Daimler. Shooting tenants from out-with Scotland did not appreciate that traditional Scottish routes through the hills and glens were considered rights of way and it was difficult to debar the public unless they committed certain offences as detailed in the Trespass (Scotland) Act. Trespass laws in England were stricter. Similar confrontations had occurred on other Highland Estates. Following the demonstration, feelings were still running high and several of Mr Schofield's dogs were poisoned by strychnine.

Balavil, proprietor of Newtonmore and the shootings, acted as intermediary. He was experienced in law having studied at Cambridge and been admitted to Lincoln's Inn. He would have been familiar with the law on either side of the border.

After that debacle, Mr Schofield became a great supporter of many activities in Newtonmore including the clay pigeon club. He gave donations to clubs, chaired many fundraising concerts, gave practical gifts (hares, venison) to the poor and supported the school at their annual prize giving. He made a small charge of "sixpence for the privilege of a day's fishing on the lower reaches of his streams, and the sum so collected he devotes to the purchase of book prizes for the school children." In return he was given honorary positions in some of the clubs including shinty and curling. By 1907, the Schofield family had moved to a big house near Harrogate called Riseley Hall. Did the many keepers who lived in Riseley, Glen Road, realise it had a Yorkshire name? Mr Schofield also supported Balavil who organised and competed very successfully in sheep-dog trials. In 1912, the Schofield Cup at the Kingussie Trials was won by J D Macpherson, youngest brother of TSM. Little did Balavil, Mr Schofield and Mr Macpherson know that in a few years time their sporting pastimes would be overshadowed by WW1 in which Balavil lost his son. Messrs Schofield and Macpherson were promoted to Captains and J D sustained a wound which would hamper him for the rest of his life.

Newtonmoracks, including the Two Cronies, felt the anxiety and sadness of WW1. Donald Campbell's youngest brother, William, was killed in Europe in 1916. In 1914, James Macdonald was appointed Chief Constable of Arbroath. "After service in France as an officer in the Cameron Highlanders, in which he was wounded, he resumed police duties. In 1935 Mr. Macdonald was awarded the M.B.E., and, in 1942, for special war-time duties, the O.B.E. was conferred upon him."[11] James had made a contribution to three major wars, starting with his service in the Fife Light Horse in South Africa. His Macdonald family had long connections to the Highland Railway. James, the youngest, spent his early years beside the railway at Etteridge. After schooling in Newtonmore and Kingussie, he worked for the railway, as a clerk in Inverness and later at Montrose. His two eldest brothers were in the police, which James joined in 1902. In 1891, another brother, John, was labouring on the construction of the Aviemore-Carrbridge section of the railway along with their father, Donald.

John Macdonald was thirled to the railway from then on: (1894 – in flying squad at Kingussie, where the layout was being enlarged and the station being re-built; 1895 – part of a gang who spent three months clearing snow at the Black Tank cutting, north of Struan; plate laying on loops including Killiecrankie in 1896, and Inshlea in 1897; late 1890s, for several years – in charge of blasting rock for the doubling of the track north of Struan.) In 1905, he was appointed Permanent Way inspector at Muir of Ord. The Highland Railway was extremely busy during WW1 with troop and equipment movements, some going as far north as Thurso, en-route for Scapa Flow. In 1915, John was appointed HR's chief permanent way inspector and in 1920, he was awarded an M.B.E. for his outstanding contribution during the extremely busy war years on the HR. He directed operations after the 1923 cloudburst north of Carrbridge which swept away bridges and closed the line for seven weeks. It was said of John, that he had walked every mile of the Highland line before he retired in 1941.[12]

John and James had two sisters. Sarah Macdonald married John Stewart and lived at Bruachville, one of the oldest houses in Newtonmore. Her "skilled joiner" husband was from Lossiemouth where he had gone to school with Ramsay Macdonald. Sarah's sister, Bella, owned Sherwood and often stayed there with her husband, Robert B Thomson. He had been the minister of the UF Church in Newtonmore. They married in 1914 after he transferred to Glenorchy. Sherwood, built in 1908, was the latest addition to a group of houses being erected in Glen Road from 1905: Parkhill (currently Neadach) for Sarah Chisholm; Clan Alpine for James Mackinnon, butler, Castle Douglas; Craigbeg for Samuel Mackenzie, retired shepherd; and Netherwood for Donald Ferguson, gamekeeper, Aberarder. There had been piece-meal development in other areas since 1895. By 1910, some of those earlier feus were being sold on.

That year, Victoria Villa was disponed by Charles Kennedy to Maria MacArthur, whose father had been the long-term tenant of the large sheep farm at Etteridge. The talented MacArthur family had been brought up near Loch Awe and Maria changed the name of her house to Inistrynich, a favourite place she could see from their hill farm at Accurrach. Several of the MacArthur siblings were accomplished musicians and Maria's skill on the piano was greatly appreciated at concerts locally and as far away as Edinburgh. For at least 20 years Maria had contributed to many fundraising concerts in Newtonmore where her rendition of Scottish music was very popular. She loaned a harmonium to St Columba's Church, Newtonmore, until they managed to buy one in 1900. That was financed by subscription with half donated from Mrs Carnegie, by then in Skibo. Miss MacArthur was superintendent of St Columba's Church Girls' Guild and helped set up a Red Cross Branch in Newtonmore.

Another talented lady, Dr Elizabeth Garrett Anderson, b. 1836, became a house-owner locally in 1910. The diminutive Dr Garrett Anderson, a feisty, determined, pioneering lady, was best known as the first woman to qualify as a physician and surgeon in Britain. She championed the cause of women in many spheres and in 1866, along with a friend, organised petitions asking that female heads of households be given the vote. It was her support of the National Union of Women's Suffrage Societies (NUWSS) that brought her to Badenoch. A group from that organisation toured the Highlands in 1909 and were well-received at a meeting in Newtonmore. The suffragists of the NUWSS wished to achieve the vote for women through peaceful and legal means unlike the more militant suffragettes. THE KINGUSSIE RECORD of 21 Aug 1909 commented on: "…the venerable personality who presided over the meeting. In the person of Dr Garrett Anderson we had … one of the oldest suffragists connected with the movement." Dr Garrett Anderson, mayor of Aldeburgh, was the first female mayor and magistrate in Britain. Alde Cottage was the name she chose for her house in Glen Road. It is now Alder Lodge.

Another hard-working lady of a similar age was mother of eight and, by 1901, sub-postmistress, Barbara Stewart. The Stewarts ran the postal services as a family concern with husband, John, listed as postman and their eldest daughter, Isabella, a PO assistant.

Their son, Peter, may also have helped during his summer holidays. He started his teaching career at Eastbank Academy, Shettleston, where his "classes in English, Latin, and French are excellently taught."[13] With the ever increasing numbers of summer visitors the PO had expanded. In 1899, the Stewarts converted their leases of the buildings on either side of 'Glenbanchor' Road to feus. Visitors in 1906 would have noticed a new PO in a taller building on the site where the single storey PO had stood for over 30 years. Telegraph facilities, installed toward the end of the century, had also brought more business to the PO. Phosa Macpherson, whose father had the nearby fish shop, remembered that the Stewarts brought in experienced telegraphers for the busy summer seasons and hundreds of people used the PO services in a day. Phosa also described her father's pre-WW1 merchandise: exotic fruits; flowers; honey; salmon from the Tay; lobsters; crabs; halibut; plaice; turbot and Dover sole. Those were brought in daily on the early morning train. Her father employed up to 13 people and they supplied about 17 shooting lodges from Blair Athol to Aviemore.[13]

As Newtonmore became increasingly popular as a health resort new and more specialised shops opened in the village. In addition to those mentioned previously, the village gained at least two butchers and bakers, a stationer and newsagent, a chemist and a few others, including a jeweller. As confidence in the economy of Newtonmore grew, the British Linen Bank, in 1906, and the Bank of Scotland, in 1908, opened branches in the village. Those were supervised by their agents in Kingussie. The 1911 census revealed a greater diversity of occupations than that of earlier times. In addition to the long-standing tradesmen and artisans there were: several gardeners; a cycle mechanic; two postmen; several washerwomen; a hotel boots; two greenkeepers; coal agents; five dressmakers; a barman; and three coachmen. The coachmen, James Logan, 23; A Macdonald (Ali Sam), 30, and Robbie Kennedy, 41, would soon have to look for other employment as the coaching era was rapidly coming to an end.

Duncan Macpherson, The Royal Hotel, Kingussie, was the first local to bring a car to the area. He intended to hire it to summer visitors. In late 1903, he bought a Daimler in Edinburgh but, on the journey home, he encountered snowdrifts at Drumochter. The car eventually made it to Kingussie towed by two horses preceded by a snowplough. Duncan was one of the adventurous children of *Rao'll a' Phleastarair,* Newtonmore.

Arthur Macfarlane, Kingussie, anticipated the need for motorised transport and bought a 20 seater motor bus in Aug 1909. He had little time to use it as he died, aged 30, at the beginning of 1910, the year in which the

Craig Mhor Hotel made provision for those with motor cars. That hotel figured in Robbie Kennedy's work when he moved on from coach driving. He obtained the tenancy of Croft Roy in 1917 and augmented his income by working for Tom Grant on his tenanted land. Earlier, Robbie had driven coaches for Cluny and for Angus James Macpherson.

That gentleman, a native of Inverness, had been a businessman in China and Japan and retired to his ancestral area in 1896. He rented Balvattan from Mrs Brewster Macpherson and after she sold it in May 1899, from Alexander Beveridge, a Kirkcaldy solicitor. When the Beveridge family decided to use the house for holidays, Angus James, moved to renting *Druimbreac* at the other end of the village. Both were big houses in extensive grounds and folk referred to Angus by the name of whichever house he was renting. Angus was "a specially good friend to the Newtonmore Shinty Club" and he supported many other organisations in Badenoch with money gifts and his business expertise. He happily undertook the duties of chairman at many village events. His obituary, in 1903, described his "lively interest in the affairs of the district, and the people of Newtonmore. To him we owe the improved postal arrangements and the additional train service at Newtonmore. He never wearied of corresponding with the authorities regarding such matters. By his

death the poor have lost a kind and unostentatious friend, and the inhabitants of the village a wise counsellor." Some of those kindnesses only became apparent after his death, perhaps because he visited folk individually. The poor, for whom it was a struggle to make ends meet, were regularly given gifts of food and fuel by the Balavil family and some of the shooting tenants, but their gifts, although very welcome, did not have the personal touch.

Paupers could claim assistance from the parish but the amounts they received were very small and could be stopped or reduced. Some help for the poor arrived in 1909 when 237 claimants in Badenoch were among the first to receive a small old age pension. That new pension for those who were over 70 was means tested; the maximum payment being five shillings per week. Other limited benefits became available in early 1913 when the National Insurance Act came into operation. Older people and the poor often suffered ill health because of their poverty. The voluntary Nursing Association provided free nursing for the poor. Such was the need for their services, they had to employ more nurses. One of those nurses may have been Christina Cattanach, a Craggan lass, who, in 1901, gave her occupation as a "monthly and sick nurse". Later, after Christina married Donald MacMaster Cattanach, her nursing skills were useful when she was employed as Matron of the Poorhouse in Oban where her husband was the Governor. Before the NHS and state benefits the Nursing Association provided a much needed service for the community.

Newtonmoracks were regularly asked to help fund-raise for various groups but some clubs were self-supporting. The winter of 1908 saw two such groups inaugurated. The Village Committee suggested that something should be "done for the young people of an improving and upraising moral tendency." That resulted in the formation of The Newtonmore Mutual Improvement Association (MI) which met on Wednesday evenings in the Public Hall. A committee was formed with the honorary posts being accepted by Balavil (president); the Rev. Mr Edwards (Established Church), Messrs Colam, Schofield and Clark (lay-preacher at the UF Church). Many clubs invited prestigious and wealthy patrons to honorary positions in hope of their financial and moral support. The week to week running of the club was entrusted to Jamie Macdonald, now a Bank of Scotland accountant, his deputy, Tom Cattanach, and a small committee of men aged between 25 and 40. The MI held lively debates, ran draughts competitions and had interesting speakers, including their honorary vice-presidents. Around the same time, Miss Grant, Craig Mhor Hotel, had been "entrusted with a sum of money and numerous games and magazines, by kind lady visitors who are interested in the well-being of the young men of the village, and are desirous of starting a pleasant meeting on Saturday evenings." Those meetings were more informal. They played draughts, dominoes and other games. An innovation, suggested by one of the sponsors, was the introduction of the energetic game of shovel-board which seemed to suit the small size of the first hall. "The young men quickly mastered [it] and very soon lusty shouts gave evidence that the game was very popular." They sometimes invited a few females to take part in that game. Competition results were noted in THE KINGUSSIE RECORD. Both groups attracted good numbers indicating that there was room in the village for the two clubs. A number of those young people were also members of one or more of the several temperance groups in the village. Along with shinty, clay pigeon shooting and curling the new clubs continued over the winter. Many of the young men had less free time in the summer when agricultural produce had to be tended.

Too much free time was often a problem in the winter, but the construction of a new road helped to alleviate that. Alexander Mackenzie, CE, Kingussie, asked for offers for: "Forming and Finishing a 10 feet [sic] Road from Station Road to Village Street [beside the school] at Newtonmore, a distance of 800 yards" to be submitted by 12 Nov 1906. As with many village-funded building projects at that time it was quickly actioned. THE KINGUSSIE RECORD of 6 Dec 1906, reported: "The new road which is now in course of construction … is already well advanced. The work is being actively carried on by Mr Grant, the contractor, who is employing a large squad of men and horses, and at this time of the year is very acceptable, as it gives employment to a number of local people who would otherwise have been

Fig 38 – Mrs Macpherson about to open the new road to the station. *(HFM.)*
L-R: Seumas Mòr, Wm Cattanach, Mrs Simpson (hotel), Mr Middlemas, ?, Mr Macgregor (Station Master), ?,
C.J.B. Macpherson, ?, ?, Robert Sellar, Tom Grant.

idle." On a lovely, sunny Saturday, 25 May 1907, William Cattanach, in a speech which recalled his ancestors' long connections with the Balavil family, called on Mrs Macpherson to open the road. Thomas Grant, the contractor, presented her with a pair of silver scissor to cut the Macpherson tartan ribbon. Thereafter: "the Laird and his lady, followed by a large crowd, drove over the New Road to the Golf House." On arrival, Balavil, in what had become an annual ritual, declared the golf course open for the season. As with several of the early 20th century projects, the new road was financed by the villagers. They were still holding concerts in summer 1908 to help clear the debt.

In contrast to those funded by the residents, projects funded by the council had to pass through various committees before being actioned. In late 1906, 14 ratepayers requested that the Council should install a five-inch water pipe on Newtonmore's main street. That was considered at a meeting of the District Committee of the County Council in early December. Their meeting at the end of March reported that the estimated cost was £262. They endorsed the project but needed "the approval of the Finance Committee and County Council" before tenders were asked for and the work could commence. Another major public work which had to go through the committee hurdles was the renovation of and additions to the school.

At a school review in April 1909, Dr Mackenzie, Chairman of the Board, asked the committee to consider his suggestions for improvements. He was in his 80th year and still enthusiastic about progressing education in Badenoch. Six months later, the board approved amended plans from the Education Department. Tenders were invited at the end of Jan 1910 and contracts awarded a month later. Four of the contractors, Messrs R and L Macpherson, A Cattanach and A Falconer, were former pupils. The masons were Alex Macpherson and his son-in-law, John Russell, who, although born near Newtonmore, had grown up at Gaskmore. Much of the finishing work was completed during the summer holidays, ready for the opening in mid-October. Prior to the ceremony, which took place outside the main door, as a new Union Jack, presented by one of the many visitors attending, was hoisted, Dr Mackenzie commented that "They all hoped that Britain would enjoy the blessings of peace for years to come, but the best way to ensure this was for the country to be prepared for war. If it went out to other nations that we were prepared for war, none of them would dare set foot on British soil … and [he] concluded by commending the defence of the country to all young men." He then invited Mrs Macpherson of Balavil to perform the opening ceremony.[14]

Following that, the smartly dressed children, teachers, members of the Board, locals from Newtonmore and Kingussie and a large number of visitors moved indoors. After the singing of Psalm 100 and a prayer, the chairman, in an interesting speech, talked about the history of the school and praised the teachers of the past. Special mention was made of the support given by the Balavil family, most recently by the gift of extra ground which had now been surrounded by a substantial wall, part of which had ornamental railings. The Rev. Dr Mackenzie also listed some of the past pupils and their achievements finishing off with "John Cattanach, who was looked upon by his fellow students as the cleverest anatomist in his class. As a shinty player he was, as they all knew, unequalled." He then invited Mrs Schofield to present the pupils with prizes for excellence, drawing and attendance. A report of 23 Nov 1910 in the school log book noted that "The old building has been thoroughly renovated and the class-rooms rearranged and brought quite up-to-date as regards heating, lighting and ventilation. The accommodation has been increased by the erection of a new building consisting of a central hall, a large classroom, teachers' retiring room, and pupils cloak-rooms … the class set apart for the teaching of Cookery will shortly be ready for occupation and the senior classroom is suitably equipped for experimental work in Practical Science."

The new headmaster, Mr Miller, and his staff were praised for making "creditable progress" with their pupils, despite "the work of the past session" being "greatly interrupted by the building operations."[15]

Those Newtonmore Public School children attended during a particularly interesting time that lasted from September 1909 to June 1911, connecting thrice to Royalty. At the beginning of the 20th century, with no radio and few taking a regular paper, the Monarchy was very remote from the people of the Highlands. The recognised start of the century was on 1 Jan 1901, but very few local celebrations were reported. Newtonmore played Grantown at shinty on the 1st. The following evening there was a concert and dance in aid of hall funds. However, the people united in sorrow when their beloved Queen Victoria, monarch for over 63 years, died on 22 Jan 1901. On Sat 2 Feb, the day of the State Funeral, the Established and UF Churches, led by the Kingussie and Newtonmore ministers, held a joint service in the Victoria Hall which was draped in dark colours. It was well attended by the local inhabitants; councillors; members of Oddfellows and Free Masons, wearing their regalia; and the Volunteers in uniform. The service ended with the singing of God Save the King.[16]

The country was in mourning and the local Volunteers postponed their annual assembly in a mark of respect. The "district final of the Camanachd Association Trophy" was postponed "on account of the Queen's funeral."[17] When that game, a local derby, was finally played at the beginning of March, the teams wore black armbands in Her memory. The new King, Edward VII, was crowned on 9 Aug 1902. Newtonmore laid on celebrations with a treat organised mainly for the children "and the aged and infirm poor." On that fine summer day, bunting decorated the village and many wore the national colours. Visitors helped with donations and assisted in running the event which began with a procession from the Balavil Hotel. The flag-waving children, accompanied by a piper, were led by *Seumas Mòr*, Robert Sellar and Angus James Macpherson in procession, down Bonanza drive to the golf course where they were presented with coronation medals by Mrs Macpherson of Balavil. After a short Divine service, tea was served by a committee of local and visiting ladies. Later there were games for all, including a married men v single men tug-of-war, which prompted much hilarity. The games were organised by Tom Cattanach, Tom Grant, George Macpherson, (James) Ian Macpherson and George Sellar. Around dusk a bonfire was lit by Mrs Kidston, a regular visitor, and many danced despite a "tremendous downpour of rain." The crowd enjoyed their salute to King Edward.

On 20 Sept 1909, the people of Newtonmore were able to salute the King in person as he motored through Badenoch on his way from grouse shooting at Tulchan Lodge in Strathspey to Mamore Forest. That was the King's fourth visit to Tulchan after his accession, but he rarely acknowledged the public on his journey. George Tod Hay commented on that in his book 'Perth and North Thereof'. Although George was born in 1892 in Ross-shire he spent many years in Alvie Parish where his family lived at Ard Insh. His grandparents farmed at Dalraddy. George wrote: "Among the notable events of the [Aviemore] junction's early days … was the halt at its main North platform of a royal train while the engine replenished its water-tank. In the train was King Edward VII, in Scotland for the first time since his accession on his way to a favourite grouse-moor at Tulchan". The many cheering people at the decorated station only saw "the long line of elegant coaches, all with drawn blinds, glide in and then in a few minutes pull out." The King had been last seen in public in Badenoch at Ardverikie in 1847. The pupils were delighted to have time off school and excited to have the chance of seeing the Monarch. Two magnificent arches of birch, rowan branches and heather had been erected outside hotels at each end in the village. At 11 am the children, with their teachers, led by piper John Macpherson, marched along the flag-bedecked street to the Balavil Hotel where the King had agreed to stop for a few minutes. At 12.55 a big cheer greeted the arrival of the Royal cars. When they stopped, George Sellar, proprietor of the hotel, introduced Mr Macpherson of Balavil who gave "an address of loyalty and welcome." The King acknowledged the salute which he received from the enthusiastic crowd by bowing and smiling repeatedly." As the Royal car drew away the scholars, joined by crowd, sang the National Anthem. Afterwards, the children were entertained to light refreshments by the laird and Mr Sellar in the hotel garden, followed by a brief speech by Dr Mackenzie.

June 1911 was a month remembered locally for its connections to royalty and to the Rev. Dr Mackenzie. The 82 year old minister had returned from the Church General Assembly looking and feeling well. His death the following week on 10 June stunned the people of the parish. Newtonmore School log book noted that on the day of the "funeral of Dr

Fig 39 – Villagers preparing to walk to the Balavil Hotel. *(HFM)*
L-R: Wm Cattanach; visitor to Simpsons Hotel; Fred Simpson, ?, Jim Macdonald;
(the lady and child might be Mrs Simpson and Arthur); John Macpherson (piper); Dr Mackenzie;
Mr Miller (teacher); Miss Cattanach (teacher).

Mackenzie", the school was closed for a half day and the flag was lowered to half-mast.

King Edward VII had died the previous May and preparations to celebrate the coronation of his successor, George V, on 22 Jun 1911 were underway in Badenoch. The school children in particular were looking forward to that as they were to be awarded a week's holiday. The village committee again undertook arrangements for the celebrations which followed a similar pattern to that of the 1902 coronation. The hard-working village committee was at that time embarking on its greatest challenge yet.

Selected further sources used in this chapter:

[1] Bel Cameron

[2] KR, 14/11/1903

[3] GB0232/CI/3/8A/8

[4] Evening Telegraph, Angus 25/3/1898

[5] KR, 27/6/1908

[6] IC, 7/12/1900

[7] The Fife Free Press, 31/5/1902

[8] DC, 3/5/1910

[9] NRS RD5/1904/3398

[10] TSM Archive

[11] CD 15

[12] Sinclair, 2005; IC, 10/1/1941; PJ, 18/1/1941

[13] BOHP, 082/B

[14] KR, 15/10/1910

[15] GB0232/CI/5/3/209A

[16] EC, 5/2/1901

[17] PJ, 9/2/1901

Many newspapers were consulted for this chapter. The local paper was first published in June 1902. Prior to that THE PEOPLE'S JOURNAL and THE INVERNESS COURIER provided much of the information.

Chapter 12

The Silver Key to prosperity?

1911–1913

"With commendable enterprise the good folk of Newtonmore
are setting about the erection of a new Public Hall."

S o stated THE BADENOCH RECORD which had been newly re-branded from THE KINGUSSIE RECORD. The new name better reflected the area it had always covered. That report of 15 July 1911 continued: "Some time ago competitive plans were invited by the Village Committee …" Members of that group were: Robert Sellar, JP, chairman; Wm Cattanach, deputy chairman; Wm Borland; Donald Cameron; Tom Cattanach; Robert Forbes; Tom Grant; Donald Guthrie; John Macdonald; Angus Macpherson; James Macpherson, JP (*Seumas Mòr*); J D

Macpherson; John Macpherson and James Tytler, their long-serving and highly-respected clerk. The chairman of the committee changed each year. You will recognise a few familiar names there. Many of those named were the men (along with some earlier residents) whose energy and foresight led to the development of Newtonmore and its facilities.

Reported suggestions about the need for a larger hall go back to 1903 at least. Although it is possible that may have been proposed earlier: "Newtonmore Public Hall" was advertised for sale in 1897. As more and more summer visitors frequented the village and the population grew, the need for a new hall became imperative. In addressing that need the Village Committee had great support from the majority of the regular visitors who gave generously to local functions. Since many of those tourists took accommodation for two or three months each summer, it was important for them to have a hall suitable for their social events.

The plan chosen was submitted by Stroneborn mason, Alexander Cattanach, The Laurels, Kingussie. His father, Donald, and his brothers, Ewen and Andrew, were also masons. Alex,

Fig 40 – Construction of Coig na Shee which was commissioned by Allan MacGillivray (left) in June 1903.
(M Mackenzie)

despite having no formal qualifications, also designed and drew up interesting plans for many local buildings, large and small, public and private. Most of the other buildings in the area were designed by Alexander Mackenzie C E, Kingussie. A rare exception was Coig na Shee. The architect was William Scott-Morton from Edinburgh with Alex Cattanach, The Laurels, employed as the plumber on that contract.

Alongside the new hall Alex suggested retaining "the wing at the back, which was erected some years ago to accommodate the local United Free Church congregation" and proposed that it should be "converted into committee and retiring rooms, with lavatories." An addition was to be made beside that wing. It would "comprise quarters for the caretaker." The original hall was to be demolished to make way for the new building. To accommodate it on the narrow site, the new hall would be nearer the street; the length of the old hall would become the width of the new. To finish it off, there will be "nicely designed turrets on either side of the front entrance, the whole being surmounted with a tower, with a flagstaff."

The anticipation of a new hall would have occupied the minds of many that summer.

Some of the holiday-makers and all villagers had an opportunity to look at the drawings and gave their approval. The hall sub-committee of the Village Committee held numerous meetings throughout the year. At their annual report, in Apr 1912, it was announced that the committee "had now the assistance of a large and influential committee of ladies." A successful sale of work had been held in October and plans were in place for a two-day fancy fair to be held in August. The summer of 1912 was to be when the bulk of the fund-raising would take place.

That was opened near the end of July with a lecture, entitled "Life in the Indian Village". The speaker, Lt.-Col. A E Roberts MD, had been in the Indian Medical Service and was a regular visitor. Clune Hope, a large house at Knock, had recently been erected for him and his wife. Like many of the regular visitors, they took a great interest in the village and offered assistance with projects. They were well liked by the local people and sent gifts to some of them at Christmas.

August and most of September were the high points of the summer season. The village and the surrounding shooting lodges were full and many fund-raising social events were held. "The Grand Fancy Fair" was carefully timed to tap into the peak season.

Behind the scenes the main players were Miss Maria Macarthur from the ladies' committee and Mr James Tytler from the village committee who were described as "the indefatigable joint secretaries." Miss

Newtonmore Hall.

The Grand Fancy Fair

in aid of the Hall Building Fund will be Opened in

THE PUBLIC SCHOOL, NEWTONMORE, on TUESDAY, 27th curt., at 11-30 a.m., by ARTHUR RAYMOND HEATH, ESQ.

C. J. B. MACPHERSON, Esq. of Balavil, in the Chair, and on

WEDNESDAY, 28th curt., at 3 p.m., by MRS. MACPHERSON of Balavil

THE RT. HON. C. SCOTT DICKSON, ESQ., M.P., in the Chair.

ADMISSION:—Tuesday—11-30 to 3 p.m., 1/-; after 3 o'clock, 6d. Wednesday—3 p.m. to 4 o'clock, 1/-; after 4 o'clock, 6d.

On Tuesday the Fancy Fair will close at 7 p.m., and on Wednesday at 10 p.m.

In connection with the above a

Grand Evening CONCERT

(organised by DR. and MR. WM. M'LURE) will be held in the

PUBLIC HALL, NEWTONMORE

On Tuesday, 27th August, at 8-30 p.m.

Admission, 2/- and 1/-

Also on Thursday, August 29, at 8 p.m., a

Grand Evening CONCERT

will be held in the

PUBLIC HALL, NEWTONMORE.

Admission, 2/- and 1/-.

Attractive Programmes will be submitted.

NEWTONMORE FANCY FAIR.

In connection with the above it is requested that all Goods for Sale be delivered at the School not later than Monday evening, the 26th inst., and also that all Collecting Cards be handed in by that date to the Secretary,   J. M. TYTLER.

(Charles Scott Dickson rented Coig na Shee. A R Heath was Balavil's brother–in–law)

The following are the names of the ladies and gentlemen who acted as stall holders:—

Macpherson Stall—Mrs Macpherson of Balavil; Mrs Macpherson of Cluny; Miss E. Macpherson of Glentruim, assisted by lady friends.

Shooting Lodge Stall—Mrs. Schofield, Glenbanchor; Mrs. Ogilvie Mathieson, Ralia; Mrs. Stancliffe, Chislehurst; assisted by lady friends.

Game Department of Shooting Lodge Stall—Mr. Schofield and Mr. de Falbe.

Visitors' Stall—Mrs. Garret Anderson, M.D., Alde Cottage; Mrs. Kidston, Cairn Dearg; Mrs. McClure, Larch Cottage; Mrs. Roberts, assisted by lady friends.

Village Stall—Miss MacArthur, Innistrynich; Miss Grant, Craig Mhor Hotel; Mrs. Sellar, Bonanza; Mrs. Macpherson, Larch Cottage, assisted by Miss Cattanach, Kingussie; Miss Sellar, Bonanza; Mrs. Gibson, Holmfield; Miss de Watteville, Kingussie; Miss Wighton, do.

Produce and Game Stall—Mrs. Macgillivray, Banchor; Miss Grant, Woodcliffe; Mrs. Macfarlane, The Manse, Kingussie, Miss Brown, do.

Refreshment Stall—Mrs. Simpson, Temperance Hotel; Mrs. Main, The Hotel, assisted by Mrs. Galbraith, the Misses Main, Simpson, M. Guthrie, J. Guthrie, B. Mutch, C. Mutch, Low, Mackintosh, and Lumsden.

Highland Stall—Mr. B. Grant, Inverness.

Amusements—Mr. Ian de Watteville, assisted by Col.-Sergt. Oakley, Messrs. Wickham, D. Macpherson, Rawson, Matthews, K. de Watteville and J. H. Tytler.

Children's Stall—Miss Roma Macfarlane, Miss Sylvia de Watteville, Master Colin Campbell.

Parcels Stall—Miss K. Macpherson and Miss Davidson.

Macarthur and Mr Tytler had each moved to Newtonmore in the early 1900s. (As well as their amazing contribution to the hall fund-raising efforts, they both worked very hard on various church committees.)

The list of stall holders showed the diversity of those involved and in many cases their residences. Some of the houses listed were owned by visitors and others were rented.

Two concerts were run in conjunction with The Grand Fancy Fair. The great effort by young and old, villagers and visitors "was successful beyond all expectations … total proceeds would be not far short of £600."

The work of the committee, visitors and volunteers, continued apace in September. Their efforts were noted in the following comprehensive report in THE BADENOCH RECORD of 21 Sept 1912:

> Since their fancy fair, the Village Committee have been busily engaged with the negotiations preliminary to the erection of the new hall. The Committee have received valuable advice from several friends among the visitors in their consideration of proposals to amend the plan of the Hall. On Monday evening of last week a meeting was held, at which, in addition to the Committee and the Ladies' Fancy Fair Committee, the following ladies and gentlemen were present, viz., Mr and Mrs Schofield, Glenbanchor Lodge; Mrs M'Clure and Mr W. K. M'Clure, Larch Cottage; Mr W. N. Colam, Ard-na-choile; Mrs Kidston, Cairn Dearg; Rev. Mr Kidston, do.; Mr G. L. Crole, K.C.; Lt.-Col. Roberts. The Rev. D. Macfarlane was called to the chair. The clerk, Mr J. M. Tytler, intimated apologies for absence from Mr and Mrs Macpherson of Balavil, Rev. Alex. Bain, Mrs Garrett Anderson, and Miss Geddes. A long and interesting discussion took place on the question of the alteration of the plans, so as to include several new features that would add to the utility and serviceableness of the hall. Several of the gentlemen present submitted practical suggestions, which were very cordially received by the Committee. The conference concluded with votes of thanks to the visitors and to the chairman.
>
> On the following evening the Village Committee met with the architect, Mr Alex Cattanach, Kingussie. It was unanimously agreed that the existing plans of the hall should be amended, and in the subsequent discussion it was evident that many of the suggestions that had been made at the previous meeting had commended themselves to the members of the Committee. It was resolved to call a meeting, at which the architect would submit amended

plans, and to which those gentlemen who had proved such helpful advisors should be invited. The clerk read a letter from Colonel Roberts, in which the purpose which a hall such as the new building was intended might serve was discussed in a very full and thorough manner. The Committee acknowledged the useful hints which the Colonel's letter contained.

On Friday afternoon a consultation was held with Mr Cattanach, at which the representatives of the Committee and of the gentlemen co-operating with them were present. Considerable time was taken up in adjusting the plans to the measurements of the feu. At last satisfactory arrangements were adopted, which will, it is confidently anticipated, result in the erection of a building which, with regard to external appearance and internal construction, will do credit to the Committee and to the architect alike. It will be seen from the advertisement columns that a sale of work is to be held on Tuesday next at which the goods left over from the fancy fair will be exposed for sale. The Hon. Mrs Pelham, of Ferniegair [now Craigower Lodge], is to open the sale, and it is hoped that all interested in the object will give it the heartiest possible support.

The Village Committee deserved highest praise for the way it steered such a diverse group to a successful conclusion. The contributions of ideas from the well-heeled, high-achieving visitors had to be skilfully acknowledged so that they would continue to contribute in cash and kind. It is interesting to note that by this time, several of those 'visitors', Col Roberts, Mr Colam, and Mrs Garrett Anderson were actually householders in Newtonmore.

The following edition of THE BADENOCH RECORD reported that the successful sale had raised £52.4s. But the end of September was also a sad time for the villagers when one of the women who had nurtured the growth of Newtonmore died at Babbacombe, Torquay. There were many tributes to Mrs Lydia Brewster Macpherson, mother of the laird of Balavil, including one from Newtonmore Village Committee.

Two weeks later, on 12 October, that hard working group were advertising for contractors to estimate for building the "NEW HALL, LIBRARY and CARETAKER'S QUARTERS to be Erected at Newtonmore." Offers were to be submitted by Monday 28th October.

At their meeting on Monday 18 Nov 1912, the following offers were accepted: "Masons, Messrs Macpherson & Russell, Newtonmore, £430; joiner, Mr Alex. McGregor, Newtonmore, £518; plumber, Mr Wm. Urquhart, Kingussie,

£129; slater, Mr Alex. Falconer, Kingussie, £124; plasterer, Mr Wm. Duffes, Newtonmore, £60.13.11d; painter, Mr Wm. M. Dunbar, Kingussie, £60.12s. That made a total of £1322.5.11d." The clerk announced that they had received a cheque for £50 from Dr Garrett Anderson and a donation from the Rev. and Mrs Macfarlane, Kingussie. Interestingly, one of the masons named had a close family connection with an original lease-holder of 1820 and shared his name – John Russell. John Russell the third, now 200 years later (in 2020), plays an active part in village life and work. As usual, with village-organised projects, things moved along quickly. The Village Committee organised a *ho ro gheallaidh* or final-fling for the end of that week, to mark the demise of the original hall. The community, and many from Kingussie, filled the building. They were welcomed with "a pleasant tea" followed by a musical selection by stalwart piper John Macpherson. The audience then enjoyed a humorous and thought-provoking talk by the Rev. John Macechern, an old friend of the community. This was followed by local men giving a short musical programme: *Jockan* on the pipes and songs from John Cattanach, John D Macpherson and John Miller, the school-master. The singing of Auld Lang Syne brought the evening to a close. The dance which followed was attended by about 30 couples and supervised by Angus Macpherson and John D

Macpherson. James Logan acted as MC and music was supplied by Miss Main and Messrs Adam Fraser and John Macpherson.

Demolition of the village hall had commenced by Friday 27 December, the date of the annual Gaelic Class Social: "The usual custom of having this treat in the Public Hall could not be carried out owing to the fact that it is at present undergoing demolition."

The Rev. D Macfarlane kindly allowed the event to go ahead in St Columba's Church. A long and detailed account of the occasion appeared in the THE BADENOCH RECORD of 4 Jan 1913. It named the performers, their party pieces and also the many prize winners. There were so many Cattanachs with similar Christian names that they were identified by name and their place of abode: Craiglea (3); Fir Grove (3); Pine Cottage (2) and Glenmore (1). The prizes were presented by a former pupil of the class and a great champion of his native language, Mr (James) Ian Macpherson, MP.

By the beginning of April 1913, with the construction of the new hall progressing well, the Village Committee authorised interim payments to some of the contractors. Although matters concerning the new hall required a lot of attention from the committee, other routine business such as road repairs, street lighting and cleanliness still had to be addressed. An unusual request approved by the committee was for the proposed erection of a slaughter-house for Messrs J and G Young who had moved from Perth to a butcher's shop rented to them by Angus Macpherson, adjacent to his own business, The Newtonmore Grocery and Provision Warehouse, at his *Cor an easan* building.

In May 1913, the said Angus was elected chairman of the Village Committee and it fell to him to lead them forward towards the conclusion of the hall project. When writing his memoirs which were published around 1954 he commented that the hall is "one of the best or perhaps the best asset that the village has got." Hall business took precedence at the July meeting of the Village Committee when the appointment of William Macdonald as hall-keeper was announced and plans for the first event in the new hall, a concert on 25 July, were finalised. Repairs to the public tennis court were noted and the hope that it would be well-patronised by visitors was expressed.

Visitors and locals flocked to the concert which was chaired by TSM who was home on furlough from the Indian Civil Service. The building still needed some finishing touches but the "attractive" main hall was able to accommodate the event. Performers included some of the regulars, some visitors and some new faces including a song from young Flora Macpherson, whose father *Jockan*, as usual, opened the occasion with a selection on the

NEWTONMORE NEW HALL

THE FIRST

CONCERT

in the NEW BUILDING will be held on

FRIDAY, 25th JULY.

Proceeds in aid of the Hall Building Fund. The Committee appeal to visitors for liberal support.

CHAIRMAN—T. S. MACPHERSON, ESQ.

A Varied and Interesting Programme will be submitted.

Doors open at 7-30.   Commence at 8 p.m.

TICKETS (2/- and 1/-) may be had at the various Shops in the Village.

pipes. The "handsome total of £20.5s." raised, gave a badly needed boost to the hall building fund. All those involved must have been looking forward to an afternoon and evening of celebrations to mark the official opening on 8 August.

Before that, many would journey to Perth on 29 July 1913 to attend a Badenoch wedding: that of the Rev. John Sellar and Miss Isabella Macdonald who had been school-mates and soul-mates at Kingussie Secondary. While many of the shinty team enjoyed the wedding, visitors used the Eilan for cricket and up to 20 locals were participating in turnip hoeing competitions.

Returning to the main event of the year in

Newtonmore: the opening of the new hall, was described by the local paper in great detail. It was designed to accommodate 500 people with the dimensions of the main hall being 46 feet x 38 feet. "Off the vestibule there are ladies' and gentlemen's cloakrooms, with a couple of entrances to the main hall, which is also provided with side entrances. The recessed platform measures 22 x 12 feet. Behind the platform are a reading room and library, with lavatory conveniences. Above are the care-taker's quarters consisting of several rooms". The total cost was about £1600 of which £554 was raised at the previous year's bazaar. Two concerts since and a few generous donations had reduced the balance due to about half the total cost. "The indebtedness of the Committee, however, is still considerable, but hopes are entertained that the deficiency will ere long be wiped off ... The formal opening of the hall door [at 3 o'clock] by Mrs Macpherson of Balavil was unfortunately slightly marred by a shower of rain. Mrs Macpherson was intro-duced by Mr Angus Macpherson chairman of the Village Committee, who also called on Mr Cattanach, the architect, to present Mrs Macpherson with a silver key." Amid cheering, Mrs Macpherson formally opened the building and "led by Mr John Macpherson playing the bagpipes, the company entered the hall, where the chair was taken by Mr Macpherson of Balavil. Accompanying the

chairman on the platform, which was tastefully decorated with palms, heather etc., as was the hall, were the following ladies and gentlemen:- Mrs Macpherson of Balavil; Mr and Mrs Schofield; Rev. D. and Mrs Macfarlane; Mr T. S. Macpherson [TSM]; Mr Crole, K.C.; and Mr Mc'Clure. A prayer of dedication was offered by the Rev. D. Macfarlane".

"The chairman [b. 1855] then delivered a short address." His first memories of Newtonmore were of "the little black new village of the moor ... Who then thought of golf courses – of drainage and water schemes – of public halls?" Newtonmore had "grown apace ... and flourished exceedingly. The trades of the builder, carpenter, plumber, labourer, and landlord have all alike bathed in the silver tide of prosperity." He praised "this fine building which we are met to open, and which we all hope may long stand as a sign-post on the road of advancement of this beautiful village."

There followed a series of speeches on different aspects of the project by most of the men on the platform and Mr Tytler. The final speech was made by TSM in Gaelic. He thanked Balavil for all his support for the current project and mentioned that for the original hall, "He had supplied a site at nominal feu duty, had headed the subscription list and 24 yrs ago had opened the old hall." He asked for applause for the Balavil family and "all who had been of assistance in building the new hall."

After tea, served by the ladies, the audience were treated to a short, highly-praised, musical programme. Two old faithfuls, *Jockan* on pipes and Miss MacArthur on piano, were joined by others including young Maggie Barnett who gave a recitation. The opening event finished with many receiving votes of thanks.

Those who master-minded the wonderful project of the hall, those who supported it and those who thronged to the opening events must have anticipated having full and regular use of the hall for many years. Sadly, within a year, Britain came to the aid of its allies and was sucked into WW1. Many who attended the opening of Newtonmore Hall would be badly affected by that war. Some of them have been mentioned in earlier chapters and short biographies of those who died have been listed in local books. Village families showed great loyalty to the cause and by Nov 1914, there were 52 Newtonmore names on a scroll "attached to the porch of St Columba's Church". Cattanachs and Macphersons predominated. Remarkably, five members of the Davidson family; four sons of *Am Bèicear Bàn*; three of Hannah's younger sons and two sons from a number of families came forward to serve their country. All three of William Cattanach's sons stood to the Colours. His youngest son, Dr Johnnie, was killed in 1915 and when William died in 1918, his remaining sons were serving in Europe and Egypt. The moneyed people who came to the village in the summer for long holidays or shooting would have served mainly in the officer classes in WW1. Officers in the trenches in that war had a life expectancy of three weeks and would have been decimated. King's Counsel, Gerald Crole's son was in the flying corps, another group with a short life expectancy. Captain Crole was awarded the Military Cross but later reported missing. He did survive, but in a German prisoner of war camp. The war caused the number of visitors coming to Newtonmore to decline sharply. With fewer people to support the fund-raising efforts, it took until 1920 before the substantial debt incurred by the building of the hall was repaid. Miss MacArthur gave sterling service to the Village Committee during the war. When her year in office as chairman finished, the local paper reported on her energy and commitment and suggested that Newtonmore should be congratulated on having "the first 'lady Provost' in the Highlands." Mr Tytler also continued his loyal service to the community despite losing two of his officer sons in the war.

In August 1913, "the indefatigable joint secretaries" must have been delighted with the evening events which followed the official opening of the hall. "Mrs Garrett Anderson M.D., a lady to whom the Hall Committee owe a great deal of gratitude for the kind and keen interest she has taken in everything relating to the welfare of Newtonmore, occupied the chair. It must have stirred every heart to enthusiasm to see the kindly old lady [aged 77] led onto the platform to the martial strains of Mr Macpherson's bagpipes." The audience were entertained by locals and visitors to a mixed selection of items including a highly-skilled exhibition of the Sword Dance. "After the concert the hall was cleared for the assembly which was to follow." People took great care with their appearance for such events. The men dressed very smartly. The women had sophisticated hair styles and elaborate long dresses enhanced by eye-catching jewellery. Young and old, locals and visitors enjoyed the dancing which in those days lasted until four or five in the morning. Were Cecilia Kidston and Rosslyn Colam one of the couples who tripped the light fantastic that evening? The extended Kidston family, which included the McClures, had holidayed in Newtonmore since 1896, while the Colam family retreated to their second home of Ard-na-coille in the summers. The young couple got engaged the following month and married

in Sept 1914 at Helensburgh, home town of the Kidstons. Capt. R Colam survived the war, but Cecilia's brother, Capt. W H Campbell Kidston succumbed to wounds he received at Ypres.

Over £49 was added to the hall fund from money raised on the day of the opening events and over £44 was raised at a concert and dance in mid-September.

The summer of 1913 must have been an up-lifting time for Newtonmore villagers whose families had struggled for so long to build a thriving community. The spirits of the people must have been soaring. The once "little black new village of the moor", had, by hard work and great foresight become a thriving village that the population could be justly proud of. They had a very good shinty team, their tourist trade was booming, and now they also had a wonderful village hall. They must have hoped that their achievement in their construction of the hall would be the foundation on which their community would continue to flourish for the rest of the, as yet, young century.

Additional note:

Newspaper cuttings from THE BADENOCH RECORD by kind permission of the STRATHSPEY & BADENOCH HERALD.

Images of the silver key kindly supplied by Allan Macpherson-Fletcher – the inscriptions on the key read – "Presented to Mrs Macpherson of Balavil 8-8-13. On the occasion of her opening the new hall buildings Newtonmore".

`An Artist's impression of Newtonmore Hall in 1913.`

Appendix 1

The Cattanach families mentioned in the book reused Christian names. To save confusion, four Cattanach families are listed below.

Please note:
- they are sorted into families by surname
- each generation is indented and rough dates, c. 1800-1870, given
- for those born pre-1855 birth date might be calculated on age at census
- only those members of a family mentioned in the book will be named

STRONE Cattanachs who migrated to Raitts and returned to Strone

1. Thomas CATTANACH [1788-1853] = Ann Stuart [1790-1853]
    2. two sons who emigrated to Australasia
    2. Ann CATTANACH [1820-1879] = Ewan MACPHERSON [1803-1889]
        3. Evan MACPHERSON [1862-1932]
            4. Ian MACPHERSON [1905-1944], the *Othaichear*
    2. Isabella CATTANACH [1823-1900] = John MACPHERSON [1817-1880], bard
        3. at least 10 children including
        3. James MACPHERSON (*Seumas Mòr*) = Ann Stewart [1843-1924]
            4. Thomas Stewart MACPHERSON (TSM) [1876-1949]
            4. Katherine MACPHERSON (Katie) [1878-1958]
            4. James John MACPHERSON (Ian) [1880-1937]
            4. John Donald MACPHERSON (JD) [1883-1960]
        3. William Cattanach MACPHERSON [1855-1930] = Jane Cattanach
    2. Janet CATTANACH [1826-1894] = Paul GRANT [1826-1883]
        children included - Janet, Paul, Tom, Maggie, William and Benjamin Grant.

STRONE Cattanachs. (John, the tailor, lived at Croft of Clune)

i. Alexander CATTANACH [d.c.1850] = Anne McIntosh, Milton. They lived in Strone
    ii. John CATTANACH, tailor [1805-1890] = Janet Macpherson [1824-1893]
        iii. Isabella CATTANACH [1848-1918] = Robert MacBean
        iii. Alexander CATTANACH [*Alaidh an Tàilleir*] [1851-1919]
            four children including Annie and Jessie
        iii. Jane CATTANACH [1855-1919] = William Cattanach MACPHERSON

    iii. Donald CATTANACH [1860-Canada]
    iii. Christina CATTANACH [1863-1931] = Donald MacMaster Cattanach
    iii. Juliet CATTANACH [1866-Canada]
    iii. Jemima CATTANACH [1868-1949] = John Cattanach [1865-1936]
  ii. Isabella CATTANACH [1809-1872] = William KENNEDY [d. bef 1851]
    iii. Barbara KENNEDY [1837-1921] = John STEWART [1836-1915]
      iv. Isabella STEWART [1864-1938]
      iv. Peter Kennedy STEWART [1876-1934] HMI
    iii. Peter KENNEDY [1841-1867]
  ii. Donald CATTANACH [1810-1869] (leaseholder SS) = Jane Cattanach, Craggan
    iii. Ewen CATTANACH (*Eòghann Clachair*) [1855-1905] b. Strone
    iii. Alexander CATTANACH [1856-1928] b. Strone, architect
    iii. Andrew [*Clachair*] CATTANACH [1860-1942] b. Strone
  ii. Alexander CATTANACH [1815-1886], one of "The Men", lived Strone and Laggan

CROFTBEG Cattanachs.

a. Donald CATTANACH [d. 1858] = Ann Mackay [d. 1865]
  b. John CATTANACH (*an t-Oighre*) [1820-1900] = Ann Martin [1822-1915]
    c. at least 9 children including
    c. Mary CATTANACH [1855-1940] = Alexander MACLENNAN
      d. Isabella MACLENNAN [1878-1962] = George SELLAR
        e. at least 6 children including
        e. Barbara Ann SELLAR [1898-1972] = Donald Campbell
        e. Marjory Jane SELLAR [1901-1974] = Donald Ralph
        e. Catherine Mary SELLAR [1906-1981] = Stewart Aitken
    c. Jane CATTANACH [1856-1944] = Gregor Fyfe
    c. John CATTANACH [1865-1936] = Jemima Cattanach (Craggan)
    c. Duncan CATTANACH [1870-1895] - Ch 9, Feb 1890, Belleville shinty
  b. Duncan CATTANACH [1825-1895] = Margaret Cameron
    c Duncan CATTANACH [1878-1949]

MILTON Cattanachs.

A. John CATTANACH [d. 1856],
  B. William CATTANACH [1801-1876], ½ brother of Ann, Donald and Malcolm
    C. Donald CATTANACH [1838-1906]
    C. William CATTANACH [1840-1918]

      D. William CATTANACH (Teela) [1879-1933]

      D. Isabella CATTANACH [1881-1967]

      D. Donald CATTANACH (Donlan) [1883-1958]

      D. Johnnie CATTANACH (Dr Johnnie) [1855-1915]

B. Ann CATTANACH [Mrs Duncan Grant] [1811-1892]

B. Donald CATTANACH (Catechist) [1813-1891] = Catherine MacMaster [1820-63]

    C. Isabella CATTANACH [1843-1895] = Alexander KINNAIRD [1842-1870]

    C. Mary CATTANACH (Mrs John MACDONALD) [1845-1893]

      D. John MACDONALD (*Seonaidh a' Mhaighstir*) Johnnie the master

      D. Katie MACDONALD

      D. Jamie MACDONALD

    C. Annie CATTANACH [1847-1930]

    C. Catherine CATTANACH [1850-1930] = John GORDON [1852-1921]

    C. John CATTANACH [1853-1919], grandfather of 'Nelson' Cattanach

    C. Donald MacMaster CATTANACH [1855-1930] = Christina Cattanach [1863-1931]

    C. Ewan CATTANACH [1857-1887] = Janet Grant [1857-1938]

      Katie, teacher, and Jessie

B. Malcolm CATTANACH [1822-1899] = Jane McLachlan [1825-1907]

    C. Ann CATTANACH [1847-1924] = Daniel MACDONALD [1838-1907]

      D. at least 11 children including

      D. Alexander MACDONALD [1870-Canada]

      D. Malcolm MACDONALD [1873-1955]

      D. William MACDONALD [1874-1945]

      D. Jane MACDONALD [1877-1907] = Thomas ROSS > Dickie & John.

    C. John CATTANACH, Am Bèicear Bàn, [1850-1932]

      D. 5 sons and 2 daughters including

      D. Alex CATTANACH, grandfather of Michael Slaney

      D. Tom CATTANACH [Tee-tee] [1894-1976]

    C. Jane CATTANACH (Auntie Sinclair) [1851-1930]

    C. Betsy CATTANACH [1853-1929]

      D. Alexander FALCONER [1871-1952]

    C. Malcolm CATTANACH [1862-1914] tailor

    C. Ewen CATTANACH [1864-1890] [=Marjory (Duffes), 1861-1955)]

      D. Malcolm CATTANACH [1886-1981, Canada]

    C. Thomas CATTANACH [1868-1945]

      D. Peggy CATTANACH (Mrs O'Reilly) [1922-2014]

Appendix 2

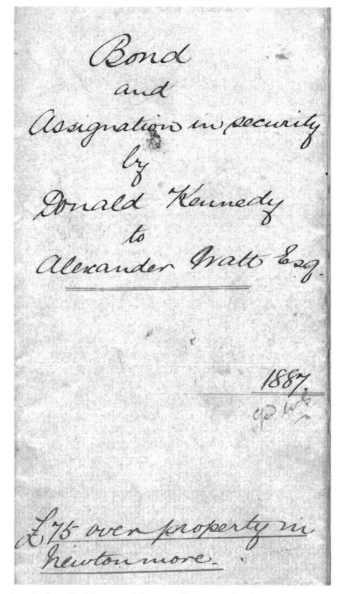

Fig 41 – Donald Kennedy, when he bought his row of four small properties, borrowed £75 of the purchase price of £130 from Alexander Watt a solicitor in Banff. The Bond of 1887 is shown here. (See p.104 and also p.159).   *(N Mccreath.)*

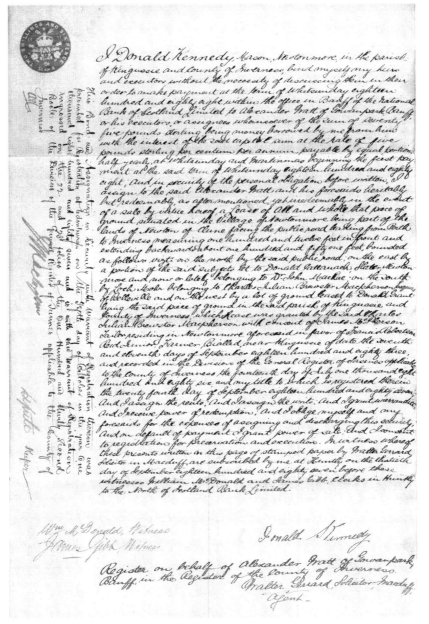

Fig 42 – Bond Details   *(N Mccreath.)*

Bibliography

Primary Sources

DOCUMENTS were consulted at:

Clan Macpherson Museum, Newtonmore [CMM]

Edinburgh University Archive. CW-50A
    Alexander MacBain, *Journal, V. 1.*

Highland Archive Centre, Inverness [GB0232]
including:
    GB0232, D1101/7/31 – Archive collected by
    Jack Richmond.

Highland Folk Museum, Newtonmore [HFM]

National Library of Scotland, Edinburgh [NLS]

National Records of Scotland, Edinburgh [NRS].
Those included:
    CENSUS ENUMERATION BOOKS for Scotland
    from 1841.
    OLD PARISH REGISTERS (OPR) for Kingussie and
    adjacent parishes, up to 1855.
    STATUTORY REGISTERS for Scotland from 1855.
    VALUATION ROLLS for Newtonmore from 1855.

Private papers

Belleville Estate papers from 1862 and 1872.

Macpherson of Biallid papers: TSM Archive

The Invereshie Book – transcription is available on
Macpherson Museum website.

MAPS AND PLANS

National Library of Scotland (NLS)

National Records of Scotland (NRS)

*Inverness Reference Library. J Mitchell, Plans &
Sections of the Inverness & Perth Junction Railway.
1860.*

Personal reminiscences

Badenoch Oral History Project, 1984, Highland Folk
Museum, Newtonmore. [BOHP]

Bel Cameron, Newtonmore

John Cameron, BR, Feb-Mar 1948

Dondo Kennedy, Newtonmore

[John Macdonald], BR, Jun 1942, Dec, 1943, Nov-Dec
1946, Mar 1947

Sandy Macdonald, Newtonmore

Malcolm Macdonald, PJ, May-Jun 1934

George Macpherson, *Memories of my Youth, By
Geordie,* New Zealand, 1982.

Jimmy Sellar, Newtonmore

The Cronies – BR, Apr 1958 – Jun 1961

Donnie Wilson, Laggan

Printed Primary Sources

Royal Commission (Highlands and Islands) 1892,
Edinburgh, HMSO, 1895. Also known as the Deer
Commission.

Evidence taken by Her Majesty's Commissioners of
Inquiry into the conditions of The Crofters and Cottars
in the Highlands and Islands of Scotland, Vol IV. Also
known as the Napier Commission: the chairman was
Lord Napier. The books of evidence, published in
1884, were digitized by Lochaber College and are
available on-line.

Sinclair, Sir John, *The New Statistical Account of
Scotland*, vol. XIV Kingussie, County of Inverness,
Feb 1835.

NEWSPAPERS AND PERIODICALS
ABERDEEN DAILY FREE PRESS
ABERDEEN JOURNAL (AJ)
ABERDEEN PEOPLE'S JOURNAL
THE BADENOCH RECORD (BR)
THE CELTIC MAGAZINE
CREAG DHUBH (CD)
DUNDEE ADVERTISER (DA)
DUNDEE COURIER (DC)
CALEDONIAN MERCURY (CM)
THE EDINBURGH GAZETTE
ELGIN COURANT (EC)
EVENING TELEGRAPH, ANGUS ((ETA)
GLASGOW HERALD (GH)
INVERNESS ADVERTISER (IA)
INVERNESS COURIER (IC)
INVERNESS JOURNAL (IJ)
KINGUSSIE PARISH MAGAZINE
THE KINGUSSIE RECORD (KR)
NORTHERN CHRONICLE (NC)
PEOPLE'S JOURNAL (PJ)
PERTHSHIRE ADVERTISER
PRESS AND JOURNAL (P&J)
THE SCOTSMAN (SC)
SCOTTISH HIGHLANDER (SH)
SHINTY YEAR BOOK (SYB)
SHINTY YEAR BOOK, 1988

Secondary Sources

Anderson, George and Peter, *Guide to the Highlands and Islands of Scotland* (London, 1834). (1st ed)

Anderson, George and Peter, *Guide to the Highlands and Islands of Scotland*, Edinburgh, Adam and Charles Black, 1850. (3rd ed)

Andsell, Douglas, *The People of the Great Faith*, Acair, Stornoway. 1998

Brown, Roy, *A Highland Village at War, NEWTONMORE*, Blurb Publishing, 2014.

Brown, Thomas, *Annals of the Disruption*, Edinburgh, 1893

Collie, William, *Memoirs of a 19th Century Deerstalker*, Bidean Books, 1992.

Duff, David, [ed.], *Queen Victoria's Highland Journals*, 1994, Lomond Books, London.

Cowper, A. S, (ed.), *SSPCK Schoolmasters 1709 – 1872*, Scottish Record Society, 1997.

Forsyth, Rev. W. MA, DD, *In the Shadow of Cairngorm*, 1900, Inverness.

Gibson, Rob, *Highland Cowboys*, Luath Press Limited, Edinburgh, 2010

Gibson, R. M. with Ritchie, R, *The Boys of the Eilan*, Newtonmore Camanachd Club, 2015.

Gibson, R. M., *The caman is their pastime,* Newtonmore Camanachd Club, 2013.

Glen, Anne, *The Cairngorm Gateway*, Dalkeith, 2002.

Gordon, M. M., The Home Life of Sir David Brewster, Edmonston and Douglas, 1869

Grant, I.F., *Highland Folk Ways*, Birlinn Limited, Edinburgh, 1995.

Grant, I.F., *The Economic History of Scotland*, Longmans, London, 1934.

Grierson, James Moncrief, Sir, *Records of the Scottish Volunteer Force, 1859-1908*, 1909, Blackwood, Edinburgh.

Gray, Affleck, *Legends of the Cairngorms*, Mainstream Publishing, Edinburgh, 1987.

Haldane, A.R.B., *The Drove Roads of Scotland,* Birlinn Limited, Edinburgh, 2008.

Hay, Geo. T, *Perth and North Thereof*, The Badenoch Printing Works, Kingussie. 1966.

Hunter, James, *The Making of the Crofting Community,* John Donald, Edinburgh, 1997.

Kerr, Derek, *Railway Sleeper Buildings*, SVBWG, Dundee 1986

Lynch, Michael [ed.], *The Oxford Companion to Scottish History*, University Press, Oxford, 2001.

[Margaret Bennett, p. 61: Temperance, p. 595]

MacGregor, Patrick, *Journal of 1833* – noted by TSM; published by Badenoch Record, Sept 1949

Fraser-Mackintosh, C. (1897) *Antiquarian Notes, Genealogical and Social, second series.* Inverness: A. & W. Mackenzie

Maclean, John, *Historical and Traditional Sketches of Highland Families and of the Highlands,* Dingwall, 1848

Maclennan, Hugh Dan, *Not an Orchid . . .,* Inbhir Nis, Kessock Communications, 1995

Macpherson, Ian, in *Scottish Country*, George Scott-Moncrieff, ed., London: Wishart Books. 1935.

Macpherson of Dalchully, *Chiefs of Clan Macpherson*, Oliver and Boyd Ltd., Edinburgh, 1947

Marshall, Peter, *The Scottish Central Railway*, Oakwood Press, 1998.

Murdoch, J., *A guide to the Highlands of Speyside*, 1852, Forres.

Newton, Michael, [ed], John, *Dùthchas nan Gàidheal, Collected Essays of John MacInnes*, Birlinn Limited, Edinburgh, 2006.

Pennant, Thomas, *A Tour in Scotland and Voyage to the Hebrides, 1772,* White, 1776.

Ross, Anne, *Folklore of the Scottish Highlands*, The History Press, Stroud, 2011.

Ross, David, *The Highland Railway*, Stenlake, Catrine, 2010.

Shaw, Lachlan, *The History of the Province of Moray*, Glasgow, 1882.

Scarlett, Meta Humphrey, *In the Glens Where I Was Young*, Siskin, 1988.

Sinclair, Neil T, *The Highland Main Line*, Stenlake, Catrine, Scotland, 2013

Sinclair, Neil T, *Highland Railway: people and places*, Breedon Books, Derby, 2005

Sinton, Thomas, *By Loch and River*, Inverness, 1910

Sinton, Thomas, *The Poetry of Badenoch*, Inverness, 1906

Somers, Robert, *Letters from the Highlands*, (1848, reprint 1985), The Melven Press.

Taylor, David, *The Wild Black Region*, John Donald, Edinburgh, 2016.

Watson, Alfred E T, *King Edward VII. as a sportsman*, London, 1911.

Withrington, Donald J., *Going to School*, National Museums of Scotland, 1997.

Youngson, A. J. *After the Forty-Five,* University Press, Edinburgh, 1973.

Historical Records of the **Queen's Own Cameron Highlanders**, Vol 11, complied by a committee. Blackwood, Edinburgh, 1909.

Index of persons

Mc and Mac are interchangeable: as are McIntosh and Mackintosh - they have been listed together.

Many names are similar: sometimes help with identification is inserted in brackets. '=' shows the name of a marriage partner: 's/o' means son of.

A

Adams, David 146
Allan, R 181
Aitken family Fig 16,130, 222
Anderson, Duncan 159
Anderson, Elizabeth (née Macpherson) 46-7
Anderson, Elizabeth Garrett 199, 213-5, 218
Anderson, George (21)53
Anderson, John (= Mary Forbes) 95-6, 143-5, 188-90
Anderson, Peter (21)53

B

Baillie, James Evan 32, 45, 52
Baillie, James Evan Bruce of Dochfour 151
Bain, Rev. Alexander 174, 213
Bain, Mary 4
Bain, Jane (wife and daughter of Donald Bain) 97
Barclay, Mr 106-7
Barnett, Maggie 218
Barnett, William 181
Bentick, Rev. Charles 111, 164
Bentick, John (= Flora Wilson) 76, 103
Beveridge, Alexander 201
Blair, Duncan Black 195
Blair, Johnnie 39, 143, 195-6
Blair, Mary (= Donald Macpherson) 196
Borland, William and Margaret 185, 209
Brewster, Sir David (= Juliet Macpherson) 29
Brewster, James 41

Brewster, Margaret 29
Brigden, Christine 14
Buie, John 55, 105
Budge, William 187
Burns, Robert 49, 149

C

Caldwell, William 27, 28, 50, 55, 68-9
Cameron, Angus (= Mary Davidson), mason and PO 55, 87-8, 112
Cameron, Angus 65-6
Cameron, Bel 131, 178
Cameron, Donald (E-end) 22, 47-8, 111
Cameron, Rev. Donald 42
Cameron, Donald (= Isabella Mackenzie) 56, 100, 109
Cameron, Donald, Laggan 170, 172
Cameron, Donald, boot maker 98, 148, 181, 209
Cameron, Donald of Lochiel 113, 174
Cameron, Duncan and Jessie McEdward 69, 105
Cameron, Ewen/Evan, Kinlochlaggan 48, 85, 90, 111-2
Cameron, Ewen, PO 88
Cameron, John 4, 97-8, 103
Cameron, John, jnr 4, 98, 102, 126, 137
Cameron, John (= Isabella Rose) 132, 134, 136
Cameron, Maggie Fig 5, 131
Campbell, Christine 21, 27
Campbell, Donald 4, 194, 198
Campbell, Donald (Dòmh'll Phàil) 32
Campbell, Donald, son of Dòmh'll Phàil 119, 141, 150
Campbell, Donald (= Barbara Ann Sellar), and family Fig 16, 130
Campbell, Donald, carter 160
Campbell family, Croftdhuac 155
Campbell, Janet (Seònaid Phàil) 65
Campbell, Lt John 170, 172

Carnegie, Andrew and Mrs 107, 153, 164, 199
Cattanach, Annie 103, 112, 177
Cattanach, Ann (née Martin) 194
Catanach, Calum 26, 28, 36
Catanach, Donull (= Catrìona) 3, 24, 26, 40, 85
Cattanach, Alexander, architect 28, 126, 146, 158, 177, 191, 210-1, 213-4, 217
Cattanach, Alexander (*Alaidh an Tàilleir*) 49, 105, 111, 125, 150, 194
Cattanach, daughters of *Alaidh an Tàilleir* 180
Cattanach, Alexander (= Anne McIntosh) 125
Cattanach, Alexander, Auchmore 143
Cattanach, Andrew (*Clachair*) 126, 155, 210
Cattanach, Donald, slater and catechist 26, 29, 36, 42-3, 55, 80, 103-4, 142-3 Fig 21, 177
Cattanach, Donald, mason, Strone 28, 55, 104-5, 126, 210
Cattanach, Donald, Croft of Clune 49
Cattanach, Donald, merchant 55, 68-9, 96, 105, 113, 149-50, 152, 181
Cattanach, Donald (Donlan) Fig 15, 124, 180, 218
Cattanach, Donald (= Ann McKay), Croftbeg 124-5, Fig 16, 130
Cattanach, Donald MacMaster (= Christina Cattanach) 177, 201-2
Cattanach, Duncan, Croft Beg 125, 141, 178
Cattanach, Duncan 187
Cattanach, Ewen (= Janet Grant) 74
Cattanach, Ewen (*Eòghann Clachair*) 126, 158, 210
Cattanach, Ewen Macpherson (= Marjory, later Mrs Duffes) 104, Fig 19, 194
Cattanach, Isabella (Mrs Kennedy) 80, 88, 109
Cattanach, Jane, Croftbeg 102, 130
Cattanach, John, tailor 28, 55, 112, 125, 151
Cattanach, John (*Am Bèicear Bàn*) 50, 105, 108, 173, 185-6, Fig 33, 194, 218
Cattanach, sons of *Am Bèicear Bàn* 186, 194, 218
Cattanach, John, slater 83, 106, 110, 177
Cattanach, John (Nelson) 104, 124, 128, 177

Cattanach, Dr Johnnie Fig 15, 124, 128, 180, 205, 218
Cattanach, John, Croftbeg and sons 125, 141, 164, 194
Cattanach, Capt John 125
Cattanach, Jane (Auntie Sinclair) 139, 195
Cattanach, Jessie 74, 177
Cattanach, Juliet 49
Cattanach, Katie 74, 177, Fig 39
Cattanach, Malcolm 24, 26-7, 36, 50, 55, 103, 108, 113, 116, 118-9, 138-9, 141, 146, 150, Fig 23, 160, 162, 165, 181-2, 185
Cattanach, Malcolm, jnr 105, 108, 116-7, 124, 186
Cattanach, Marjorie (*Marsag*) 38, 126
Cattanach, Mary 4, 39, 82
Cattanach, Peter L 86
Cattanach, Thomas 162, 181, 202, 206, 209
Cattanach, William, slater 26-7, 36, 47, 49, 55
Cattanach, William (= Ann Kennedy) 96, Fig 15, 146, 181, Fig 31, 190, 193, Fig 38, 204, Fig 39, 209, 218
Cattanach, William (Teela) Fig 15, 124, Fig 31, 218
Cattanach, Baillie William 77, 85-6
Chisholm, Donald 109
Chisholm, Sarah 199
Cockburn, William 108, 133, 181
Colam, William N 202, 213-4, 219
Collie, William 132, 138
Crole family 213, 217-8

D
Davidson, Alexander 28, 55, 108
Davidson, James 28
Davidson family 218
Dewar, Rev. Neil 80, 141, 143, 154, 174, 195
Druim an Staink 178
Dobie, Rev. Prof John 146
Duffes, Marjory (= Ewen Cattanach, later William Duffes) 104
Duffes, William 182, 194, 215
Dunbar, William 215
Duncan, Alexander 63

Duncan, Jane (née Macdonald) 114-5
Duncan, John 82

E
Eason, John 26

F
Falconer, Alexander 124, 139, 177, 204, 215
Farquharson, James 86
Ferguson, Donald 199
Forbes, Duncan 28, 94, 114, 151, 163
Forbes, Isabella 56
Forbes, James 21, 26-8, 47-8, 94, 130
Forbes, James 94, 95, 106, 187-8
Forbes, John (= Winwood) 94
Forbes, John (s/o Duncan) 117, 161
Forbes, Robert 21, 36, 94
Forbes, Robert 75, 111, 116, 161, 188, 209
Forbes family 95, 117
Fraser-Mackintosh, Charles 4, 118-9
Fraser, Adam 215
Fraser family 129, 130
Fraser, Duncan 142, 143
Fullerton, Catherine and Joseph 112
Fyfe, Affleck 60
Fyfe, Gregor 102-3, 174, Fig 29, 177

G
Geddes, Miss 213
Gibson, Thomas (= Isabel Macpherson) 57
Gibson, Thomas, jnr 84
Grant, Benjamin 74, 190
Grant, Duncan (= Ann Cattanach) 29, 55, 104
Grant, Edmond 96
Grant, Lachlan 164
Grant, Maggie 74, 117, 191, 202
Grant, Paul (=Janet Cattanach) 55, 68, 73-4, 96, 190
Grant, Paul, jnr 74, 107, 117, 152

Grant, Tom 74, 107, 117, 148, 165, 181, 183, 190-1, 201, 203, Fig 38, 204, 206, 209
Grant, William 74, 143, 155
Grant family 117
Gordon, Alexander 27
Gordon, Alexander 16
Gordon, Duchess of 10, 32
Gordon, Duke of 15, 17, 19, 26, 124, 155, 195
Gordon, Duncan 55, 68
Gordon, Rev. Evan 17, 22
Gordon, John 16-7, 24
Gordon, John 104, 177
Gordon, Robbie 127
Gordon, William 16-7, 24
Gray, John 28, 110, 143
Guild, Jimmy 39, 128
Guthrie, Donald 209
Guthrie, Jimmy 38-9
Guthrie, John (= Margaret Young) 113
Gwyer, C F 113-4

H
Halliday, Catherine 55, 108-9
Halliday, Francis 27-8
Harrower George 161
Hay, George Tod 206
Herd lads and lassies 178

I
Innes, Mrs 194
Iverach, Prof James 152

J
Jeans, Isabella 84

K
Kennedy, Alexander (*Ruadh*) 49, 126, 158, 179
Kennedy, Andrew 196

Kennedy, Angus (*Ruadh*) 47, 49, 158
Kennedy, Ann (née McIntosh) 161, 162
Kennedy, Charles (*Ruadh*) 49, 158, 160, 199
Kennedy, Charley (*Ruadh*) 123, 140-1
Kennedy, Christina (*Ruadh*) 49
Kennedy, Christina (née Macpherson) 55, 108
Kennedy, *Ceit Dail a' Chaorainn* 105, 196
Kennedy, Donald 22, 27, 133
Kennedy, Donald, *Dòmhnall Ruadh* 75, 105, 111, 127, 139, 160-2
Kennedy, Donald, mason 104, 110, 224, 225
Kennedy, Donald, Drumochter 128
Kennedy, Dondo 14
Kennedy, Duncan 123
Kennedy, Ewen 110
Kennedy, James 83
Kennedy, *Seumas Dail a' Chaorainn* 105, 196
Kennedy, John 22
Kennedy, John, carrier 28
Kennedy, John, Moor of Strone 105, 123
Kennedy family, Moor of Strone (Duncan, Johnnie, Katie, May) 123, 178, 195
Kennedy, John (Honnie) 128
Kennedy, Robert (*Ruadh*) 123, 179
Kennedy, Robbie 200-1
Kennedy, Peter 80
Kennedy, Peter T 117, 146-8, Fig 22
Kennedy, William, *Uilleam Dail a' Chaorainn* 85-6, 105, 196
Kidd, J M 191
Kidston family 206, 213, 219
King Edward VII 187, 206-8
Kinnaird, Isabella (née Cattanach) 103-4

L
Leslie, John 187
Leslie, William (= Marjory Cameron), 83, 195
Logan, James 39, 40, 200, 215
Logan, Lachlan 117
Logan, Kenneth 114, 164

M
MacArthur, Maria 116, 163, 199, 211, 213, 218
MacBarnett, Donald 31
MacBarnett, Misses 27, 50, 68, 90, 103, 109
McBain, William 32
Macbean, Donald and Isobel 22, 27
MacBey, Peter 72, 94
M'Clure family 213, 217, 219
McCook, George 50, 56
McCook, Hannah 50, 56
McCook, Joseph 50
Macdonald, Alexander (*Alaidh laochan*) 104, 126, 137-8, 160, 161
Macdonald, Alexander (Dan) 186-7
Macdonald, Angus (s/o Unie) 82, 136, 137
Macdonald, Angus 123
Macdonald, Angus, railway 129, 158, 159
Macdonald, Annie (= John Macdonald) 71, 95
Macdonald, Ann (= John Morton) 135
Macdonald, Catherine (née Rose) 102, 112, 134-5
Macdonald, Daniel (= Anne Cattanach) 102-3
Macdonald, Donald, mason 102, 112, 123, 134-5, 136, 177, 192
Macdonald, Donald, Craggan 109, 159
Macdonald, D, postman 39
Macdonald, Donald, Easterton 123, 134
Macdonald, Duncan (s/o, *Alaidh laochan*) 107, 126, 180
Macdonald, Duncan (= Catherine Rose) 123, 134, 136
Macdonald, Duncan, Lakefield 155
Macdonald, Elsie 105
Macdonald, Grace (*Gracag* = Alister MacKintosh) 100, 129, 159
Macdonald, Isabella (née Clark) 21, 27, 72, 95
Macdonald, Isabella, Ralia 195
Macdonald, James 4, 173, 198

Macdonald, Jamie 128, 177, 186-7, 202

Macdonald, Jim Fig 39

Macdonald, John 179, 198

Macdonald, John (= Mary Cattanach) 4, 80, 82, 84, 161, 179

Macdonald, John (Johnny the Master) 4, 39, 75, 106, 143, 161, 177, 186-7

Macdonald, John (= Isabella Stewart) 26, 123, 134, 136, 162, 195

Macdonald, John (*Bàilidh* = Margaret Davidson) 28, 90, 109, 114-5, 123, 139, 162, 164

Macdonald, John, mason 102, 112, 123, 134-5, 137, 177, 181, 192, 209

Macdonald, John (= May Kennedy) 123, 158, 195

Macdonalds, Strone, (Donally, Johnian, Maggie, Duncan, Alister, Robbie, Angie, Betty) 123

Macdonald, Malcolm (Ackie Dan) 103, 105, 121, 128, 178, 186, 195

Macdonald, Margaret (*Mairead a' Bhàillidh*) 115, 123

Macdonald, Samuel 97, 103, 109, 124, 127, 139, 140, 141, 143, 145-6, 148, 178, Fig 31, 189, 192-3
  'the Sams' 124, 128 (Sam), 180, Fig 31, 188 (Sam) 193, 200

Macdonald, Unie 110, Chapter 8

Macdonald, Victoria Alberta 95

Macdonald, William (Dan) 170, 173, 178, 186-7, 216

Macdonald, Sarah and Michael, Moor of Strone 186

McDonald, Allan 27,108

McDonald, Rev 31

Macdonell, Forbes James 19-24, 27-8, 50, 76, 89, 90, 97,121

MacFadyen, Helen 96, 114

MacFadyen, Neil 96, 114, 116

Macfarlane, Arthur 200

Macfarlane, Rev. D 213, 215, 217

MacGillivray, Allan 149, Fig 40

MacGillivray, John 106

MacGregor, Alexander 148, Fig 38

MacGregor, Dr, (MP) 149-51

MacGregor, Patrick 38

McGregor, Alexander 189, Fig 36, 214

McIntosh, Charles 68, 74, 112

McIntosh, Donald, Moy Cottage 55

McIntosh, Donald (= Elspeth Macpherson) 123, 126, 130

McIntosh, Finlay, keeper 50, 116

McIntosh, Finlay (= Mary Cameron) 55, 96, 112

McIntosh, Jane 17

McIntosh, John, mason 28, 34, 55, 112-3

McIntosh, John (*Uncail sa' Chreagan*) 162

McIntosh, John 170, 172

McIntosh, Paul (= Annie Fyfe) 123,130

McIntosh, Thomas 75

Mackintosh, Aeneas 123

Mackintosh, Alistair 123

Mackintosh, Edward 94

Mackintosh, William 94

Mackintosh, Winwood 94

Mackintosh, William 94

Mackintosh, Shaw 94

Mackay, Rev. Angus 174, Fig 29

Mackay, Duncan 15, 23

Mackay, John 29

Mackenzie, Alexander 119

Mackenzie, Alexander, CE 171, 193, 202, 211

Mackenzie, Rev. Dr Kenneth 68, 80-1, Fig 9, 84, 107, 111, 115, 143, 163, 173, 177, 204-5, 207-8, Fig 39

Mackenzie, Sir Kenneth 113-4, 118

Mackenzie, Samuel 199

McKenzie, Donald 55, 76, 97

McKenzie, Margaret 27, 28, 97

Mackinnon, James 199

Maclean, Allan 126

Maclean, James 47, 49, 55, 109

Maclean, Jimmy 49, 109, 194

Maclean, Sandy 109

Macleod, Cameron 103

Macleod of Macleod 118

MacMaster, Catherine 103

MacMaster, John 39, 42, 77, 78, 79, 82, 195
Macpherson, Alexander, drover 14
Macpherson, Alexander, Craggan 27
Macpherson, Alexander, (Burke and Wills) 48
Macpherson, Alexander, teacher 77
Macpherson, Alexander, (*Alaidh Bàn* = Hannah
   McCook) 50, 102, 106-7, 146, 155, 182, 194, 204, 214,
   218
Macpherson, Alick (Hannah) 171-3
Macpherson, Alfred 170, 172
Macpherson, Andrew of Banchor 12, 19, 75, 85
Macpherson, Angus 4
Macpherson, Angus (*Aonghas a' Phleastarair*) 48, 55,
   83, 112, 179
Macpherson, Angus *(Aonghas Bàn)* 107-8
Macpherson, Angus, piper 4, 111, 181, 183-5, 209, 215-7
Macpherson, Angus (= Margaret Sellar) 155
Macpherson, Angus James (A J) 165, 173, 201, 206
Macpherson, Miss Ann of Belleville 22-4, 27-9, 31-2, 41,
   43, 52, 65, 74
Macpherson, Charles J B of Belleville 95, 106, 107,
   118, 141, 148, 152, 154, 197, 201, Fig 38, 204, 206-7, 213,
   217
Macpherson, Duncan of Cluny 20
Macpherson, David Edward of Belleville 68, 80, 82, 86, 94,
   98, 118, 152, 164-5
Macpherson, Donald (= Ann MacGregor) 16, 23
Macpherson, Donald (= Kate MacGregor) 29, 47, 49, 104
Macpherson, Donald (= Mary Blair) 41, 196
Macpherson, Duncan (s/o Ranald) 48, 200
Macpherson, Evan 20
Macpherson, Ewan (= Anne Cattanach) 29, 74
Macpherson, Ewan of Cluny 145
Macpherson, Ewan George of Cluny 173
Macpherson, Ewen, (Old Cluny) 41, 43, 48, 52-3, 55, 60, 64,
   67, 71, 117, 160, 162
Macpherson, Finlay 21, 24, 26-7
Macpherson, Geordie (NZ) 98, 105, 128, 158, 179, 194

Macpherson, George (Hannah) 170-3, 178, 206
Macpherson Ian (*Othaichear*) 29, 50, 70
Macpherson, James (*Seumas Bàn*) 9-10, 12, 20
Macpherson, James, jnr (Belleville) 10, 14-5, 17-8, 20-2,
   28, 30-1, 75
Macpherson, James (*Seumas Mòr* = Ann Stewart) 3, 102,
   107, 110, 146, 181, Fig 38, 206, 209
Macpherson, (James) Ian 13, 103, 122, 127, 152, 164, 180,
   206, 215
Macpherson, James (s/o Ranald), tailor 48, 55, 70, 104,
   112, 160
Macpherson, James Stewart (JS) 104, 185, 194
Macpherson, John (= Isabella Cattanach) 13, 68, 74-6
Macpherson, John 22, 27
Macpherson, John (Johnny the Sports) 48, 178
Macpherson, John, tollman 96
Macpherson, John D (JD) 103, 197-8, 209, 215
Macpherson, John (Jockan) 183-4, 206, Fig 39, 209, 215-9
Macpherson, daughters of Jockan - Phosa 200; Flora 216
Macpherson, Juliet 29
Macpherson, Lachlan 27
Macpherson, Capt Lachlan (Old Biallid) 32, 125, 162
Macpherson, Lachlan, plasterer 48-9, 126, 177, 192, 204
Macpherson, Lt Lachlan of Corrimony 64, 66, 153
Macpherson, Col Lachlan of Glentruim 114, 145
Macpherson, Lucy of Balavil (née Baxter) Fig 38, 204,
   206, 217
Macpherson, Lydia Brewster 98-100, 106-7, 110, 115,
   117, 153, 201, 214
Macpherson, Niall Malcolm Stewart 4, 99
Macpherson, Ranald (*Rao'll a' Phleastarair*) 28, 47-48,
   112, 162
Macpherson, Ranald (s/o Angus, s/o *Rao'll*) 48-9, 126,
   162, 177, 192, 204
Macpherson, Ranald (s/o James Macpherson & Ann
   Gray) 126, 155, 195
Macpherson, Robert of Glentruim 55, 64-5
Macpherson, Sarah 178

Macpherson, Sophia 16
Macpherson, Thomas Stewart (TSM; Sir Stewart) 3, 4, 5,
    13, 21, 97, 99, 103, 106, 122, 124, 125, 127, 164, 196, 217
Macpherson, William Cattanach 13, 70, 97, 103, 109, 112,
    114, 116, 161, 169, 183
MacRae, Rev. Alexander 164
MacRae, Donald 13, 73, 76
MacRae, Donald, Ballallan 119, 151
MacRae, John, PF 43
MacRae, Dr John 67, 69, 70, 80, 90, 109
Main, George 193
Main, Miss 215
Matthewson, Rev. J 21
Meldrum, Gordon 42, 79, 80
Middlemas, John 106, 108, 155, 158-9, Fig 38
Middlemas family 100, 117, 129, 178
Miller, John 205, Fig 39, 215
Ministers in the 1890s 152-3
Mitchell, Alexander (= Christina Macpherson) 194
Mitchell, Joseph 52-4, 61, 96
Murray, John 45-6

O

Orchard, Edward (Boysie) 67
Orchard, Edward 67
Orchard, John 67, 113-4, 139

P

Parker, Robert and family 147, 154
Pelham, Hon Mrs 214

Q

Queen Victoria 71-2, 74, 116-7, 165, 169, 172, 205-6

R

Ralph family 129, 130
Rao of Cutch 115-6
Reade, Mary 94

Reid, Francis Robertson Reid 104, 173
Ritchie, William 167, 173-4
Roberts, Lt.-Col and Mrs 211, 213-4
Robertson, Alexander (*Alasdair Mòr*) 96-7
Robertson, Jane 95, 116
Robertson, Rev. John 42
Rose families, Unie and her many relatives Chapter 8,
    131-138
Rose, Alexander (= Janet Macpherson) 22, 55, 108, 133,
    136
Rose, Alexander, monitor 82-3, 139
Rose, Alexander (s/o Lachlan) 90, 133, 138
Rose, Alexander (s/o William) 108
Rose, Aeneas 138
Rose, Donald (= Ann Kennedy) 42, 131-32, 136
Rose, Donald, jnr 82, 134
Rose, Ewen 82, 133
Rose, Lachlan 47, 49, 90, 131, 138
Rose, Janet, widow 82, 133-4
Rose, Sarah 39, 40, 138
Rose, Rev. William 132, 133
Ross, Donally 179
Ross, John 152
Ross, William 105, 110, 152
Rusell, James 21-2, 26, 51
Rusell, John 21-2, 26-8, 51, 133
Russell, John 204, 214-5
Russell, John 215

S

Schofield, George and Mrs 196-7, 202, 205, 213, 217
Sellar, Andy 127-8, 179, 180
Sellar family 100, 125, 127, 130, 155, 222
Sellar, George (s/o Robert) 123, 206
Sellar, George (bro/o Robert) 173, 187-8, 207
Sellar, Jimsie 127, 170, 173, 178, 180, 194
Sellar, Rev. John (= Isabella Macdonald) 127-8, 179,
    180, 216

Sellar, Robert (= Barbara Riach) 102-3, 107, 111, 146, 148, 153, 155, 165, 168, 181 Fig 38, 206, 209
Shepherd, Rev. George 42-3, 45, 78-80
Simpson, John and Mrs 96, 181, 185, 188-9, 192, Figs 37-9
Sinton, Rev. Dr Thomas 4, 5, 15, 59, 77
Smith, Isabella and John, Achnahatnich 134
Smith, John 159
Snug, Charlie 105
Stevenson, Robert Adam 188
Stewart, Ann 3, 102
Stewart, Alexander (*Alaidh Mòr*) 182
Stewart, Duncan 104, 125
Stewart, Isabella (= Angus Cameron) 48
Stewart, Isabella (PO) 199
Stewart, John (= Barbara Kennedy) 88, 107, 109, 113, 117, 164, 182, 199, 200
Stewart, John (= Sarah Macdonald) 198
Stewart, Neil 64
Stewart, Peter K 199
Stewart, Robert 77
Stewart, William (*Uilleam Mòr Stiùbhart*) 47, 49, 55, 104, 107, 113
Strone Crofters 54

T
Tawse, John 78-9
Taylor, John 57, 63, 99
Thomson, Alexander 68
Thomson, Peter 70
Thomson, Robert B 198
Tod, William 19
Turnbull, Bill 128
Two Cronies 4, 86, 97, 103-4, 109-10, 112, 125-8, 139, 160-1, 178-9, 181, 193, 196, 198
Tytler, James 112, 181, 209, 211, 213, 217-8

U
Urquhart, George 79

Urquhart, William 214

W
Warren, Charles 22
Warren, Robert 22-3, 27
Watson, David 29, 111
Watson, Peter M 173, 181, 194
White Well members 100
Williamson, Thomas 158, 160
Wilson, Alexander 28, 36, 41, 55, 76, 97, 111, 164
Wilson, Donnie 50
Wilson, Ewen 96, 97
Wilson, Flora (Mrs Bentick) 103, 111, 188
Wilson, Lachlan 97
Wolfenden, William 173

Y
Young, Alexander Waugh 112
Young, A & G 216